GAME
CHANGER

GAME CHANGER

BOB WHITSITT

An Insider's Story of the Sonics' Resurgence,
the Trail Blazers' Turnaround, and the Deal
that Saved the Seahawks

FLASH
POINT

Published by Flashpoint™ Books, Seattle
www.flashpointbooks.com

Produced by Girl Friday Productions

Photo credits: page 44, courtesy of Bob Whitsitt; page 106, Randall Polliard, as originally published in the *Seattle Times*; page 138, Jeff Johnson Artworks/www.cartooniversity.com

ISBN (paperback): 978-1-959411-26-0
ISBN (ebook): 978-1-959411-29-1

Library of Congress Control Number: 2023905958

Printed in China

First edition

For the Sonics faithful, the Seahawks 12s,
and Rip City, because you were game changers.

CONTENTS

The only place success comes before work is in the dictionary.

—Vince Lombardi, NFL Hall of Fame
coach of the Green Bay Packers

PREFACE

PEOPLE ARE ALWAYS ASKING ME to share anecdotes about my decades in professional sports, to tell the stories *behind* the stories. They want to know how the sausage is made. *What are the players really like? How do you know which coach to hire? What does a general manager actually do? How do you get a job in professional sports? Will Seattle get another NBA team?*

That insatiable curiosity inspired me to write this book, to capture all in one place the questions I've answered and the stories I've told countless times. The pages ahead offer honest glimpses behind the front-office curtain—the backstory of franchise-defining draft picks, trades, and other moves that shaped three crown jewels in Pacific Northwest sports: the Seattle SuperSonics, the Portland Trail Blazers, and the Seattle Seahawks.

There's something infinitely fascinating about sports—with its phenomenal displays of athleticism, the fierce rivalries, the big personalities, the riveting drama of wins and losses, and the billions of dollars that fuel the whole business. As I look back on my career, so much has changed since the late 1970s, when I got my foot in the NBA's door. From that moment forward, I had a front-row seat as the NBA evolved from a stodgy, low-budget league run by old-timers who dismissed the three-pointer as a "terrible idea," to an entertainment empire of 30 teams that topped $10 billion in revenue in 2021–22.

I started below the bottom rung of the sports management ladder, as an intern making $500 a month and sleeping on a friend's couch. This was back when pro basketball games were aired on tape delay after late-night news. Some teams (including the Pacers, where I interned) struggled to make payroll.

Then came Magic Johnson, Larry Bird, and a rivalry that electrified the basketball world. Suddenly, arenas started filling up with fans. TV networks started paying the NBA lots of money to broadcast their games—in prime time! It was exciting! I was thrilled to be making a living in the middle of it all—both back then and throughout my career as a sports executive. I've always considered my career one of the great privileges of my life. As hard as I worked, day in and day out, it often didn't feel like work to me. I love sports that much. I always have.

Growing up in Madison, Wisconsin, I played every sport I could as a kid—baseball, basketball, football, swimming, hockey, and volleyball. There wasn't a day of the week, year-round, when I wasn't busy with whatever sport was in season at the time. I was a good athlete, but athletic skill wasn't my biggest asset. My biggest assets were heart and hustle.

The same attitude, work ethic, and passion for sports guided me during the early days of my career, when I became the youngest president of an NBA franchise at 30 years old. I showed up early and stayed late every day. I said yes to every opportunity to learn and gain new skills. I figured things out, for the most part, with little or no guidance (usually the latter). Through it all, I learned to trust my instincts and stay calm in a crisis, to expect the unexpected, to adapt and anticipate—all things that great athletes and business leaders do.

Ultimately, the most rewarding and challenging aspects of my job as president and GM involved big, bold risks. The more people thought a risk was bound to fail, the more homework I did to make sure it was not just a chance worth taking but that I had solid reasons to swing for the fences. Early on, if I swung and whiffed, I had a good chance of getting fired. If I belted one out of the park, I would get another chance to take a big, bold risk.

There are a lot of books out there with helpful advice about risk-taking, how to build confidence in your decision-making process, how to win arguments, how to influence people, and how to get what you want in a negotiation. I touch on these and a lot of other business-leadership topics in the chapters ahead as I share stories about the most memorable moments in my career.

If you're a die-hard fan of the Sonics, some stories will transport you back in time to the first glimmers of the team's mid-1990s glory days. If you're a Seahawks fan, you might get the shivers realizing how close Seattle came to losing its beloved NFL team and what a series of long shots it took to keep the franchise in Seattle. If you're a Sounders fan, maybe you'll gain deeper appreciation for the world-class stadium where your Major League Soccer team plays in front of wildly supportive sold-out crowds. If you're a Trail Blazers fan, you might wonder how a guy from Seattle who devoted almost a decade to rebuilding the Sonics could suddenly switch allegiance to their archrivals. The answer is simple. When Paul Allen called, he gave me the same kind of opportunity that drew me to Seattle: to lift a struggling franchise out of a deep rut and get it back on track, in position to win another championship.

If you're not much of a sports fan when you start this book, you might become one by the end. There's really no other form of entertainment quite like sports. When you see a movie, the cinematography, sound effects, and suspense might mesmerize you, but you're not on set, watching it all unfold right before your eyes like you do when you watch sports live. The actors might deliver Oscar-worthy performances, but they're not part of your community. The pro athletes on your team(s) form a cast of characters you get to see over and over, week after week, for an entire season. You sit shoulder to shoulder with fans who share your passion for the sport, your loyalty to the team, the adrenaline rush of a come-from-behind victory, the gut punch of losing a decisive playoff game.

When you go to a game, it's an inclusive experience—a chance for folks who never made it on to a varsity team in high school to experience a kind of exhilaration like no other. When you talk about your home team, it's "we" not "they." They're part of your community. You might see them at your kid's school or in the grocery store, at the car wash or in a commercial for a local business. They feel like family to you, and you feel like family to them. That's the kind of relationship teams have with their loyal fans. When you and the sold-out crowd around you cheer so loudly, you drown out opponents as they're trying to coordinate plays, you give your home team an undeniable advantage—enough so that when they win, you feel like you were part of it. Because you were.

Die-hard fans never give up on their teams, no matter how bleak things get. For 21 years straight, loyal fans of the Seattle Mariners hung in there with their team during one of the longest playoff droughts in history. Then, in 2022, the Pacific Northwest got fired up when the M's started winning again. You could feel a deep sense of pride swell after two decades of dormancy. The Mariners didn't win it all, and they didn't have to. Their success gave their fans a long-overdue sense of hope and confidence that the tide was starting to turn.

There's nothing quite like the transformation of a losing team into a juggernaut with the right mix of talent, grit, and character capable of winning a championship. It takes a lot of effort, year after year, to climb the ladder high enough to make it into the playoffs. The teams I managed achieved that almost every year. It wasn't a fluke. After the long look back I took to write this book, I'm convinced the success that the Sonics, Trail Blazers, and Seahawks achieved from my rebuilds is repeatable. It worked, it worked, and it worked. I feel pretty good about that—good enough that I'd like to do it again with another team. Because it's never too late.

CHAPTER 1

REIGN MAN

N O ONE LIKES GETTING BOOED, but you can't avoid it when you're in the business of running a professional sports franchise. You need thick skin, a sky-high tolerance for nonstop stress, the confidence to take bold risks, and the courage to stand by them—especially ones that get you calls at home from angry fans who shout f-bombs you can hear halfway across the room when your toddler picks up the phone.

One of the most memorable choruses of boos I ever received came one midsummer afternoon in 1989, when hundreds of Seattle SuperSonics fans packed into a downtown hotel banquet hall to be the first ones to find out which up-and-coming players we would get in the NBA draft. We had two first-round picks that year: 16th and 17th. I announced them back-to-back. First, Dana Barros, a point guard from Boston College, one of the school's all-time leading scorers. Next, Shawn Kemp, a six-foot-ten-inch phenom from Indiana, one of the top players in the country when he'd graduated the previous year . . . from high school.

Booooooooooooooo!

There were no TV clips showing how fiercely Shawn could dunk, no impressive stats and accolades from college coaches. He was the only player in the draft that year who hadn't played a day of college ball. This was well before Kevin Garnett, Kobe Bryant, and LeBron James and more than a decade since a few other players had dared to go pro right out of high school.

There was Moses Malone, drafted in 1974 by the Utah Stars of the American Basketball Association (ABA). Malone made Rookie of the Year and the All-Star team his first season in the ABA, the scrappy, flashy league that later merged with the NBA. A future Hall of Famer, Malone won the NBA's Most Valuable Player award three times, made the All-Star team 12 years in a row, and led the league in rebounding for five consecutive years.

The next two prep-to-pro players had less illustrious careers. Drafted a year after Malone, Darryl Dawkins warmed the bench for most of his first two seasons with the Philadelphia 76ers. Bill Willoughby, drafted the same year as Dawkins, started out with the Atlanta Hawks and played unremarkably for six teams during his eight-year run as an NBA journeyman.

First off, most coaches don't like draft picks to begin with. They want veteran players who can help them win right away, not kids who might take years to develop, at which point said coaches may have moved on to other teams. Coaches have to win now, or they get fired. GMs have to make good choices and win, or *they* get fired.

In 1989, we needed a point guard, so I assured Sonics coach Bernie Bickerstaff that I would draft Dana Barros, who was not only a solid point guard but also a strong shooter who could spread the floor with his limitless range. "Give me what I need," Bernie said, "and you can do what you want with your second pick. . . . Way to get another pick, by the way. How'd you *do* that?" (Normally, all a team gets is one first-round pick per year, but I'd acquired an extra one through a previous deal. I knew it would give me some great leverage when I needed it.)

In the lead-up to the 1989 draft, I sent scouts to Los Angeles, where Shawn had moved for the summer, to watch him play. They liked what they saw, so I flew him to Seattle and organized some games with local Amateur Athletic Union (AAU) and college players. I had our coaches and scouts sitting with me in the stands there at Seattle University. You could tell how much he loved the game. Shawn was thrilled to get out on the court and show his stuff. He was clearly a powerful and versatile player with tons of potential. He outdribbled and outran everyone on the court. He dunked, blocked shots, sank three-pointers, and grabbed rebounds with stunning ease.

I could also tell he was a good guy. I liked him. I liked his work ethic. He didn't come to town with an agent or an entourage, as many players do. He wasn't preprogrammed with all the canned answers. He loved getting into the gym and playing. The guy just wanted to compete. He wanted to play against the best and see how he compared.

When he asked if he would get any playing time in Seattle, I said, "We never dictate who gets to play. The players decide that. You practice, you play, and we play the best players. If you're one of the best players, you play. If you're not one of the best players, you keep working until you *are* one of the best players." He said that was all he wanted to hear. The coach for another team had given him a brutal answer to the same question: "We're not going to draft you, but if we did, you'd never play."

Shawn was one of the top players in the country in 1988, his senior year of high school. He was heavily favored to win Indiana's Mr. Basketball honors until he declared his intent to play for the University of Kentucky—a major blow to his home-state Hoosiers and Bobby Knight, their infamously hot-tempered coach. Shawn had to sit out his first year at Kentucky because of low SAT scores that fell short of NCAA eligibility standards. Within a matter of months, he got ensnared in a scandal involving two gold chains, which his teammate Sean Sutton, son of Wildcats coach Eddie Sutton, had reported stolen. No charges were ever filed, though the accusations were still grabbing headlines when Shawn packed up and left Kentucky. He moved on to Trinity Valley Community College in Texas, where he would continue sitting out his first year, this time because he'd transferred from another school.

Shawn then declared his eligibility for the 1989 NBA draft. He'd been out of sight, out of mind for most of the past year. Some questioned why this brash 19-year-old who hadn't played competitive basketball for most of an entire year thought he was ready to jump straight into the NBA. Most people I talked to about him told me I'd be foolish to draft him, but I sensed Shawn had the raw talent and potential that the Sonics needed to catapult to the next level.

"Look, here's my philosophy," I said as I made my case to Sonics owner Barry Ackerley. "If we're ever going to win a championship, we've got to hit one big. This kid is not going to change the franchise tomorrow, but if he becomes the kind of player I think he can become, he'll be a combination of Dominique Wilkins and Charles Barkley. He can jump out of the building. He can dunk. He can do all these unbelievable things that Wilkins can do. Yet he's a powerful guy like Barkley. He won't be either one of those guys. He'll be *both* of them."

Barry wasn't buying it. "Absolutely not. I don't know who this guy is. The fans don't know who he is. My friends don't know who he is. He won't sell a ticket because nobody knows who he is. So, no, we're not going to waste a first-round pick on him."

I wasn't about to give up. It took a lot of back-and-forth with Barry to win him over. At one point, I asked, "Are you telling me I can't take him?"

"No, I'm telling you I don't *want* you to take him."

After I made my case again and again, he finally gave me the closest thing to a yes: "If you feel that strongly, I won't overrule it," he said. "If it works out, great. If not, bye-bye."

Not that he needed to point out my job was on the line. That was the case with everything. You make a mistake in this business, you're gone. That's it. Pack your bags, and hope some other team will hire you, which could be a long shot if you haven't had a chance to prove yourself. This is why a lot of GMs play it safe. They don't swing for the fences. Sometimes, they don't swing at all, watching pitch after proverbial pitch go by. For them, there's no difference between striking out looking and giving it all they've got to hit one out of the park. Either way, it's a failure, and they'd rather stay employed.

I was in my early 30s, married just a few years, with two little kids at home, a mortgage, and a boss who seemed to take immense pleasure in reminding me he'd dump me in a heartbeat. I had a great feeling about Shawn's potential, but still, I knew there was a chance he would never make it in the NBA. Or he'd be unbelievable. As silly as that sounds now, it was a real hit-or-miss kind of thing. Most players either become average or pretty good. With this kind of deal, he was going to be great or he was going to be terrible.

I've always believed you have to be willing to take chances like this to propel a franchise to championship caliber. If you take a chance and know what you're doing—which you should if you've done your homework right—you build confidence that you can make things work. Sure, there's always the risk that things *won't* work. You might fail because you hired the wrong coach. You might fail because you couldn't manage your owner well enough. You might fail because guys get hurt.

Oftentimes, you make a move because you have other great moves lined up for later that will ultimately lead to success. When you make that first move, it might look pretty silly on its own. You might get a lot of criticism. You know what you're doing, yet you can't tell people, "Trust me. I'm gonna make a few other moves down the road, and it'll all make sense." You won't be able to get those deals done if you tell all in advance. The thing I never wanted to do was wake up one day and say, "Gee, I had my chance, but I didn't have the courage to do what I believed in. And I'll never know if it would have worked, because I didn't have the guts to go for it." I've taken a lot of carefully calculated risks throughout my career, and most have turned out pretty well.

Getting a great draft pick is one thing. Getting a great draft pick to sign a contract that's an exceptionally good deal for your team is another. Shawn Kemp was a home run on both counts. He turned out to be every bit as talented as I thought he could be—and then some. He also agreed to a six-year, $4.1 million contract, the first three years guaranteed, then three years nonguaranteed. Most first-round picks get a four-year fully guaranteed contract, which is what Shawn and his agent had wanted.

If Shawn had flopped, we could have cut him at the start of year four without having to pay him anything because the latter half of his contract was not guaranteed. Players usually push hard to get every year of their contract guaranteed so they will still be paid if they get injured or cut by their team. Shawn made more than $1 million in the final year of his contract but was arguably worth much more. It was an outstanding deal for the Sonics and the beginning of a remarkable career for a star who stands out as one of the best bets I took during my 25 years in the NBA.

Throughout his rookie season, Shawn worked hard to prove he had what it took to play NBA ball. He rose to the challenge I'd given him back when he'd interviewed: "Go compete. Earn a spot. Earn some minutes. Show the coach you belong." He played in 81 games his first season, all but one, when he was out with an injury. He only started one of those games, but many rookies barely play their first year.

We had to teach Shawn a lot of fundamentals. He'd been a man among boys in high school—big, fast, and overpowering. In the NBA, he had to learn how to maneuver around players who were just as big, if not bigger, just as quick, if not quicker, just as physical, if not more physical than he was. No matter how stellar a shooter you are in high school or college, when you're new to the NBA, it feels like you can never get off a shot because you can't get open. Guys are grabbing you, holding you down. You expect the refs to call a foul, as they did in high school or college. Not in the pros. That's not even a love pat in the NBA.

Early on, Shawn would be so excited to dunk, he'd get the ball in the low post and do a spin move so fast that he would often travel. We had to teach him to slow down. And even when he slowed down, he was still extremely quick. It was part enthusiasm, part adrenaline. He was just so excited to play, he'd get ahead of himself or try to force a play that wasn't there. Eventually, he learned that when defenders were all over him, he could throw the ball out to a guard, wait, and the ball would come back to him five, six, seven seconds later. Then he'd have a better advantage to attack the basket.

He also had a knack for getting into quick foul trouble. Sometimes, it was for plowing through a couple of defenders to shoot. Sometimes, it was because he wanted to block every shot—which even the best defenders can't do every time. After Shawn blocked a shot, the next time, a player would pump fake, Shawn would jump out of the building, then the guy would just lean into him, drawing a foul. Shawn had to learn that, sometimes, he just had to play his position and hope the guy missed. He probably would've gotten more playing time his first season if he hadn't racked up so many fouls so fast. We didn't get too bent out of shape about it. It's all part of the learning process.

Usually, you learn a lot of this stuff in college, but even if Shawn had played in the NCAA, he would have spent a lot of his first few years working on fundamentals. For new players, basketball isn't just a game anymore. It's a job. It's a profession. It's a career. And it's demanding. Eighty-two games a season (one hundred when you count pre- and postseason), ten-day road trips, coaches throwing terminology at you that you've never heard of and don't understand—it's both physically and mentally exhausting. There are playbooks to study, and the coach isn't going to stop practice and walk you through a step-by-step tutorial. You just have to figure it out. Fast. Then adapt without skipping a beat the second the defense changes things up.

Really good teams have a core group of players who have been together for years and have a system that runs smoothly. Everyone knows it inside out. They could do it blindfolded. The coach will add a little of this here, a little of that there, and players adjust seamlessly. The Sonics were building toward that when Shawn arrived. They were a decent team—not nearly as good as they would become a few years later, but strong enough to relieve the pressure from Shawn to dominate as one of our main guys. Young phenoms in the high draft picks typically go to bad teams, then flame out, overwhelmed by the expectation that they carry the team right away. Who could blame them?

It's not unusual for young players to struggle as they adjust to life on their own. The rigors of the NBA, their newfound wealth and fame, so much changes so fast it can make their heads spin. At 19, Shawn was the youngest Sonic by several years, and he held his own. In fact, he showed more maturity than many older players I've seen. He'd been through a lot. He'd gone from being one of the greatest things that had ever happened in Indiana basketball to almost villain status because he'd chosen to go to Kentucky over Indiana. He'd dealt with scandal and harsh media criticism. Learning how to endure scorn and scrutiny made him more circumspect, more resilient. He never came to my office complaining. He just kept his head down and focused on improving his game.

Shawn became fast friends with his co-rookie, Dana Barros, a really good guy, four years older, also coming to a new market for the first time. They spent a lot of their time off-court together. They were pretty much inseparable. One of our top scorers, Xavier McDaniel, nicknamed X-Man (or just X), took Shawn under his wing that first year. He gave Shawn a lot of valuable guidance. Same with Coach Bernie Bickerstaff. Veteran players often give rookies the cold shoulder. Why root for some newcomer who might take your spot on the starting lineup? But between his talent, his work ethic, and his patience about paying his dues, Shawn earned the respect of veteran teammates, who showed no qualms about doing their part to help him develop as a player.

He impressed teammates when he would take hard hits in practice without making a big deal about it. When an aggressive player like X-Man clobbered him, there would be no, "Hey! You really pounded me on that one!" Shawn wasn't one to mouth off. His talk was his play. The guys learned that if they banged on him, they better watch out. A couple of plays later it would be *BOOM!*—Shawn giving it right back, just as physically.

During his second season, I made a bold decision to trade Xavier McDaniel, easily our best and most popular player. He was about to become a free agent, and I didn't have a big enough budget to get him signed. Another GM might have fought for more money, anything to keep their shining star from leaving. I saw X's forthcoming free agency, combined with persistent knee injuries, as an opportunity to let him move on, opening up more playing time for Shawn.

In his first two games after X left, Shawn scored 49 points, shooting 61 percent, grabbing 18 rebounds, and blocking 5 shots. "I was ready," he told the *Seattle Times*. "I thought I'd get a starting position sooner or later, whether it was this week, this year, two years from now, or whenever. I was determined enough to do whatever it took to get that role."

Shawn went on to become one of the Sonics' best and most beloved players of all time. His nickname was Reign Man, for how spectacularly he reigned over his opponents in a city famous for its rain. He went on to make the All-Star team five times during his eight years in Seattle (plus one last time with the Cleveland Cavaliers). Only two other players in Sonics history made more All-Star appearances: Jack Sikma (seven) and Gary Payton (nine). Fred Brown, who played on the Sonics' championship team in 1979, made the All-Star team just once in his 13 years with the team. Of the 48 players who have represented Seattle as All-Stars, most did so just once or twice.

Back in 1989, when I was the only one talking up Shawn, everyone else was saying, "No way. Not this kid. Too big of a risk." They changed their tune when he became an All-Star. "Geez, why didn't *we* draft that guy?"

Scouts and general managers also have a knack for rewriting history, claiming they led the charge to draft this or that star back before anyone could've guessed how good they would become. One time, after the Sonics beat the Denver Nuggets, their general manager, Pete Babcock, went off in a news story about how he'd known Shawn was going to be a phenomenal player and that he would've drafted him if only Shawn had been available. He's lucky no one fact-checked him. Shawn *was* available during Pete's turn to pick. I drafted Shawn 17th, two picks after Pete drafted Stanford's Todd Lichti. (Lichti played decently for the Nuggets for two years, then knee injuries held him back for the rest of his short and unremarkable NBA career.)

I called Pete to refresh his memory. "Come on, Pete. What if a reporter actually looked it up and saw that you *could* have drafted Shawn but didn't?"

"Well, I'd be screwed," Pete said. "Thanks, I better not say that anymore."

Shawn's extraordinary success paved the way for future NBA stars who went pro without going to college: Kevin Garnett, Kobe Bryant, Jermaine O'Neal, Tracy McGrady, Amar'e Stoudemire, LeBron James, Dwight Howard, and many more. Then in the late 1990s and early 2000s, as more and more 18-year-olds entered the draft, NBA commissioner David Stern called for raising the minimum age of NBA draft eligibility to 20. He and others argued that players were being scouted too young and that too many were launching their careers before they were mature enough to fully appreciate that pro basketball isn't a fail-safe path to fame and riches. The players' union pushed back and eventually agreed to a minimum age of 19, plus one year out of high school.

I think it's best for players to go to college, get an education, and develop as basketball players. That way, if they don't succeed in the NBA, they will have a college degree to fall back on as they pursue other careers. We always read about the LeBron Jameses and the Kobe Bryants and the Shawn Kemps, but there are many more players you never hear about because they never made it, and they missed a great opportunity to get a college education, to grow up, to gain intelligence in nonathletic areas, to have relationships, and all that.

That said, I also believe players should have the right to go straight to the NBA out of high school if that's what they want. Most who go that route will fail, fizzle, they'll be out of the NBA in a couple of years. It will be devastating, and they'll probably feel lost, but they should have the opportunity to make that choice for themselves.

Ultimately, I don't think one year will make or break this conversation. If it were up to me, I would allow them the opportunity to enter the NBA after high school and set up a strong counseling system to help steer them toward making good decisions, what's right for them.

It would be nice if every kid saw college as the invaluable opportunity it is. But the truth is, college isn't the best option for everyone. If players have no interest in learning, never go to class, and are only there to play basketball, they might as well have the opportunity to become a professional as soon as they want. They'll either make it or they won't. Not everyone has what it takes to be the next Shawn Kemp.

CHAPTER 2

THE INTERN

MY CAREER IN PROFESSIONAL SPORTS began with a phone call that never rang.

I had played basketball during my freshman year at the University of Wisconsin-Stevens Point, also four years of baseball, and one year of football in my fifth year. I was a good small-college player. Not good enough to play pro, which is why I decided to pursue a career on the management side of sports. I had no other job prospects when I applied for a three-month internship with the Indiana Pacers. I learned about it from a director at Ohio University, home to the nation's first master's program in sports administration, where I had applied the previous year but hadn't gotten in. Determined to wait a semester and reapply, I went back to Stevens Point, enrolling as a fifth-year senior and taking classes to earn a teaching credential. Teaching and coaching seemed like a solid fallback career if sports management didn't pan out. I also tried out for the football team. It was an unconventional idea but a strategic one. I wanted to show the folks at Ohio University how passionate I was about sports. Playing football seemed like a great way to impress the admissions office at a school with one of the top college football programs in the country.

I hadn't played since high school, and the University of Wisconsin-Stevens Point football program was one of the best National Association of Intercollegiate Athletics (NAIA) teams in the country. I also couldn't work out with the football team all summer; I was fighting off mono. Two weeks before practices were scheduled to begin, I flunked my physical. My white blood cell count was too low. I got healthy enough to pass the physical only three days before the first practice, which began in the stifling August heat. I blacked out a couple of times while standing up. I worked my tail off and made the team, probably because one of the assistant coaches had also coached me in baseball. Rather than outright cutting me, they told me I would be a tenth-string tight end. I bet they hoped I wouldn't take it, but little did they know that *any* spot on the team was good enough for me, so I kept grinding away.

One day, during intrasquad scrimmaging, our All-American quarterback Reed Giordana got frustrated when a tight end dropped a pass. He spotted me on the sidelines and shouted, "Whitsitt! Get in here!"

I caught every pass. It was the turning point that earned me my spot in the starting lineup. During our season opener in Detroit against Wayne State, I set a stadium record for receiving yardage (170 yards) and scored a touchdown. Not bad for a fifth-year senior who had just barely made it on to the team. We had a great season. The Pointers led the nation in passing and won the Wisconsin Intercollegiate Athletic Conference. Our team was ranked third in the nation and was one of four teams selected to play in the NAIA college tournament. We made it to the semifinals, losing to the eventual national champion, Abilene Christian.

After the football season, I reapplied to the program at Ohio University and also applied at Ohio State, which had just started a master's program in sports administration. I got accepted at both schools and chose Ohio State because it was a much larger and more well-known school in the world of sports. I started the program in January 1978.

A couple of times a month, I would head down to visit some friends at Ohio University, about an hour southeast of Columbus. I would volunteer at high-profile sporting events, each time meeting people and shaking hands, always looking for potential job opportunities. I didn't know anyone in the sports business back then. I had no rich uncle or family friend who could get me a job interview. I had to build my network.

I learned a lot working at the Mid-American Conference commissioner's office while in graduate school. The office was based in Columbus, not far from the Ohio State campus, and represented schools in Ohio, Michigan, Indiana, and Illinois. Working there helped me figure out that I wanted to work in professional sports, not college sports, which felt slow moving and bureaucratic. Too much red tape. Better job security, but fewer opportunities to try new things quickly. In pro sports, all you'd have to do is ask an owner for permission to implement a strategy, and if your idea got the green light, you could make it happen immediately. The idea of working in a government agency, which is what a college sports program at a public university basically is, sounded stifling, like being a small cog stuck in a giant wheel.

It was late summer in 1978. I was 22 and had just finished my classes in graduate school at Ohio State University. All I had left to do to earn my master's degree in sports management was get an internship. I had completed all the other requirements for the two-year program in less than a year, packing my schedule with a heavy course load during the academic year, then taking classes in the summer while working at the school's prestigious Eldon Miller basketball camp, named after the Buckeyes' head coach. I didn't make any money teaching kids how to dribble, post up, and make layups. I did earn free room and board, though. That was good enough for me.

As I was completing my master's and it came time to apply for jobs, I mailed hand-typed letters to every team in the National Football League (NFL), National Basketball Association (NBA), Major League Baseball (MLB), and National Hockey League (NHL), also many arenas and stadiums, in case nothing panned out with the pro sports leagues. There was no internet back then, of course, so I thumbed through phone books, called around for names and addresses, cranked out earnest letters on a creaky old typewriter, stuffed them in envelopes with my thin résumé, and mailed them off. I racked up quite a collection of rejection letters. It got to a point where getting a firm rejection in the mail felt better than never hearing back at all. For years, I kept those letters stuffed in a box. That collection reminded me that, sometimes, it takes no after no after no to break through and get your foot in the door.

The director of Ohio University's sports management program knew me because I was probably the first applicant they'd ever admitted who had turned them down. He was the person the Pacers usually called when they were ready to hire an intern each fall. That year, though, no Ohio University students wanted to intern with the Pacers, so the director said, "Call Ohio State. This kid Whitsitt's looking for an internship." Two of my Ohio State classmates also got invited to interview for the internship. (Lucky them. All those hours I put in volunteering and networking at Ohio University paid off for them, too!)

After my interview, the Pacers told me to expect a call by the following Friday, right before Labor Day weekend. I didn't have a phone in my dorm room, so I gave them the number of the phone down the hall. I waited for that phone to ring the entire day. It was hotter than hell. No air-conditioning. Everyone was clearing out for the break between summer and fall, everyone but me, sweating my butt off as I paced the hallway, staring at that phone as if I could will it to ring. I called the Pacers' front office a few times that day, to no avail. Eventually, I sauntered out to my dark-green Buick Skylark, loaded up all my things, and hit the road for a long and lonely drive home to Madison, Wisconsin. I figured the Pacers had given the internship to one of the other guys.

Indianapolis was on my way home, about three hours west on Interstate 70, so I pulled over, headed to the Pacers' office, which looked closed, and found a pay phone to make one last-ditch call. No one answered. For the final eight hours of my drive home, I figured that was it. I had struck out again. I pulled into my parents' driveway late and didn't quite know what to say when my dad asked, "Well, what are you gonna do now?"

I had no plan B.

My father had never thought of professional sports as a promising career path for anyone except athletes. He wasn't into sports much at all. Except for football, which he loved. He and my mom went to the University of Wisconsin Badgers football games every Saturday, leaving my older brother in charge of me and my younger sister at home. The whole family would watch the Green Bay Packers play every

Sunday after church. He played football himself, during his first year in college at Wisconsin State College-Superior, hurt his knee, then never played again.

My dad, Raymond Whitsitt, was a self-made man, a hardworking doctor, who'd met my mom, Dolores, in 1950 at a Milwaukee hospital where they both worked. He was doing his residency in obstetrics and gynecology, and she was a labor and delivery nurse, equally driven and self-motivated. She had grown up on a dairy farm in central Wisconsin, out in the middle of nowhere, the oldest of four children. Mom, her two younger sisters, and a younger brother had milked cows and shoveled manure every day before walking a couple of miles to a one-room schoolhouse. It's what all kids on farms in the rural Midwest did back then. Families needed lots of kids to work their farms. That wasn't the life Mom wanted, so she left as soon as she graduated from high school and never looked back.

My mom and dad were both the first in their families to go to college. They had no money when they ventured out on their own. They put themselves through school doing whatever odd jobs they could find, my mom working as a maid, cleaning homes, and my dad working construction and as a lifeguard. They worked hard, never taking anything for granted. My father suffered his first major heart attack when I was ten years old. He was just 41 and went on to have six more heart attacks over the next two decades. After that first one, he was racing against the clock to pay off the mortgage on our family home and provide financial security for my mom and us three kids.

Mom and Dad wasted nothing and made sure that my siblings and I knew that just because we wanted something didn't mean we would get it. I wore nothing but my older brother's hand-me-down clothes for most of my childhood. Scott was two years older and a lot bigger than I was, so his clothes always hung loose on me. The first pair of new shoes I remember getting were Converse Chuck Taylor high-tops, a splurge my dad promised me if I made the ninth-grade basketball team. I wore that pair of Chucks for two or three years, turning them into low-tops when the high part started to unravel. For the rest of my high school basketball career, I settled for the cheapest sneaker available, usually a tennis shoe. It was what we could afford, and as long as I could play, I didn't fuss about not wearing the latest, greatest gear.

I played a lot of basketball growing up. I enjoyed the game as a team sport but also because I could play on my own for countless hours. All you need is a basketball and a hoop, not even a playground. When I was 13 years old, my parents put up a hoop in our backyard. I loved dribbling and shooting at all times of the day and during every imaginable kind of weather. In the middle of an unforgiving Wisconsin winter, I'd go outside, shovel away as much ice and snow as I could, and shoot until I could barely feel my fingers.

I played a lot of sports, all year long. I was always on the go. I swam competitively through most of my childhood, taking the bus to the YMCA pool in downtown Madison after school, coming home with bloodshot eyes, then heading off to baseball practice. I played hockey for years and tried volleyball one year in high school, eventually giving up both because they conflicted with basketball. On the football field, I was usually the youngest, skinniest kid on my team because I was a year younger than everybody else in my grade; I had skipped kindergarten when I was five. My brother, Scott, on the other hand, was one of the biggest players on his teams, a star fullback and defensive lineman on his ninth-grade team. When you're the biggest kid, you're always the best, then at some point, everyone else gets bigger, and it all levels out.

I was a good player, and what I lacked in natural talent, I more than made up for with hard work. It's the way I've shown up for every role I've ever played, in sports, in school, in business, in my family life. Scott didn't value hard work, nor did he ever do much of it. He was the guy smoking cigarettes in his uniform on the edge of the football field until the whistle blew for practice. The coach would yell at him not to smoke. He'd shrug it off like he did whenever he and his buddies got into trouble. He did things his own way, unapologetically. One day, coming out of church, I overheard my dad arguing with the football coach, complaining that Scott didn't get the ball as much as he should. The coach cut to the chase.

"Scott has all the talent in the world, and he'll use only 70 percent of it," he said. "Bob's the opposite. He's a decent player, not the best, but he'll put in 100 percent every second he's out there on the field."

By the time my parents started a family, they had made big strides toward their dream of giving their kids a more comfortable life than they'd had growing up. They both worked when they were first married, my dad as an OB-GYN in private practice based out of Madison General Hospital and my mom as a registered nurse at University Hospital in Madison. They rented a small apartment on the east side of Madison until my younger sister, Pam, was born. Having a third child required more space, so the family moved into our first house, a three-bedroom home on Woodburn Drive on the west side of Madison.

When I was in second grade, we moved into a house my parents built, where I would live until I graduated from college. Our home on Sherwood Road was in a typical middle-class neighborhood. My next-door neighbor's dad was an insurance salesman, and my best friend lived down the street. His dad was a carpenter. My friends and I attended public school, and my graduating class at West High School had about 750 students.

After four years of working as a nurse, my mom stayed home to take care of the kids full time. My dad worked long hours, usually six days a week, taking off Saturday afternoons for Badgers football games and Sundays for church and Packers games. He was a serious man and made sure we all understood that if we wanted something, we had to work for it, to earn it fair and square.

I'll never forget the first lesson he taught me about business. I had started mowing our neighbors' lawns, charging five dollars a pop—big money for a kid in junior high back then. One day, I returned home from a lucrative afternoon with a proud grin on my face and told him about all the money I'd made.

He took a good long look at the mower caked in grass, the tank empty, and said, "You know, son, the lawn mower is not very clean. There's no gas in it. So . . . you're using *my* lawn mower, *my* gas. You're putting wear and tear on it, and you're keeping the five bucks!"

I clearly hadn't thought about the costs that went into running this enterprise.

"Normally, you'd rent a mower from a guy like me *and* buy the gas for it. You're young, but I just want you to understand how business works. Those are called expenses."

For a second there, I thought he might start charging me mower rent and making me pay for the gas.

"Here's what I'm gonna do," he said. "I'll buy the gas, and all you've gotta do is clean the mower when you're done. I want it to look like it's brand new. You've gotta turn it over, clean out all the grass, clean the top, and fill it up."

My father was not the kind of guy who would've laughed if I'd said something like "Aw, come on, Dad. Aren't you being a bit of a hard-ass here?" He commanded respect. Plus, after I thought about it, I realized I was getting a pretty good deal. I wouldn't always have someone covering my expenses, so I agreed to my dad's terms and got good at cleaning that mower to a spit shine.

That conversation with my father, and many others we had over the years, influenced me greatly. It taught me the importance of showing up with a good attitude, working hard, and doing my best to exceed expectations. Those values have guided me in every job I ever had, from umpiring Little League games (one of my favorites) to scrubbing the filth out of apartments that college students had lived in for the school year (one of the worst).

The day after I made that long, sad drive home to Madison from grad school, I was shooting baskets in my backyard when my dad stepped out to say a woman named Sandy Knapp from the Indiana Pacers was on the phone, asking for me. I ran inside, my heart pumping fast. Sandy was the head of public relations for the Pacers, the woman who was supposed to call me the day before. She apologized for not getting back to me, saying she'd had a busy day, then gave me the great news I thought they'd given to someone else: I got the internship. I'd make $500 a month for three months and start at nine o'clock Tuesday morning. It was a Saturday, which gave me barely enough time to line up a place to live—on a friend's living room couch. I packed up my car on Labor Day, made the eight-hour drive to Indianapolis, and showed up for my first day well before the office opened, eager to get started.

The Pacers were entering their third season in the NBA when I joined the team in the fall of 1978. Two years earlier, four American Basketball Association (ABA) franchises (the New York Nets, the Denver Nuggets, the San Antonio Spurs, and the Indiana Pacers) had become part of the NBA during the merger of the two leagues. The NBA was the older, more established league. The ABA was younger, scrappier, and flashier, known for its freewheeling style of play, red-white-and-blue ball, and introduction of the three-point shot. The Pacers thrived in the ABA. Sportswriter Terry Pluto called them "the Boston Celtics of the ABA" in his book *Loose Balls: The Short, Wild Life of the American Basketball Association.*

> No ABA team drew more fans, won more games, won more titles or had more stability than the Indiana Pacers. They won ABA titles in 1970, 1972 and 1973. They lost in the 1969 and 1975 finals, so they played for the title in five of the ABA's nine years.

It was a different story in the NBA. They finished their first season with a 36–46 record. They struggled financially. The NBA had charged each former ABA team a hefty $3.2 million entry fee and barred them from earning any share of national TV revenues for three years. The year before I got there, Coach Bobby "Slick" Leonard and his wife, Nancy—the first woman to serve as GM of an NBA franchise— organized a Save the Pacers telethon, raising more than $2 million to keep the team in Indianapolis. The Pacers didn't even have a sales department when I started my internship.

It was a small office, just 10 or 15 full-time employees, which meant that even a lowly intern could come to weekly staff meetings, sitting at the same table as the general manager and everyone else. We had nobody in charge of selling tickets, so we were all expected to do our part. John Jewett, the team's chairman—who had spearheaded a campaign to keep the Pacers in town during the real threat that they would move—would take off a shoe, pound it on the table, and yell, "I want you to wear down the soles of your shoes, people! Knock on the doors of every office building in Indianapolis! Pound the pavement! Wear out your shoe leather. Sell season tickets!" Despite Mr. Jewett's edict, nobody was selling season tickets.

I did a little of everything as an intern. A lot of everything, actually. I was the go-to delivery and pickup guy for anyone in the office who needed anything. The gofer's gofer. Whatever the bottom rung of the ladder was, I was below it. I didn't mind, though. I had my foot in the door and was taking my first steps toward a career in professional sports. A lot of the work I did was tedious, like stamping checks and entering check numbers on thousands of cards we kept on file for each season ticket holder. Nobody wanted to do that, so I did it.

I also looked for opportunities to contribute in more interesting ways. At one point, I noticed a lot of teams had newsletters, so I proposed that we start one for season ticket holders. I got a thumbs-up from the publicity director and started researching and writing articles, which came pretty naturally; I had been a communications major in college. I got the printing company we used for game programs, business cards, and other materials to print the newsletters at no cost. We sent it out with our season ticket mailings. I got a pat on the back from the publicity director, who gave me shout-outs at staff meetings, saying, "If you have anything for the newsletter, talk to Bob." It made all the gofer duty and lunch deliveries a bit more tolerable.

I was the first one in the office every day and the last one to leave. I didn't know a soul besides the friend whose couch I was sleeping on, so all I did was work, work, work. On game nights, I'd have dinner in the press room and wouldn't get home until midnight or one o'clock in the morning, reporting back to the office at seven. I had no money. My roommate and I lived on hot dogs, bologna, bacon, and chili that he got free from his job at Oscar Mayer. How we dodged heart attacks is anyone's guess.

I learned a lot about logistics while working for the Pacers. The grunt work of last-minute scrambles to pull things off usually fell on me, the guy who gladly did any job thrown his way. One time, we landed this great promotion with Coca-Cola. We'd give away Coke-branded basketballs to the first 5,000 kids who showed up at a Saturday-night game. It was a big deal. The Pacers never had the money to do this kind of promotion, with such a premium giveaway item. Everyone said, "Boy, we're going to sell out the building this night because everybody's gonna bring their kids to get these basketballs!" Everything was coming together.

In a meeting the day before the game, the promotions director turned to me and told me to get the balls to each of the arena entrances. I asked where the balls were being stored and got nothing but blank stares from everyone in the room. They'd all been so excited, no one had fully thought through an important detail: how the basketballs would get from the Coca-Cola warehouse to Market Square

Arena. It became my job to figure it out. I can't tell you how many trips I made during the next two days to and from that warehouse with boxes of promotional basketballs stuffed into a Pacers van, floor to ceiling.

I was still sliding boxes of balls to the entrances as fans poured into the arena. No one with a full paycheck seemed the least bit worried about how close we came to having no basketballs to give away when people showed up for the game. No one gave me an "Attaboy!" for busting my butt to get the job done. They were too busy high-fiving each other for pulling off a great promotion that the fans loved.

There were other last-minute scrambles early on in my career, like the time I had to sub as the public address announcer for a Kansas City Kings game. Nobody had thought about a backup plan in case the regular announcer called in sick. I did OK filling in, but it wasn't the best use of my time and skill set as an assistant general manager. When 18,000 people are paying a lot of money to come see an NBA game, they don't want to listen to some amateur stand-in who's never announced a game in his life. You have to think about every last detail of every game and have contingencies in place in case something falls through. Because, at one point or another, it will.

My three-month internship with the Pacers gave me the last few credits I needed to complete my master's degree in sports administration. My dad was proud that I'd earned a graduate degree but still didn't think working in professional sports would give me the kind of financial stability he and my mom had worked so hard to achieve themselves. Just as the Pacers didn't have a sales department back then, even the NBA didn't have a marketing department. It was nothing like the $10-billion-a-year business it is today. Games typically aired on tape delay after the eleven-o'clock news—even the NBA Finals! There were few job opportunities, not with the league and not with teams, especially at the entry level, where I was. Still, I could tell this was the right career for me to pursue.

After my three-month internship concluded, I was determined to convince the Pacers to hire me as a full-time employee. I asked if I could stay on and sell season tickets on a commission-only basis, echoing the chairman's demand to get more season tickets sold. They told me they had to think about it, as if there was anything to think about. They'd seen how eager and hardworking I was. They needed to sell more tickets, and here I was offering to do it for next to nothing. If I didn't sell tickets, I would go broke fast, so they let me stay. I was thrilled.

At first, I had no clue what I was doing. And no one taught me how to sell a ticket. When I made a call and someone said they weren't interested, I would just hang up and move on to the next phone number. This happened over and over until I talked to a guy working at the gas station where I always filled up my car. When he said yes after my pitch, I wasn't sure what to do next, so I told him I'd have to call him back.

I hated selling tickets, but after a while, I got pretty good at it. I'd tell folks how lucky they were to have an NBA team right in their hometown, how they could see the greatest athletes in the world playing ball about 20 feet away because, as season ticket holders, they'd be guaranteed the best seats in the house.

"It's better than the ballet," I'd say. "It's better than live theater. It's better than the movies, better than football, where you're a mile away from the action. It's better than baseball, quicker and more exciting."

My first "real job" with the Pacers, selling season tickets on commission, was a slight step up from the $500 a month I made as an intern. Ticketing was a manual job back then, a lot of hard work. There were these big books filled with the names of every ticketholder for every full or partial season ticket sold in the arena. It was a tedious job from start (phone calls and door-to-door sales) to finish (printing and mailing out all the tickets). Not very fun, but it paid the bills—for the Pacers and me.

I got my first full-time, salaried position by taking over the business and ticket manager's job after she left on maternity leave. She'd been there awhile, and I knew she made about $20,000 a year. They offered me $12,000 a year to do the same job. My dad thought I was foolish to even consider it.

"How can you live on $12,000 a year?" he implored. "You got your *master's* degree! Are you sure this is the business you want to get into?" He thought I was more valuable than that.

On one level, I knew I was getting screwed. But I also had enough humility to realize that I was new, had a lot to learn, and didn't deserve to make as much as my predecessor, who'd been doing the job for years. The reality was I needed a job. And I knew they needed me, so I came back with a counteroffer. I would take it if they increased my salary to $14,000 a year. They said OK, playing it like they were doing me a big favor.

During my second year in Indiana, the owner was trying to sell the team. Money was tight, so tight that at one point, none of us got a paycheck for six weeks. It wasn't a huge deal for me. I wasn't making that much to begin with and had no problem living frugally. But a lot of people with families and mortgages quit. Those vacancies presented one opportunity after another for me to move up the ladder, taking on more responsibilities with each step. They wouldn't replace the employees who left. They just gave me and anyone else who stayed more to do. I learned a lot about every level of the business from the bottom up that way.

When you're young and single and doing something you love—the games, the business, all of it—you don't really think, *Am I ever going to make enough to support myself?* There was no road map to making a career in pro sports, other than if you were a player. It's a lot different now. Professional sports offer many good jobs today—and a lot of people want them, which makes those jobs hard to land. But if you're good at it, the ladder you climb is pretty tall. You can make a good living. Back then, if you were good and you climbed that ladder, there was no guarantee the career path you charted would lead to financial stability or professional success. It's probably good that I didn't overthink it.

QUICK CLIMB

E VERYTHING I DID DURING MY four years with the Pacers, I learned on the fly. And it wasn't just on-the-job learning. I had to figure things out on my own because with each rung of the ladder I climbed, I replaced someone who'd left because they couldn't afford to keep working for a franchise teetering close to financial collapse. One promotion after another, they would jazz up my title a bit, but they never paid me much more. My biggest bump up the ladder came when Sam Nassi, a businessman from Los Angeles, bought the Pacers. He named his lawyer, who had negotiated the purchase of the team, as acting general manager.

Bob Salyers didn't know a thing about basketball and had no shortage of work on his plate with his full-time law practice, so he promoted me from director of business affairs and promotions to assistant general manager. He basically said, "OK, Bob, I'm going to promote you to assistant general manager. You'll get to do all this stuff you want to do someday. It'll be great!"

The Pacers weren't about to anoint a 25-year-old as their top front-office executive. They didn't have the money to pay me as much as other teams' GMs made, and I was way too young for that title. I didn't care about the title, and Bob didn't want the director of business affairs and promotions to be negotiating contracts. It was a win-win. The Pacers got a screaming deal on a hard-charging top executive who gave it his all without demanding a raise.

Bob Salyers was the closest thing to a mentor I had during my career in pro sports. He didn't exactly take me under his wing and teach me. He let me get involved in the process of negotiating contracts. It was kind of like a seasoned pilot telling a novice to fly a plane, one he wasn't licensed to fly yet. Instead of flying beside me and instructing me as his copilot, he expected me to create my own manual, read it cover to cover, learn everything, then fly. Solo. I experienced a lot of that at every stage in my career. It was frustrating, yet it also pushed me to figure things out fast, make full use of whatever resources I had available (often not many) to get the job done, and move on to the next thing.

Long before it was officially part of my job, I volunteered to scout players, just to get experience. I watched a ton of game tapes. I drove to nearby college games to check out up-and-coming players. I wrote up scouting reports. The coaches would thank me, let me know what observations were helpful, and give me tips on what I could do better. They didn't always use the reports, and I didn't expect them to. I just liked getting out there to develop an eye for talent. I also took trips on my own up to Chicago to watch our upcoming opponents play the Bulls, the only NBA team within driving distance of Indianapolis. I watched the games closely and took notes on all their plays, what signals the coaches used. I learned a lot about the Xs and Os of pro basketball that way. It deepened my understanding of the game from a technical perspective. It gave me a sharper view of our team's strengths and weaknesses, which helped me get better and better at scouting.

Early on in my self-education in scouting, I took several trips to Terre Haute, where a fifth-year senior named Larry Bird was having one heck of a final season at Indiana State. The Celtics had drafted him in 1978, when he was a junior. Because he had transferred to Indiana State, he could play one more year of college ball. Boston's legendary general manager, Red Auerbach, bet big on Bird, using a first-round pick on a player exercising his final year of NCAA eligibility. The Celtics would have to wait an entire season before Bird could actually sign a contract. And if he didn't do so by April of his senior year, he could reenter the draft, and another team could take him.

Like most who scouted Larry Bird, I could definitely tell he was NBA material. In his last year leading the Indiana State Sycamores, he averaged 28.6 points and 14.9 rebounds per game. The team started the season unranked and finished number one in the nation. The only game they lost was the NCAA championship against Earvin "Magic" Johnson and the Michigan State Spartans. The Hick from French Lick was named National Player of the Year, but not everyone was sold on him.

What I couldn't tell yet about Larry Bird was whether he'd be a starter, much less the superstar he became. He was a skilled passer and an amazing shooter. I thought he could play both big forward and small forward for any team but wasn't sure if he was quick enough defensively. I wondered if the competition he played against at a school as small as Indiana State was up to par with the level of talent he would face in the NBA. And he was a fifth-year player. Normally, if a guy's been in college five years, he won't get that much better, whereas if you see him in his first year, you might say, "Hey, that guy's going to get a lot better because he's still got more years to develop."

For a while, it wasn't clear if Bird would sign with the Celtics. He eventually did, and the rest is history. The more I saw him play—especially close up on the Pacers' home court—the more I realized that it's not all about how fast you can run or how high you can jump. What Larry Bird lacked defensively in foot speed and lateral quickness—the things that caused so many scouts to underestimate him—he made up for with basketball smarts. He was an extremely smart player. A basketball savant. Some players are incredibly gifted athletically, but no matter what lengths you go to when teaching them offensive and defensive plays, they don't get it. You can write it down and explain every maneuver step by step. You can go out on the court and walk them through it. They're listening to you, but they still don't get it.

With guys like Larry Bird, Michael Jordan, and other Hall of Famers, you don't even have to show them. They understand plays instinctively. That intangible skill is hard to scout and measure. Players who really know what they're supposed to be doing, what the other team is trying to do, too—that's a rare gift. Not only do they know *their* team's plays, but they know exactly what the competition is about to do. So when the coach yells, "Play two!" they beat the player to the spot where the pass is going and steal the ball. And they make it look easy.

In 1979, the year Larry Bird entered the NBA, I watched him in awe as he developed into a prime-time ball player. As I continued to hone my scouting skills, I remembered him and the "it" factors he had that are harder to spot and even trickier to measure: intuitive basketball smarts, passion for the game, competitiveness. I didn't beat myself up for underestimating Larry Bird. Everybody but Red Auerbach had.

Scouting is tedious work. Being a good talent evaluator is part science and part art. You have to have a feel for it, which takes time and lots of practice. Great scouts have good instincts, do their homework, and possess the courage to make bold predictions about which players will succeed and which will fail. *Most* scouts can't put all three of those pieces together. Even if they can do the first two, they may not have the confidence to make a stand and say, "I think that guy can play, and here's why" or "I don't think he can play, and here's why." The vast majority of people in this business—scouts, coaches, general managers, anyone involved with recruiting players—do their fair share of sitting on fences. "Well, he could really be good if . . . ," or "He might fail if . . . ," and so on. They answer it both ways so that whatever ends up happening down the road, they can say, "I told you so."

An accomplished GM like Red Auerbach will miss on a lot of first-round picks during his storied career. He could afford to make mistakes. He was the original godfather of the NBA. Before leading the Celtics as GM, he had proven his worth many times over as one of the most successful coaches of all time. He led Boston to nine NBA championships during his 16 years as the Celtics coach in the 1950s and '60s. A lot of Red's first-round picks turned out to be nothing, but the ones who did work out were grand slams: Larry Bird, Robert Parish, Kevin McHale, Danny Ainge. All icons of basketball who played pivotal roles on incredibly talented and successful teams.

I had zero clout in my early days as a general manager, which made it pretty nerve-racking to go up against the likes of Red Auerbach, Jerry West, and other established GMs when drafting or trading players. I was just 25 when the Pacers made me the top front-office executive.

The first big contract I negotiated was for Clark Kellogg, a power forward from Ohio State who had earned All Big-Ten Conference and Most Valuable Player honors in college. He was our first-round draft pick in 1982 (eighth overall).

Clark's agent, Everett Glenn, tried to rattle me the first time we spoke about his contract. "Bob, don't take this the wrong way, but I've never heard of an assistant general manager negotiating a first-round pick before."

"Well, don't feel bad, Everett. There are a lot of general managers who have never negotiated a first-round pick." Back in those days, owners would often take the lead in negotiating first-round picks. I'd never done one, so he was trying to knock me back on my heels. I tried to level the playing field a little bit by telling him, "I'm just like all these other guys, and I'm the guy you're dealing with, so let's get on with it."

I didn't have a lot to work with. My budget was $1 million over five years. Clark was easily worth twice that. He knew it, his agent knew it, and I knew it, but I had no wiggle room.

The owner had kept things simple. "We have $1 million total," he told me, "$200,000 a year. That's all the money we have. We don't care if you sign him. We don't care if he ever plays. That's the most we have, so good luck."

At times, Glenn and I were screaming at each other on the phone. At times, we talked for hours. Ultimately, I got Clark Kellogg signed far below his market value. Clark's only other option was to sit out a year and reenter the draft, which no player had ever tried. Between my determination, my persistence, and the reality that we truly didn't have more money, I wore his agent down. When you don't have anything else to give, it's a lot easier to hold your ground. It was great to get Clark signed, but to this day, I feel kind of bad about it. He should've gotten more money, even though I gave him all we had.

The year before, I had negotiated some second-round picks, a big deal for me. Agents chewed me out, calling me every name in the book, trying to get in my head and prey on my inexperience. They told me I would screw up so badly that I would singlehandedly ruin the franchise, I'd be the reason nobody would come to the games. It was pretty intimidating stuff for a guy in his mid-20s to be treated like such a punching bag, but taking all those hits had given me amazing experience. I relished it as a crash course in negotiating fundamentals.

Some of the wisdom I gleaned early in my career had nothing to do with basketball, like the time I had to break up a fight between the two girlfriends of one player. It happened in the stands of a Pacers home game. The player approached me before the game with a request: that I seat one of his girlfriends on one side of the arena and the other one on the opposite side. My job was to handle it discreetly, to make sure neither knew the other was there.

I thought I had pulled it off, but during a time-out, one of the girlfriends, dressed like a supermodel, walked across the court, then up the aisle toward the section where I sat with my friend and Pacers marketing director Basil DeVito. "Oh no. This can't be good," I said right before the woman dumped a giant cup of beer on the other girl-friend's head, just a few rows behind us.

Basil and I scrambled to the feud, pulling the women aside and escorting each in a different direction, the whole arena watching with bated breath as we tried to defuse the situation. From that day on, whenever anyone spotted me and Basil together, they'd say, "Look! There go Starsky and Hutch!"

It was the first time I had to interrupt a fight between women our players were dating (or married to), but it wouldn't be the last. It was pretty common for players to have more than one romance in their lives at any given time. I didn't enjoy playing a behind-the-scenes role in players' love lives, but I did have a job to do: minimize the risk that any drama would upset a player and throw him off his game. Like a lot of my on-the-job learning, there was no training manual for this. I never expected to have to break up a brawl between girlfriends, wives, or even players themselves, like I'd do years later in Seattle, when two of our stars had a fight so fierce it spilled out from the lobby of our front-office building into the street—right in front of the radio station that covered our games (more on that in chapter 9). In the heat of the moment, there's no time to do anything except follow your instincts, act quickly, and do all you can to straighten out whatever's going sideways.

I was always ready to jump on a job that got thrown my way, even if it wasn't in my job description. A few times, I got invited to sub in at practice when players were sick or nursing injuries and they needed an extra body for a five-on-five scrimmage. Back then, we had only one assistant coach, unlike teams today, which typically have ten or more, many of them former pros just a few years out from playing in the NBA.

Our lone assistant coach, George Irvine, had played in the NBA for several years but was all banged up and a chain smoker, so Head Coach Jack McKinney turned to me. At six foot three and 200 pounds, I was probably the only guy on staff who had the size and athleticism not to get killed in a scrimmage with NBA players. I had played basketball only one year in college (my first), but I loved the game, so I stayed in shape and kept my basketball skills sharp by playing in some pretty competitive city leagues.

Coach McKinney set some ground rules for me when I subbed in. First and foremost: no shooting. If I had an uncontested layup, I could take it. Otherwise, my main jobs were to push the ball, play defense, and pass. Now and then, one of the guys would gripe, "Shoot the ball!" when I'd pass instead of taking an open shot. I'd just shrug it off with a smile and keep swimming in my lane.

Running full speed up and down the court with NBA players was a lung-burning thrill. Going toe to toe with these guys gave me a whole new level of respect for how strong, fast, and fluid they were. Some guys were so graceful, so explosive, they could get by me so quickly I didn't even have a chance to foul them. Sometimes, I'd be pushing with all my strength, but the guy I was defending wouldn't budge an inch. Then he would turn around, give me a shove like he was swatting a fly, and move me five feet back. I was playing like it was the fourth quarter of a championship game, and they'd be giving it their just-got-out-of-bed half speed, which was still incredible.

A few years later, in Kansas City, I played on a semipro team that regularly drew a couple thousand fans excited to watch NBA players up close in the off-season. Kings forward center Ed Nealy was the best on my team. I held my own, usually scoring ten or so points a game, mostly three-pointers. I rarely went inside the paint. The guys were too big. I knew I had a better chance of taking an elbow to the nose than making a shot if I tried to drive to the hoop. Now and then, I'd make a rare exception.

Once, we were playing a team with two Kings starters: center Joe C. Meriweather, one of only a few NBA players who ever managed to block ten shots in a single game more than once, and Larry Drew, a guard who averaged 20 points a game and eight assists during his best year with the Kings. At one point during the game, I started barreling in, stopped shy of Joe C. Meriweather to avoid his notoriously powerful block, then lobbed a teardrop so high I thought it would be an air ball. When the floater swished, Meriweather chuckled and shook his head. "Damn, boss. Not bad!" We finished third in a league of 12 teams that summer.

During my first year with the Sonics, I came in one Saturday morning to watch a couple of draft prospects run through drills and scrimmage. We didn't have enough guys to get a five-on-five game going, but when I walked in wearing sweats and gym shoes, Coach Bernie Bickerstaff asked if I could play a little two-on-two with the two prospects, Derrick McKey and Olden Polynice, and our video coordinator, Paul Woolpert. I was 31 by then, not as quick as I'd been during my time with the Pacers and Kings, but still good enough to hold my own for a 15- or 20-minute half-court game. I remember Polynice defending me pretty hard, his left arm wedged firmly against my back as I tried unsuccessfully to post up. By the end of the workout, I was drenched head to toe and headed home impressed with both prospects. When I got home from the workout, my wife gasped as she saw blood all over the back of my sweatshirt.

"Bob! Are you hurt?" she yelped. I had no idea what she was talking about, then remembered that our video coordinator had been wearing a watch that had scratched Polynice on the arm while we were playing. He wasn't bleeding profusely, but it was enough to cover just about every inch of the back of my sweatshirt with dabs of red. It looked like I had backed into one hell of a bar fight. That might've been the last time I went shoulder to shoulder with NBA players. I had more than enough on my plate as president and GM at that point, toward the end of my first season with the Sonics.

This would never happen today, of course. Most teams have so many assistant coaches, they'd never run short if extra bodies were needed. And no matter how good you might be, chances are the front office wouldn't want anyone without an NBA pedigree working out anywhere near their multimillion-dollar assets. Nor would they want to risk having their multimillion-dollar assets injure some guy who's never played pro ball.

Lucky for me, I got into NBA management back when it was scrappy enough for me to go up and down the court with these phenomenal athletes. It deepened my appreciation for just how elite you have to be to make it into the NBA. I thought I knew the game pretty well, and I did, having played it for most of my life. Yet something about the experience of running alongside players like George McGinnis, Joe C. Meriweather, Derrick McKey, and Olden Polynice helped me better understand just how amazing these athletes are, the exceptional strength, speed, and talent I needed to look for as I set out to build winning teams.

CHAPTER 4

TRAIN WRECK

THE SONICS WERE A TRAIN wreck when I first got there in the spring of 1986, nothing like the fabled franchise that had won Seattle's first and only NBA championship seven years earlier. For two years straight, they had won just 31 games, the second-worst record in the NBA in 1984–85 and the following season. They'd missed the playoffs both years, too. The team was losing money. Fans had stopped going to games, furious at owner Barry Ackerley for making one mistake after another. He didn't re-sign Gus "the Wizard" Williams, a beloved and high-scoring member of the 1979 championship team, trading him for Ricky Sobers and Tim McCormick, neither of whom had done much of note for the team during their two years in Seattle.

Another big loss for the Sonics occurred in 1984: "Downtown Freddie Brown," who had captained the championship team, retired after 13 spectacular seasons. Freddie had played more seasons with the Sonics than any player in franchise history at the time, but Ackerley thought he was no longer an asset to the team, so one day, he told Freddie he wouldn't renew his contract after it expired.

While the Los Angeles Lakers and Boston Celtics regularly sold out their arenas as fans flocked to see Magic Johnson and Larry Bird,

Seattle ranked close to dead last in the NBA for attendance, averaging 7,300 seats per game—just half of Seattle Center Coliseum's capacity. The team was in horrible shape financially, losing millions of dollars during Ackerley's first two years of ownership. That was what bothered him the most. He made that clear from the get-go.

"I don't want to lose any more money," he told me as he interviewed me to replace him as president. Understandable. No one likes losing money. But I was curious. How important to him was it for the Sonics to start winning more games? He made his priorities clear: "The first thing is I don't want to lose any more money. After that, I want to win games."

Barry Ackerley was in the advertising business. Billboards, radio, TV. He bought the Sonics in 1983. Few NBA team owners appoint themselves as president because they want someone with experience scouting talent, negotiating contracts, managing coaches and players, securing sponsorships, all the things it takes to run a winning, profitable team. It took Barry two years to figure out he wasn't the right guy for the job. He invited me in for an interview when I was second in command with the Sacramento Kings. We first met when I was the point man for the team's relocation from Kansas City. He served on the ownership committee that reviewed and approved the Kings' move in 1985.

Moving a team is a big deal. It's difficult to pull off—complex, often controversial, the threat of lawsuits looming every which way. I led the Kings' relocation effort, which was very challenging but also presented a great opportunity for me professionally. It gave me the chance to meet movers and shakers in the NBA, to make a name for myself as an earnest up-and-comer with the work ethic, business savvy, and confidence to close difficult deals.

The Kings were a struggling franchise when I joined the team as vice president of marketing in 1982. The following year, an investment group from Sacramento bought the team, publicly pledged to do everything they could to turn things around, restore the team to profitability, and keep the Kings in Kansas City. But the team continued to lose money, so partway through the 1984–85 season, owner Gregg Lukenbill and general manager Joe Axelson announced they would not be renewing the Kings' lease at Kemper Arena and put me in charge of making the move to Sacramento.

As I made my pitch to a committee of NBA owners, half of them were looking at me like, *Yeah, right. Your team's lousy in Kansas City, and it's going to be lousy in sleepy Sacramento. You're just giving us all these rosy projections because you've got to show us you'll do a better job there than you're doing here, or we won't allow you to move.* Nobody said we had no chance of succeeding, but they made it clear they had their doubts.

No one talked about Sacramento in the context of professional sports. They'd been the on-again, off-again hometown for a minor league baseball team—the Sacramento Senators, later the Solons—until 1976, when the team moved south and became the San Jose Missions of the Pacific Coast League. That was about it. To root for a "home" team, Sacramento sports fans had to drive 90 miles to San Francisco or Oakland. Sacramento was a ripe, untapped market that welcomed its very own NBA franchise with unbridled enthusiasm.

I moved out to Sacramento a few months ahead of the team to start the enormous amount of work required to get a franchise off the ground in a new city. On very short order, I hired every employee for the business operation—all while we were still playing in Kansas City. There was so much to do and no blueprint to follow. I hired, then trained, the stats crew. What's a turnover? What's an assist? When do you change the 24-second clock? Every detail of an operation that I was used to other people doing. But at the time, when you started a team someplace new, nobody knew anything, so you had to start at square one. You had to negotiate agreements to broadcast games on local radio and TV. You had to set ticket prices. You had to hire and train your sales staff to sell seats.

For a while, I held pretty much every job in the front office. Not a day passed that I wasn't making a speech to a civic or community group or a potential team sponsor, not to mention never-ending requests for media interviews. As if all that wasn't enough, Sacramento had no arena suitable for an NBA game, so we had to build our own. It was a lot, but in the end, we got it all done. We sold out every home game that first season—a streak that would last 12 years, almost 500 games. We improved our record to 37 wins and made the playoffs, and even though we got swept by the Houston Rockets in the first round, it was a thrill for our fans that we were in the playoffs with the league's best teams. (The Houston Rockets went on to face the Boston Celtics in the NBA Finals, losing in six games.)

It was quite a franchise turnaround. We went from losing money in Kansas City to ranking fifth in the league in revenue our first season in Sacramento, in large part because of an arena naming-rights deal I spearheaded—the first of its kind in professional sports. Unlike publicly financed arenas, often named after politicians and civic leaders who helped secure the funds to build them, the Kings' arena would be built with private money. One day, owner Gregg Lukenbill asked if we could call the arena anything we wanted.

"Yeah," I said. "You can name it Kings Arena. You can call it Lukenbill Palace!"

He came back a few days later and asked, "How about we put a corporate sponsor's name on it?"

"I don't see why not," I said.

We hired a marketing firm to take the first crack at finding us a title sponsor. Gregg offered them 10 percent of whatever deal they lined up. They worked on it and worked on it and, after several months, came up with nothing. No bites. That was how the naming-rights deal got added to my already-overflowing plate, but I wasn't about to say no to a groundbreaking opportunity like this. I did an enormous amount of homework developing the concept. The only other corporate sponsorship naming-rights deal I could find was the Carrier Dome at Syracuse University, named after an air-conditioning company that had helped finance the stadium's construction.

I had to get NBA approval before pitching any potential naming-rights sponsors, and they pushed back hard. TV networks paid big bucks to broadcast games, and the league didn't want any sponsors to get "free advertising" by having their name on the arena, on the court, in the news. They said no at first, but I kept negotiating as I made one cold call after another. I must've pitched 20 different companies. In a lot of cases, the amount we were asking—$1 million a year, as I recall—was more than their annual advertising budgets. Each team that heard my pitch responded with some version of "This is a lot of money you're talking about. And no one's done this before. What makes you so confident it'll be worth our while?"

Honestly, our asking price felt a bit out of our league, too. The biggest sponsorship we'd had in Kansas City was $50,000 a year. Most companies turned me away, definitively not interested. I got some traction with Apple and Toyota. I joked that not every company would be suitable for this kind of sponsorship. Think about it: Who would want to go to Preparation H Arena?

The most promising inroads I made were with Atlantic Richfield Company (ARCO). After multiple meetings with the oil and gas company's advertising agency, they invited me down to their headquarters in Los Angeles, where I made my pitch to a roomful of executives. Most of them looked intrigued, in a good way, until Chairman Lod Cook started drilling me with lots of questions, telling me to speed up my presentation because he had to leave to catch a plane. He said he didn't like the idea and put his staff on the spot, asking for someone to speak up in support of this newfangled naming-rights deal. Silence.

I felt sure I was going down in flames, but as the meeting ended, he came up to me and said, "Walk with me." As we headed out of the room, he said, "I assume everyone who works for me likes this. Otherwise, you wouldn't have been able to get a meeting with me."

"Yeah," I said. "Clearly, they *loved* it!"

"Yeah," he said, "but as soon as I don't love it, you see how quickly they don't love it? Look, we're going to do a deal, but here's what you need to understand. Everything you told me was about marketing and impressions and cost per thousand—typical advertising stuff, all the exposure ARCO would get. I want you to tweak some of that.

"Here's the reason I'm going to do it: Here I am in Los Angeles. I'm a large oil company. You're up in the capital of California . . . I'm paying 18 full-time lobbyists, who sit up in Sacramento and lobby the politicians about every piece of legislation that involves the oil industry. California state government is hugely important to our company. If this arena naming-rights sponsorship can give us some recognition for helping bring the Kings to Sacramento and we have use of the venue to schmooze and entertain politicians, I would support this more from a government affairs angle than a marketing angle. But don't get me wrong, I need them both."

I reworked my pitch, came in strong with the community and political affairs angle, and landed the deal: $7 million over ten years. That's how the home court of Sacramento's NBA team became ARCO

Arena. At first, the media refused to call it ARCO Arena in print or on the air. We pushed back, and so did they. In a meeting with the editors and publishers of the *Sacramento Bee*, they said ARCO spends a lot of money on advertising—money the paper stood a good chance of losing if ARCO got all this "free advertising." The NBA also kept pushing back hard. After a lot of back-and-forth, the league reluctantly let us move forward with the deal, provided we did not put the ARCO logo on the stadium floor. We compromised and agreed to use only the words "ARCO Arena"—no logo. Then we had to negotiate camera positions so ARCO's name wouldn't get overexposed. Who would've guessed it would be easier to get California's Department of Transportation to put ARCO Arena on highway signs than it would be to get permission to use the name inside our own building?

Since then, naming rights have become standard for major sports venues. They've grown a lot more valuable, too. In 2021, the Los Angeles Clippers and financial software maker Intuit sealed a 20-year naming-rights deal, reportedly worth at least $500 million, which would be more than one-third of the projected $1.2 billion cost of their new arena. Not to be outdone, the Los Angeles Lakers sold the naming rights to their existing arena, the Staples Center, to cryptocurrency platform and exchange Crypto.com. The 20-year deal is reportedly worth $700 million. Twenty years ago, Staples paid $116 million for the naming rights to the same arena.

When we landed the ARCO deal, Gregg Lukenbill called me into his office, ecstatic and eager to reward me for my efforts.

"I want to do something for you, Bob," he said, praising me for all the hard work I had put into closing this innovative deal. He credited me with essentially saving the Kings 10 percent of the revenue they would have had to pay a consulting firm to do what I'd done as a sala-ried employee, without extra pay.

I liked where he was going with this. Ten percent of $7 million would be a life-changing bonus for me!

"I'm going to buy you a Mercedes," Gregg said.

I did not own a car but was happy using a promotional car Toyota provided as part of its sponsorship with the team. I didn't need or want a flashy car of my own.

"Gee, Gregg, that's generous," I said. "But honestly, I'd rather have the cash. In fact, you could pay me less than what the Mercedes will cost and save money!"

"No," he said. "I want to make a statement. I want everyone to see that when you go above and beyond, the owner will take care of you."

So he bought me a 420 SEL Mercedes, a fancier car than I cared to drive. I didn't hold it against him. It was nice to be acknowledged for doing a job well.

This all went down during Barry Ackerley's second year as the Sonics' owner. As he was running his team into the ground, he saw me take the Kings from the outhouse to the penthouse financially. Not only did I make good on all the promising projections I had pitched the NBA regarding the Kings' proposed move to Sacramento, but I also put together what amounted to the greatest billboard deal ever, only instead of a billboard, it was a building with the sponsor's name on it, sitting at the junction of two of Northern California's busiest highways: Interstates 5 and 80. Ackerley must've been thinking, *Wow, I've never dreamed of a billboard like that before.*

I was visiting Seattle frequently at the time, dating the Sonics' vice president of marketing and broadcasting. Jan Sundberg and I met at an NBA business meeting in Salt Lake City while I was with the Kings in Kansas City. She had moved to Seattle after working for ABC Sports in New York, and Barry hired her shortly after he bought the team. Jan and I had recently gotten engaged, and she planned to move to Sacramento, but before the 1985–86 season ended, Barry asked Jan if I would be willing to meet him on my next visit to Seattle. At our first meeting, he told me he wanted a new president. He saw me take a bad Kansas City team and turn them into a gold mine in Sacramento and wanted me to do the same thing in Seattle.

I was in line to become the number one guy in Sacramento, but there was no telling how long it would take for Joe Axelson to give up the reins as general manager. The chance to be the number one guy in Seattle—at age 30—seemed like a golden opportunity. Jan was from Seattle. She had family and friends in Seattle. She wanted to stay. And I wanted the chance to rebuild an NBA franchise, to give the city a team to be excited about again. So I asked Gregg Lukenbill if he would let me out of my contract in Sacramento, and he obliged. I then negotiated with Barry, shook hands on a three-year deal to replace him as president, and moved up to Seattle, determined to get a wrecked train repaired and back on track.

Before agreeing to take the job, I wanted to make sure that the Sonics GM, Lenny Wilkens, would be OK with me as his boss. Coming into a high-level job as a young guy, I didn't want to ruffle the feathers of a future Hall of Famer. Lenny was a legend in Seattle. I had great respect for him. He had played for the Sonics in the late 1960s and early '70s, had played *and* coached from 1969 to 1972. He had been head coach for the Sonics in 1979, when they'd won the NBA championship. After missing the playoffs in the 1984–85 season, he had been fired as head coach and reassigned to the front office as general manager. When I asked Barry what Lenny thought of me taking over as the Sonics' president, Barry assured me Lenny was on board.

"I told him, and he's happy about it. He's excited!" Barry said.

To get off on the right foot, I wanted my first meeting to be with Lenny and for Barry to be there, too.

"Great," Barry said. "Let's meet Saturday at the Sonics office. You, me, and Lenny. We'll have a great meeting."

That Saturday, as I walked toward the Sonics office on Queen Anne Avenue, I saw Lenny coming down the sidewalk, and he cheerfully said, "Hey, Bob, what are *you* doing here?"

"What do you mean what am I doing here? Has Barry talked to you about me?"

"No," Lenny said. "About what?"

During a short and awkward elevator ride, I let Lenny know Barry had approached me about replacing Barry as president and that I was interested as long as I wouldn't be stepping on Lenny's toes.

When we got up to the Sonics office on the second floor, Barry greeted us briefly, said, "Well, you both know each other. Why don't you finish your meeting, and, Bob, call me later?" Then he walked away.

We couldn't believe it. A professional to his core, Lenny listened intently as I shared highlights of everything Barry and I had talked about during the interview process, my vision for transforming a slow, walk-it-up-the-court offense to a fast-paced, athletic game.

Lenny liked the sound of it, especially the part about me taking over as president. "Bob, I don't want to be the general manager. The only reason I am is that Barry fired me as coach and said I'd have to serve as GM to get paid for the rest of my contract. I'm not a GM. I'm a coach."

When I asked if he would like to coach again, he said, "Absolutely!"

I told him I'd see what I could do.

As we wrapped up, he said, "By the way, Bob, I'd rather have you as a boss than Barry, any day. If I can't find a coaching job and I stay here as GM, I'd love to learn from you and work with you. Boy, it'd be a lot better than working for Barry. The only time Barry ever meets with anybody is when he's mad at you or wants to fire somebody."

During my first week or so in Seattle, I made some calls around the league. Wayne Embry was the new general manager of the Cleveland Cavaliers and was looking for a coach. When I told him Lenny really wanted to coach, Wayne said, "You're kidding. I love Lenny Wilkens!" Lenny was equally excited.

Barry was not. He didn't want to let Lenny out of the end of his contract.

"Look, Barry," I said, "we're going to let him out if he wants to go."

And we did. Lenny went on to coach the Cavaliers and several other teams over the next two decades, retiring in 2005 as one of the winningest NBA coaches of all time.

Once Lenny left, I told Barry I wanted to hire a new general manager. His answer was no. "*You're* the general manager."

The president's job was a lot, in and of itself. I was running the entire business operation, with oversight of everything from ticket and sponsorship sales to accounting, event management, and public relations. As general manager, I would also be responsible for selecting every player and coach for the team. As GM, I would have to spend an enormous amount of time scouting college and NBA players while also running the entire business. By letting Lenny out of his contract, Barry wouldn't have to pay his salary anymore, yet he didn't offer me more money, just more responsibility. It was clear he would be a tough owner to work for, but I agreed to take on the GM job. I would learn a lot. And if I did the job well, I would make a positive impact on the team, the fans, and the city I would call home for many years to come.

I worked around the clock during those first several weeks. There was so much to do. My first priority on the business side was to become profitable and draw fans back to the games, excited about the Sonics again. Seattle is a great sports town, but the fans had little appetite to support the brand of basketball Barry was selling. The draft was in less than a month. I was moving at warp speed and barely had time to be bothered that Barry kept dodging me when I asked him about my contract, which remained in handshake limbo. We hadn't signed anything. He kept promising me it would happen, and at a certain point, I realized the only way it would get done was if I did it. With a lawyer's help, I drew up a simple, straightforward contract, putting everything we'd agreed to in writing, and set up a meeting at Barry's corporate office. When I presented my contract, he looked it over, saying "Yep, yep, yep . . ." as he read each line. Then, when he got to the terms, he grabbed his pen, crossed out year three, and initialed it.

"Barry, what are you doing? We had a three-year deal!"

I'll never forget what he said as he looked up and pushed the contract across the desk. "I'll know if you're any good after *two*."

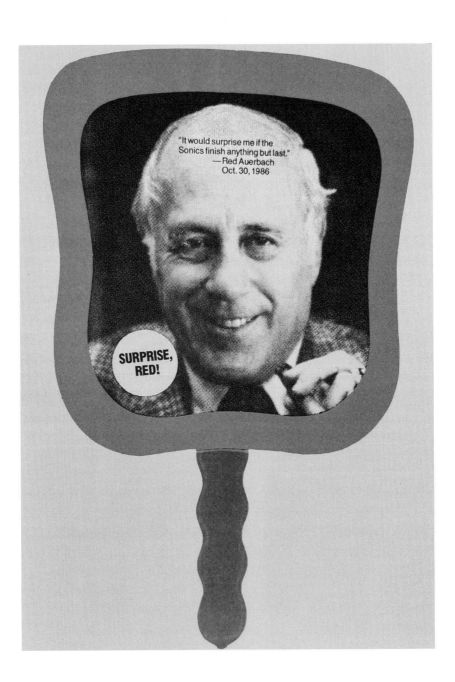

CHAPTER 5

CLEANING HOUSE

THE FIRST TIME I WAS dispatched to a meeting with high-level NBA executives and GMs, I had no business being in the room. It was 1980, my second year with the Pacers. I was 24, working hard, and moving up in the organization, which was going through some serious upheaval under new owners who didn't want anyone from the old regime representing the Pacers anymore. So when it came time for an NBA Competition Committee meeting to discuss the state of the game, potential rule changes, referees, and other business, acting general manager Bob Salyers—who knew nothing about basketball—told me, "You're coming with me, Whitsitt."

As we headed up to Chicago, he made it clear he wanted me to contribute to the conversation, to share my opinions on issues of importance. We weren't going just to sit there and listen. He would introduce us, but then it was up to me to serve as the face and voice for the Pacers. Me, the 24-year-old kid who'd been the gofer intern two years before. I had only recently started making enough money to move off my friend's living room couch and into my own apartment. If I'd had any choice in the matter, I would've kept quiet out of respect for the seasoned pros who could speak from decades of experience.

But I had my orders, so when the three-point shot came up for discussion, I worked up the nerve to chime in. "The three-pointer is the most exciting play in basketball," I said. "It gives coaches additional in-game strategy, and fans love it. The NBA should adopt it."

All the old-timers in the room glared at me like, *Who the hell does this chump think he is?* I had spoken up right after Celtics GM Red Auerbach had argued against the three-point shot, calling it a gimmick. It had originated in the ABA, one more reason NBA traditionalists hated it. While I had the floor, I also questioned why we gave players three attempts to make two foul shots or two attempts to make one.

"It's stupid," I said. "It makes the game longer. College players don't get an extra free throw, so why should the best basketball players in the world need an additional attempt? If our guys are such bad free throw shooters, maybe we should get better players."

On the trip back to Indianapolis, Bob Salyers commended me for speaking up, especially as the youngest one in the room. "You made some good arguments," he said, "but you've gotta be more forceful." It was good advice that I took to heart and followed dutifully in the years to come.

The NBA *did* adopt the three-pointer, first on a trial basis at the start of the 1979–80 season, when Larry Bird and Magic Johnson came in as rookies. It's been part of the game ever since. And the extra foul shot became a thing of the past beginning with the 1981–82 season. Maybe I *did* belong in that room, after all. It was the first of many opportunities I seized to make forward-looking arguments that challenged the status quo—and prevailed.

I got used to being the youngest one in the room for the next decade or so. Soon after joining the Sonics as the youngest top executive in the NBA, I learned that Barry had hired me without realizing I was only 30. He figured it out after my age came up in a radio interview. A lot of people thought I looked older than I was. I'd never met anyone my age who had anywhere close to the depth and breadth of experience I had gained in the first eight years of my career. I was driven and disciplined and had a lot of hands-on knowledge about the inner workings of struggling NBA franchises, which gave me the confidence to go about transforming the Sonics, starting with the roster.

I had very little time to prepare for my first NBA draft in 1986. I joined the team in May, and the draft took place in mid-June. The time crunch was a big enough challenge on its own. An even bigger disadvantage: I had no first-round pick. Ackerley had traded it to the Celtics the year before for Gerald Henderson, a mediocre player who had famously stolen a pass and scored a game-tying layup in Game Two of the 1984 NBA Finals against the Los Angeles Lakers.

It was an unquestionably outstanding play and impressed Ackerley so much he decided that Henderson would be worth more to the Sonics than a future first-round pick (which turned out to be the *second* pick overall). If Ackerley had taken a step back and looked at the big picture, he might have seen Henderson's brilliant steal in that pivotal game for what it was: a dazzling fluke by a pedestrian player.

This is why owners of professional sports franchises have no business being general managers. They often make bad decisions based on starry-eyed, rash judgments. And their teams pay the price. Gerald Henderson played as unremarkably in Seattle as he had in Boston. The Sonics finished the 1984–85 and 1985–86 seasons 31–51, missing the playoffs both years and ranking among the bottom six teams in the entire league. I traded Henderson six games into the 1986–87 season.

(The Celtics had expected great things from Len Bias, the All-American forward they drafted with the pick Ackerley had traded away. Instead, they mourned his tragic death from a cocaine overdose two days after the draft.)

The lack of a first-round pick in 1986 definitely held us back in my first NBA draft, but the North Carolina State point guard we selected 30th overall in the second round became a fan favorite who played his entire career in Seattle. In his first season, Nate McMillan tied Ernie DiGregorio's NBA rookie record for assists in a single game (25). McMillan started at point guard for the next four years, ranking among the league's leaders in assists. Nate was an excellent floor general and a superb defensive player. Defense became the hallmark of our great Sonics teams in the early to mid-90s, anchored by McMillan and Gary Payton. Each led the NBA in steals for a season, and together, they created havoc on opposing backcourts. McMillan retired as a player in 1998, then coached in Seattle for another seven years, first as an assistant under Paul Westphal and later as head coach. He went on to coach the Portland Trail Blazers, Indiana Pacers, and Atlanta Hawks, but in Seattle, he's still known as "Mr. Sonic" for the 19 years he dedicated to the Sonics.

One of the most challenging trades I had to make that first year (1986) was for our last remaining superstar from the 1979 NBA championship team, who had demanded it before I got there. Jack Sikma had played every game of his nine-year career for Seattle, but after the Sonics missed the playoffs two years in a row, he wanted out. There were only a few teams he was willing to be traded to, and I assured him I would do everything I could to work out a deal with one of them. It was the least he deserved. After talks with several teams, I zeroed in on the Milwaukee Bucks as the best option for both Sikma and the Sonics.

The Bucks had been doing well in the regular season but kept falling short in the playoffs because they needed a stronger center. In exchange for Sikma, I wanted Milwaukee's Alton Lister (a defensive center) and two future first-round draft picks. They countered with Lister and two *second*-round picks, probably figuring I would cave. But I held my ground. I knew those two first-round picks could prove valuable as I rebuilt the team, whether I was drafting players or negotiating trades. We went back and forth a few times, and I wound up getting exactly what I wanted: an up-and-coming center and those two first-round picks.

The deal worked out well for the Sonics. Lister was athletic enough to play the kind of faster-paced game that I firmly believed would lift Seattle out of its rut. More than just a tall guy who could score in the paint and grab rebounds, Lister could run and block shots, contributing both offensively and defensively. The best season of his 17-year career as an NBA player was his first in Seattle. And those two first-round picks? They got us two players who became important assets in the formation of a fantastic team: Derrick McKey in 1987 and Shawn Kemp in 1989.

I traded most of the roster during my first few months in Seattle, the spring and summer of 1986, pretty much everybody except forwards Xavier McDaniel and Tom Chambers. I brought in veteran players like Clemon Johnson (Philadelphia's backup center) and Maurice

Lucas (a power forward the Lakers had recently cut and placed on waivers). Both had championship experience, an important part of my strategy. You need veterans who have had success, who know the difference between regular season and playoff basketball and can impart that wisdom and work ethic to the younger players. To get Clemon from the 76ers, I traded two marginal players, Tim McCormick and Danny Vranes. Neither had done much for the Sonics. As part of the same deal, Philadelphia also gave me a first-round pick in 1989.

It all sounds like a no-brainer, right? Get rid of bad players, trade them for better ones, squirrel away draft picks to improve the team in years to come, repeat. In some ways, it's simple. In other ways, it's anything but. There's an art and science to rebuilding a roster fraught with unknowns. If you make a big enough mistake early on in your career, it could likely be your last. I knew I was on a short leash, one that Barry Ackerley had unceremoniously shortened from three years to two. I also had a lot of confidence in my decisions. One trade at a time, I did my homework, came to every conversation prepared, put in the time, and negotiated with confidence, balancing the need for talent that could help us win today with maneuvers that would improve our odds of acquiring difference makers down the road.

In another trade that worked out extremely well for the Sonics my first year, I got rid of Al Wood, who had come into the NBA five years earlier as the fourth overall pick. He'd never quite lived up to the hype, though. You would be surprised by how many high draft picks turn out to be overrated. The player I traded him for was just the opposite: Dale Ellis, who'd been an All-American for the University of Tennessee Vols, was undervalued and warming the bench in Dallas.

The Mavericks had drafted him with the ninth pick in 1983, despite drafting Mark Aguirre and Rolando Blackman two years earlier. Dallas loved players who played small forward and shooting guard and had drafted Detlef Schrempf two years after Ellis. The Mavericks had used four lottery picks to fill two positions, and Ellis had become the odd man out. I could tell he had what it took to be a great player. He just didn't have the opportunity to stand out on a team that had too many guys who played the same positions. After scoring only seven points a game in Dallas, he blossomed with the Sonics and became an All-Star. He earned the NBA's Most Improved Player Award in 1987 and All-Star honors in 1989, when he averaged almost 28 points per game.

I got creative with some deals, like when I traded Gerald Henderson to the New York Knicks for a future second-round draft choice (1990), plus the right to exchange either of our two first-round picks in 1987 for the Knicks' first rounder that year. It was a complex deal, one of the first in the NBA involving lottery protection. If New York wound up in the lottery and drew one of the first three selections, they would not have to swap first-round picks with us; instead, we would have the option of getting their first-round choice in 1989. That scenario seemed unlikely because the Knicks were considered championship contenders that year.

When you make deals like this, you don't know how valuable those future picks will be. It depends on how well or poorly the team you're making the deal with does in the coming season. If they have a great season and make the playoffs, they'll pick low in the next draft. If they have a bad season and miss the playoffs, they'll get a high pick.

I had another big job to do besides making smart draft picks and trades. I had to figure out how to get people to buy tickets again. I met with the head of Seattle's chamber of commerce and asked for his help with the business community. A lot of them had been big Sonics supporters but had stopped coming to games.

He could tell I was earnest, listened to everything I had to say, and told me he would get back to me. A week later, he cut to the chase. "Look, nobody in the business community likes your owner at all. They have no interest in supporting him. I'd recommend you just win a lot of games, and people will show up."

Based on my own experience with Ackerley, I wasn't surprised he was unpopular in Seattle. It stayed that way for the nearly two decades he owned the Sonics. He spent a lot of time entangled in legal disputes over things like chopping down trees in front of his billboards without the proper permits or not paying bills. The *Seattle Times* once wrote, "Running a modern business involves litigation but Ackerley . . . almost needs a luxury box at the King County Courthouse."

By the time training camp started that first season, I had reshaped the Sonics with players who all fit into my vision for playing a more fast-paced game. I'd taken the time to speak one-on-one with virtually every player. Same thing with the coaching staff, led by Bernie Bickerstaff. It was important to me to earn their trust and respect. When you're young and new to an organization, you can't just say, "Hey, I'm the boss. You've got to listen to me."

Addressing the team and coaches for the first time during training camp, I felt ready for the job, confident that my changes would turn things around. I handed out the rule book and laid out clear expectations that it was time to pick up the pace and play hard. Our two best players, Xavier McDaniel and Tom Chambers, were great runners, so we were going to run, run, run, push the fast break, extend the floor defensively, exciting stuff. The coaching staff was on board, so now it was up to the players to embrace the up-tempo philosophy.

Things felt like they were falling into place as we got closer to the start of the season. We held a competitive training camp, and the players loved the new style. We had athletes who excelled in the open court, and the new system highlighted our best players' strengths.

Then Boston Celtics president Red Auerbach rather publicly predicted that the Sonics would be the worst team in the NBA that year during an interview on the *Today* show. I couldn't believe it. It was such an easy question to deflect diplomatically: "Oh, I'm not going to trash-talk other teams. Basketball is best when all teams are playing great." But when one of the interviewers took a break from fawning over how phenomenal the Celtics were with Larry Bird and asked Red which team he thought would be the worst in the league, Red didn't skip a beat: "It would surprise me if the Sonics finished anything but last."

There I was, a young president and GM. I'd been working my tail off for months to develop community support and get our season started, and now, the guru of professional basketball goes on national TV and unequivocally declares that we're not only going to suck, but we're going to suck worse than any other team in the NBA. This was long before 24-hour news networks or the internet, so a statement like this, on national network TV, from a guy like Red, garnered a lot of attention.

I called him up after the show and said, "Come on, Red. Why'd you have to do that?"

He answered as matter-of-factly as he had on TV: "Well, that's what I think."

We went on to win 39 games that season, eight better than the two prior seasons and enough to make the playoffs. X-Man, Chambers, and Ellis each averaged over 23 points per game, five points higher than the Sonics' leading scorer had achieved the previous season. No one expected us to make it into the postseason, including our landlords at the coliseum. The city of Seattle didn't reserve our own arena for a potential playoff run, so we had to play our first series games in Seattle at Hec Edmundson Pavilion, home court of the University of Washington Huskies. A full house packed into the 8,150-seat arena for the third and fourth games of the first series against the heavily favored Dallas Mavericks.

For that first home game, I had 10,000 paper masks on sticks with Red Auerbach's face and his disparaging prediction, which fans gleefully hoisted throughout the arena. I called him up the week before the game to let him know about it. He was a public figure, so I didn't need his permission, but I felt I owed him the respect of giving him a heads-up. At first, he gave it a hard no.

I didn't want to tell him, "Too bad, Red. We've already got 10,000 of them in a warehouse, and we're doing it." I had a week to get him on board, so I FedExed him one.

It took a bit of cajoling and flattery to get him on board. "Come on, Red. It's a really good picture. You look ten years younger! It'll be fun. Everybody respects you, and fans will love it."

"All right, I'm OK with it," he relented. "On one condition, though. Send me a dozen more so I can give them to my friends."

A GM'S JOB

During my tenure as an NBA president and GM, I oversaw both the business and basketball operations of the franchise. Most teams, then and now, had their president run the business, leaving basketball operations to the GM. People tend to be much more interested in the moves that make or break rosters than they are in team finances, so I field a lot more questions about what GMs do than presidents.

Here's a brief overview of a GM's job:

- **Talent evaluation:** GMs are responsible for every player acquisition that happens through the draft, a trade, or free agency. This requires hiring and training a scouting staff to evaluate draft prospects worldwide and NBA players eligible for free agency or acquisition via trade. Building and developing a championship team with winning chemistry and character happens over years, and each acquisition must be well thought out. As GM, you need to know the personnel of every NBA team as well as the players on your own team.
- **Hiring coaches:** GMs hire the coaching staff, so the head coach and assistant coaches must buy into the type of team their GM builds. Teams perform at their best when their coaches believe in the system they're hired to implement. The head coach sets the culture, but all coaches need to be good communicators and motivators willing to develop younger players.
- **Negotiation:** You need to be a skilled dealmaker to succeed as a GM. It takes salesmanship and savvy to make player trades with other GMs. Pursuing (and hopefully acquiring) free agents can be especially challenging because you not only have to determine their market rate, but you also have to convince them to become part of the team you're building.
- **Manage salary cap:** The salary cap is a very nuanced revenue-sharing agreement with players that determines how much teams can spend on their player payroll each season. Salary-cap rules determine how player trades can be made and penalize teams that exceed spending limits. As a GM, you have to understand the collective bargaining agreement inside and out to manage player rosters and cash budgets.
- **Administration:** Many facets of a GM's job go unnoticed but are very important, such as scheduling summer league games, preseason games, training camps, and

regular-season games. GMs oversee the maintenance and upgrading of practice facilities and inventory of practice gear and training supplies. On game day, the GM makes sure the stats crew is prepared and the scoreboards function properly. The GM checks with arena management to ensure backup basket standards, shot clocks, basketballs, and other essential equipment are on hand. And as a GM, it's on you to hire the right people for the many essential support roles: public and media relations, doctors, nutritionists, psychologists, counselors, trainers, strength-and-conditioning experts, security, equipment managers, and administrative support staff.

- **Analytics:** Data, statistics, performance models, and other forms of analytics play an essential role in player and coaching evaluations. GMs must hire and effectively use an analytics department in all aspects of basketball operations decision-making. Analytics are also an important part of the business operations used in many departments, such as variable ticket pricing and concessions and merchandise selection and pricing.

- **Community relations:** The GM usually serves as the face of the franchise. This time-consuming role requires excellent communication skills as well as patience for a steady stream of calls and emails from season ticket holders along with daily conversations with the media. As a GM, you have to be fair and honest while "staying on message." You also need to have thick skin, take responsibility when things don't go well, and shield ownership from negative publicity.

- **Organization:** GMs need excellent people skills to motivate a team on the court and employees in the front office. Staff members look to their leader for vision, messaging, and guidance. The example a GM sets will make professionalism and accountability a core element of the organization.

- **League relations:** Maintaining a good working relationship with the league usually involves serving on committees (in my case, the NBA Competition Committee, which governed the rules of the game; also, the senior Men's Basketball Committee, which picked the members of the international and Olympic basketball competitions; and in the NFL, the stadium and relocation committee). GMs evaluate referee performances throughout the season, which partially determines which officials work the playoffs. GMs are responsible for all league operations mandates, including the referees' locker room, visitors' locker room, security, game tickets, visiting players, corporate partners, and referees.

- **Ownership:** GMs must regularly communicate with ownership. An owner should never first hear big news about their team from the media (trade rumors, off-court issues, NBA fines or suspensions, lawsuits, etc.). And owners should not be caught by surprise if the GM is doing their job. Building a championship organization requires close collaboration between GMs and owners, whether it's developing and updating salary-cap and financial models or executing simultaneous short- and long-term plans.

You must be organized to do all of this well! And it helps if you love sports enough to watch as much as I did before, during, and after my front-office career. By a conservative estimate, I have watched more than 10,000 live NBA basketball games in person or on television over the past 45 years, and I continue to do so to this day. This means I have spent about 3.5 years of my life watching NBA games live. I've also seen every Super Bowl live, either in person or on TV—57 years straight!

CHAPTER 6

CINDERELLA SURPRISE

No one thought the Sonics belonged anywhere near the NBA playoffs in 1987. Yet we eked our way in, seeded seventh out of eight Western Conference teams that made it to the postseason. We would face the Dallas Mavericks in the first round, a formidable opponent that a lot of people expected to win it all. The Mavs had won 55 games during the regular season, including all five we'd played against them. They'd beaten us by double digits each time. They'd have home-court advantage in the playoffs, of course, so we would play our first two games to a sold-out crowd in Dallas's Reunion Arena, in front of 17,000 fired-up fans salivating for a repeat of the Mavs' victory over the Sonics in the first round of the 1984 playoffs—the last time we had made it to the playoffs. All this, plus our starting center, Alton Lister, was out with a broken foot.

The odds were stacked tall against us, but we had some things going for us, too. Dale Ellis was having a stellar season, leading the team in scoring with almost 25 points per game. We couldn't wait to see him play like the star Dallas never let him become by keeping him benched. We had just beaten the Lakers 110–104 in the final game of the regular season. Xavier McDaniel had scored a phenomenal 39 points in that game, boosting his scoring average north of 23, in line with our second-leading scorer, Tom Chambers.

"With those three going at full blast, the Sonics will be a problem for any team in the playoffs," Lakers guard Michael Cooper told the *Seattle Times* after the game.

In the lead-up to Game One, the coaching staff and I reminded the guys they had earned the right to be in the playoffs. Every pep talk we gave centered on some version of "We belong here. Be proud." We talked about how different the playoffs are from the regular season, how we would get to adjust from one night to the next as we played the same team three to five times in a row instead of many weeks apart. We would study each game, learning from mistakes (ours and theirs) and fine-tuning plays. We would focus not just on playing our best but playing our best against this specific opponent. We had a couple of guys with championship chops, Clemon Johnson and Maurice Lucas. And the young players who were gearing up for their first NBA postseason listened earnestly to everything the veterans had to say about what to expect—how the game slows down and gets more physical, how playoff refs (the best in the league) like to keep games going, so they might not call an elbow here or a hack there. You have to play through it and not let it rattle you. We went into Game One knowing we were the underdog of underdogs, hungry for an upset.

Round One, Game One
The Mavericks obliterated us. As soon as we'd get the ball, they'd swarm us, forcing bad passes and turnovers that electrified the Dallas fans. It looked like a game of hot potato. *Oh no. Here comes another double-team. I better get rid of the ball!* Our young guys panicked. We turned the ball over so many times. It was the biggest blowout I'd ever seen. Dallas won 151–129. The Mavs had never scored so many points in a single game. They still haven't. As bad as the score was, the game, as a whole, was even worse. At one point during the fourth quarter, they had a 38-point lead and let their starters rest on the bench for the remainder of the game.

Seattle Times columnist Steve Kelley bashed us ruthlessly for the loss: "The Sonics not only lost last night's first game of their best-of-five playoff series with the Mavericks, they had their confidence stripped away like paint off a weathered home. Stripped. The way Dallas guard Derek Harper undressed Sonic rookie Nate McMillan." A lot of people probably thought Kelley was right when he piled on, saying Dallas "won the war. And broke the Sonic spirit."

But nothing about our spirits was broken that night. Not even close. We did no head-hanging or hand-wringing in the locker room. No finger-pointing or self-blame. Every member of the team exuded fiercely focused toughness, a competitive itch to get back on the court and play the kind of basketball that had gotten us *into* the playoffs. We were all livid and embarrassed, but we didn't feel sorry for ourselves. We knew we were better than the pitiful game we'd just lost. We knew we could beat this team. I didn't give much of a spiel that night, aside from reminding everyone that one win in a best-of-five series is just that. One win. That's all Dallas had done. Now it was up to us to win *our* first game. Then two more.

At practice the next day, we focused on adapting our response to Dallas's press, the defensive adjustment the Mavs had made so effectively in Game One. We wouldn't let it unnerve us again. During walk-throughs, we had six guys playing defense against a five-man offense. We started out at half speed, practicing different ways to anticipate the press then break past it. Once we did, we would often have an offensive advantage, with three Sonics on two Mavericks as we barreled toward the basket. This wasn't rocket science. They'd all been doing various versions of this since junior high. We hadn't seen Dallas run anything close to that kind of defense at any point during the regular season. In hindsight, we realized the Mavs had overwhelmed us with a defense that we knew how to break. They had just caught a young team off guard. They'd rattled our nerves. So had the hometown's roaring so loudly we could barely think straight. We wouldn't let that happen again.

Round One, Game Two

With the whole world sure it was over for us, we showed up for Game Two determined to play quick, smart basketball and prove that we were worthier opponents than we'd appeared to be the night before. In addition to the adjustments we made to break through Dallas's press, we made some important changes to *our* defensive strategy.

Tom Chambers would take the lead on defending two-time All-Star forward Mark Aguirre, instead of Xavier McDaniel, who struggled to defend him on his own in Game One; X-Man would play more of a roving defense and slide into the lane whenever Aguirre got the ball, double-teaming him with Chambers. Sometimes, Clemon Johnson would join in for a triple-team.

It was clear within the first few minutes that we weren't going to let the Mavericks destroy us again. Instead of getting flustered and rushing passes that Dallas picked off, we patiently made an extra pass to break the press and get the ball into the frontcourt so we could attack the basket.

"I could tell we were in trouble in the first three minutes when Seattle handled our press so well. It didn't bother them at all," Dallas coach Dick Motta told reporters after the game, which was competitive from start to finish.

We led 35–34 by the end of the first quarter, then trailed by two at the half and two by the start of the fourth quarter. The lead changed 25 times. Clemon Johnson scored a season high of 20 points, making 9 of 13 shots from the field. He hadn't taken more than six shots in any game all season. He had taken one shot in Game One and missed.

It was especially gratifying for Dale Ellis to play so well against the team that had so grossly underestimated him. He led our team in scoring with 32 points, including a game-tying 18-footer with 1:30 left and a pair of free throws with seconds left on the clock after two controversial calls against Dallas.

The first came with four seconds left. Derek Harper was called for traveling on an inbounds pass. I can count on one hand the times I've seen an NBA player do this and get called out for it during my 25 years in the NBA. Referee Jack Madden deserves a lot of credit for making the right call against the home team, in a game that would give the underdog a stunning upset to tie the series.

The second call came two seconds later. The Mavericks triple-teamed Ellis in the right corner as he caught Nate McMillan's inbounds pass and hurled the ball toward the paint. The ref (Jack Madden again) called Dallas's Sam Perkins (on the triple-team) for a foul as Ellis fell out of bounds. The question about the call was this: Was Ellis shooting or passing when it happened? If he was trying to pass, we would have gotten the ball out of bounds. But the ruling on the floor was that Ellis was trying to shoot, which gave our ex-Mav two chances to make a game-winning free throw against his former team. He drained both.

"This is what I had dreamed of, coming into this building and doing something like this," Ellis told reporters after the 112–110 victory. The game "was the first close one we've played against Dallas all year. We knew we had to have it. Now we are going home with a split, and that's exactly what we wanted."

The crowd that'd had the building buzzing the entire game fell silent as we celebrated the stunning upset. The *Dallas Morning News* devoted a full article to the second disputed call, saying Sonics coach Bernie Bickerstaff had apparently agreed with Dallas coach Dick Motta that Ellis was fouled while trying to throw the ball to center Clemon Johnson, who was wide open in the lane. Ellis himself told a gaggle of reporters right after the game that he was trying to pass to Johnson inside. When one of the writers pointed out it was actually a shooting foul, Ellis reportedly stared across the room for a moment and said, "Then I was trying to shoot," first straight faced, then breaking into a laugh.

Right or wrong, the call went our way, and we held our heads high, knowing we had earned every point in a spectacular win.

"I can't even put the words to it," the Mavs' Mark Aguirre told *Dallas Morning News*. "Incredible. They just had a great game. It takes it for that team to win. They're going to have to keep playing like that in order to beat us."

Steve Kelley, the *Seattle Times* columnist who had declared our spirits broken after Game One, praised us effusively in his analysis of the game: "From the pits," Kelley wrote, "they rose to the penthouse."

Walking off the court, I felt a surge of excitement, sweet vindication for all the hard work I'd put into rebuilding this team. When I saw the Mavs' president and general manager, Norm Sonju, walking toward me with Rick Sund, the team's vice president of basketball, I got ready to relish the moment, to shake their hands and thank them as they commended Seattle for the victory. As quickly as Norm congratulated me, he said something along the lines of "How great that you didn't lose all three games of this series. This will give you something to build on next year."

I doubt Norm meant to condescend. He's a good guy. So is Rick. They probably thought we'd gotten lucky and didn't stand a chance of winning again. I told the team about it in the locker room, adding fuel to their fire for two more wins as we headed home to Seattle for Games Three and Four.

Round One, Game Three

We didn't quite have home-court advantage in Games Three and Four. The coliseum was booked for a home show, and the Mariners were playing in the Kingdome, our alternate arena, so we had to play at UW's Hec Edmundson Pavilion. Seven years earlier, as defending NBA champs, the Sonics had infamously lost Games Three and Four of the 1980 Western Conference Finals to the Los Angeles Lakers at Hec Ed, with just over 8,500 fans crammed into the building. Former Sonics captain Fred Brown described Hec Ed as having "a boxy, claustrophobic feeling from what we were used to. It felt like a road game during the exhibition season."

Both those losses in 1980 came as big blows, but it was Game Four that would go down as one of the most miserable days in Sonics history. *Seattle Post-Intelligencer* columnist Art Thiel called it "the Hec Ed debacle that sent the franchise into the void." The Sonics had held a commanding lead at the half (57–39) and maintained an almost 20-point advantage well into the third period, then it had all fallen apart quickly, as the Lakers had unleashed a blistering fast-break offense led by rookie point guard Magic Johnson. The Lakers won the game 96–93, beat Seattle again in Game Five, and went on to win the NBA championship, the first of five titles Magic Johnson would win with the Lakers.

We weren't obsessing over any ghosts of playoff-collapses past as we headed into Game Three against the Mavs. We weren't bemoaning how much smaller the crowd at "What the Hec Ed" would be. We'd have played them in the parking lot if we had to. We were fired up and ready to build on the momentum we'd snatched from Dallas in Game Two. We knew we had to dial in our focus even more. We had to be even hungrier for our second win. We knew in our heads and hearts that we could beat these worthy opponents again, this time in front of our home crowd.

The 8,150 fans who packed into Hec Ed were Sonics diehards. They were thrilled about their hometown NBA team, as excited as they'd ever been in the years since the franchise had started unraveling after the 1979 Championship. Whatever they lacked in numbers (being about 6,000 shy of our usual crowd), they more than made up for in fervor.

Just like we had diligently practiced, then executed the night before, we worked around Dallas's press with quick pass-and-cut ball movement. We also blitzed them with the same level of defensive pressure in the first half, allowing Dallas only 15 points in the first quarter. We outscored them again in the second, leading 55–37 at the half. We outrebounded them. Dale Ellis dominated once again, leading the team with a career-high 43 points. He hit 18 of 28 shots from the field plus all 5 of his free throws, and grabbed 14 rebounds. Dallas narrowed our lead in the third and fourth quarters, but not enough to close the gap. We won the game 117–107.

Days after publicly trash-talking Ellis, saying he "couldn't beat [Mavericks guard Rolando Blackman] if he was here for 10 more years," Dallas coach Dick Motta gave some credit where credit was overdue. "I'm happier than hell for Dale," Motta said. "Did he only have 43? I thought he had 60."

I knew long before Motta that we'd gotten the far better end of the deal that brought Ellis to Seattle and sent Al Wood to Dallas. The Mavericks thought otherwise. In fact, they had been so enthusiastic about Wood, they'd insisted I extend his contract from one year to three years as part of the trade. Wood wound up not starting a single game during the Mavericks' regular season. He averaged less than seven points per game, what little he did play. And he sat out the playoffs, not playing a single minute. The Mavs released him the following November, paying him *not* to play for those two years they had strongarmed me into adding to his contract. And that was it for Wood's NBA career. As we celebrated our win, a banner hanging from the Hec Ed rafters said it all: "Nice trade, Dick."

Round One, Game Four
I could see fear in the Mavericks' eyes, both during and after Game Three. I didn't dare say it to anyone but my wife, but I had a feeling

the series would end with Game Four, right where we wanted to be. In Seattle. "There's no way in the *world* we're going to lose this game," I told Jan. "I can *feel* it!"

Some people wonder if the kind of momentum we captured in Games Two and Three is real, something that can make stars align for one team and throw another so off kilter they choke. I'm telling you, it's as real as real can get. When you have it, you *feel* it. Sports psychologists have countless theories about how players and teams get momentum, how they keep it or lose it. It's hard to quantify. It's like an invisible smell. You don't know where it comes from, but suddenly, you can smell it. Dallas had all the momentum in Game One. They never expected we'd take it away from them, yet we did.

In a column before Game Four, Randy Galloway of the *Dallas Morning News* declared that losing this playoff series to the Sonics would be "socially unacceptable," something that could get the Mavericks "laughed out of the league."

By the time we were done with the Mavs, no one in Dallas was laughing. We clobbered them, winning 124–98. A team with the fourth-best regular-season record in the league (55–27) became the first second-seeded team ever eliminated by a seventh seed. Our fans started celebrating well before the game was over, chanting "Beat LA! Beat LA!" just as Dallas fans had in Game One.

To this day, I'm as proud of this group of players and coaches as I've ever been of any team I've led as a GM. They worked so hard. There were no divas. No matter the challenge, they would just roll up their sleeves and get after it. In one way or another, everyone on that team— myself included—had legions of doubters. And we all seized this improbable opportunity to show those doubters we belonged. Before this series, everyone had written us off as hopelessly outmatched. Yet every step of the way, we believed in ourselves. We brought out the best in each other. And we earned the right to face another exceptionally strong team in round two: the Houston Rockets, reigning Western Conference champions.

Round Two, Game One

We had won three of four regular-season games against Houston, one of them 136–80; at the time, that was the largest margin of victory by a visiting team in NBA history. But we knew the team we'd face in the playoffs would be harder to beat. The "Twin Towers"—Ralph Sampson (seven foot four) and Hakeem (then known as "Akeem") Olajuwon (seven feet)—were back in the starting lineup, healthy again after injuries had forced them to sit out much of the season.

"We're jumping out of the frying pan and into the pot," Coach Bernie Bickerstaff said. He admitted the Rockets were a better team, but this was the playoffs. All bets were off. Anything could happen.

We were hoping Alton Lister could get back on the court in the second-round series opener, but the broken bone in his right foot was still causing him too much pain. So Clemon Johnson would continue to start at center. There was a lot of talk about how tired we'd be for the first game in Houston. This was back in the days when we flew commercial, and we had to catch a 6:45 a.m. flight to Houston the morning after we'd eliminated the Mavericks in Seattle.

Exhausted as we might have been, we played a solid game, both offensively and defensively. We periodically pressed Houston, forcing 21 turnovers, 14 in the first half. Dale Ellis had yet another great game, scoring 34 points, including a three-pointer with 14 seconds left in overtime. The Rockets, by contrast, missed several easy layups, a lot of free throws, and played so poorly overall that one of their hometown sportswriters wrote that they "sleepwalked like zombies," when *we* were supposed to be the ones trudging out there "looking like the cast of *Night of the Living Dead.*"

We won the game in overtime 111–106.

The *Houston Chronicle* writer Fran Blinebury called us the Lone Star party crashers. "This is a team that Red Auerbach labeled the worst in the league at the beginning of the year," he wrote, "one that is now making an Alysheba longshot run at showing up in Boston for the NBA Finals and blowing cigar smoke back in the old man's face. Yes, the Sonics are for real."

Then came the infamous nightclub incident that briefly landed two of our players in jail. It happened at the Ocean Club in Houston after the game. Kevin Williams allegedly punched an assistant manager, and Dale Ellis grabbed the officer trying to handcuff Williams. I learned about it in the wee hours of the morning after Game One. I had a ton of work to do at the office, lining up all manner of details for the business side of the playoffs, so I had gladly accepted Sonics owner Barry Ackerley's invitation to fly home in his private plane. It must've been one or two in the morning as we landed in Seattle. When I got home and checked my answering machine, it was blowing up with messages. Of all the things I was prepared for, I never expected that two of our players would wind up in jail.

So much for all that work I had to do. I jumped on the first flight back to Houston a few hours later and shifted my focus to damage control. After almost a decade in this business, I'd learned a lot about putting out fires, but nothing until now had been remotely this stressful. With the whole world watching, it fell on me—a 31-year-old in my first year as GM—to get this giant distraction under control. From the get-go, I told Ackerley as little as possible. He was so thrilled with how well we'd done so far (not to mention all the money he'd made as owner each time we advanced in the playoffs), he basically left it to me to handle everything. He didn't need to know all the details.

As soon as I returned to Houston, I went to see Dale and Kevin and asked them the first and most important thing—the same question I ask my children when anything goes sideways: "Are you OK?"

I could tell they hadn't gotten physically hurt, and as they talked about what had happened, I listened closely to get a sense of how they were coping emotionally. Back then (and still in a lot of cases today), NBA players didn't exactly jump at the chance to talk about their mental health. Sure, they knew what it meant to have their "head in the game," but they often didn't want to admit when they were so anxious or stressed that they were having a hard time thinking straight.

As they each filled me in on their perspectives of what had happened, I parsed out what seemed to be consistent with each of their stories and hired a Houston lawyer to represent them. I made sure they both knew we had hired a really good attorney and that we had their backs. We helped them prepare for the white-hot media spotlight. If they or anyone else said anything wrong, it could easily be misinterpreted and make matters worse.

It seemed pretty obvious that the fight, the arrests, the charges (resisting arrest for Williams and hindering arrest for Ellis) were a setup to throw us off our game. But nothing good could come from public finger-pointing, so we advised everyone on the team to say "Hey, we're here to talk about basketball" if they were asked for a comment about the Ocean Club snafu.

As a rising star who had shined so brightly in the series against his former team, Dallas, Ellis would get the most attention. He was a pretty quiet guy, not very comfortable talking to the media, but we encouraged him to spend some time with reporters, answering their questions calmly, without getting into the play-by-play of what had happened. It's always better to deal with a situation up front, all at once. Sometimes, all you can say is you can't answer this or that question, but that's better than trying to run away from the situation. If you avoid it, you'll have three reporters stalking you at the hotel, five looking for you at the restaurant, others calling your room in the middle of the night. Dale did as we advised, spending a good half hour with the horde of reporters hounding him with questions.

"I have a job to do," he said, as our PR director and I stood nearby. "I'm not going to let this bother me." He even predicted the incident might push him and the team to focus more.

Tom Chambers agreed. "If anything, it will make us come out and play better. It will make us concentrate on our game and play harder. I know Dale. He'll be better."

Round Two, Game Two

A hostile Houston crowd loudly booed Ellis as he was introduced before Game Two. Some fans held up signs that read, "Free Drinks at the Ocean Club." Some signs showed Dale in prison garb and handcuffs. The Rockets' overtime loss in Game One combined with the nightclub incident had Rockets fans in a fever pitch before the game even started. Ellis hit just two of his first seven shots, then got back into his groove and went on to score 30 points. The Rockets were up 97–94 when Ellis narrowed their lead to one, hitting his fourth 20-foot jumper of the game with 1:50 left, then a three-pointer that clinched our 99–97 win. After the game, Ellis said he was surprised the crowd went so easy on him. "I was a little disappointed," he said. "I thought they would've given me a little more grief."

Round Two, Game Three

Only four teams in NBA history had ever come back to win a best-of-seven series after losing the first two games. Houston coach Bill Fitch struck a decidedly doubtful tone as the Rockets arrived for practice the day after Game Two. "We're either all through or it's just starting," he said. "It doesn't look good."

It wasn't win or go home for Houston, but the pressure to win Game Three loomed large. If we prevailed, we could win the Western Conference semifinals in Seattle. On our *actual* home court. With more than 14,500 screaming fans packed into the coliseum, the Rockets pounded Ellis defensively, who missed 14 of his 19 shots. As a team, we missed six of our eight free throws in the first half, which ended with Houston up 56–33. Hakeem Olajuwon and Ralph Sampson were dominant. The Twin Towers had 35 points and outscored our entire team in the first half. We shot just 39 percent for the game and never got closer than 15 points in the second half. We lost 102–84, and the Rockets let out a collective sigh of relief. "This is the kind of game I was expecting us to play at home—to beat them by 15–20 points," Olajuwon said.

Our fans seemed unfazed, among them Jack Becker, who told the *Seattle Times*, "I'm not worried. We're still up and we're still home. I've been coming to these games since they started, and this feeling has been a long time coming. This is still heaven to me."

Round Two, Game Four

Whatever mojo slipped away from us in Game Three, we got back in Game Four, once again in front of a sold-out coliseum crowd. Alton Lister's return to the starting lineup helped offset Houston's inside game; he grabbed 17 rebounds. Tom Chambers scored a playoff career-high 38 points and Dale Ellis added 32. Nate McMillan played a solid floor game, finishing with ten assists. Olajuwon finished with 20 points and was limited to just 27 minutes—only 10 in the first half—because he got into foul trouble. Sampson also got into foul trouble, scoring just 18. We scored eight unanswered points at the start of the fourth quarter, including a three-pointer by Ellis that put us up 89–83 with not much more than eight minutes left. We took a three-to-one lead in the series with a 117–102 victory.

Round Two, Game Five

Home-court advantage is big in Game Five of a best-of-seven series. Yet as we headed back to Houston, just one win away from advancing to the conference finals, we didn't have the slightest doubt that we could win on the road again. We'd done it twice in Dallas and twice in Houston. Only four teams in league history had ever come back to win an NBA playoff series after falling behind three to one.

We also knew nothing would be easy about eliminating the defending conference champions on their home court. We set out to beat them with quickness. They would try to beat us with size. Both teams were determined to force their will on the other, creating a classic playoff game chess match.

Coming off a win and up three to one in the series, we didn't want to tweak anything too much. We just wanted to keep doing what we were doing, using our speed and athleticism to pick them up full court because their guards were not great ball handlers. They would lose precious seconds on their shot clock, trying to advance into the frontcourt. As they tried to set up their half-court offense, defenders like Kevin Williams would ball hawk them with in-your-face pressure. We'd make it hard for them to get the ball to their Twin Towers down in the post, where they were pretty hard to stop. Our defensive scheme was to push them farther out on the floor, out of position, where their shooting percentage wouldn't be as good. We'd work to get fast breaks on them so they couldn't set up defensively.

Even though we trailed by 21 points at three different times in the first half, nothing about Game Five shook our confidence. We lost 112–107, but it wasn't a drubbing. Tensions simmered, for sure. At one point, the game got so physical Xavier McDaniel and Jim Petersen exchanged shoves, and both benches emptied onto the floor. No one threw any punches, but both head coaches were yelling at each other so viciously that Houston forward Ralph Sampson intervened and separated them. When the game resumed, we outscored Houston 14–4, narrowing their lead to eight points. With 7:11 left in the game, a three-pointer by Tom Chambers put us ahead 97–96. We led one more time after X-Man dunked with 4:23 on the clock, and got within one point three more times, but it wasn't enough. We played a good game. Not great, but we competed.

It's always a bit of a gut punch when you lose a close playoff game. Then again, every playoff game *should* be close. In the locker room after the game, there wasn't a twinkle of doubt that we could take this series. We never expected to sweep the defending conference champs, nor did it surprise us that they squeaked out a win in their own arena teeming with hometown love.

"It's hard to put somebody away in the fifth game when their backs are against the wall and they're at home," said Maurice Lucas, who came off the bench to score 13 for us. "I think we showed them that, if they plan to win this series, they'll have to fight us."

Our confidence was right where we needed it to be, and we were right where we wanted to be. Up three to two and heading home.

Round Two, Game Six

The pressure for us to win Game Six was intense. A loss would tie the series at three to three, and Game Seven would be in Houston. Our Seattle crowd was so fired up, so loud. You could just *feel* their energy.

It's hard to beat a team when one of its stars scores 49 points, grabs 25 rebounds, and blocks six shots like Olajuwon did in Game Six. He played a phenomenal game, but we won the final showdown of the Western Conference semifinals 128–125 in double overtime. It took everything we had. We trailed by five points with 55 seconds left in regulation. With Houston up 107–102, we executed our half-court offense to perfection, freeing McDaniel for a dribble drive into the lane. X-Man drained the ten-foot jumper, cutting the Rockets' lead to 107–104. As the clock wound down, Houston's point guard, Dirk Minniefield, tried a crossover dribble at the top of the key. McMillan poked the ball loose and threw it ahead to Ellis, who made a layup while getting fouled. Dale's free throw tied the game at 107, forcing the first overtime.

The lead went back and forth in the first overtime, as Olajuwon and Tom Chambers kept trading baskets. Trailing by two, Chambers completed a three-point play with 15 seconds left, giving us a 115–114 lead. Sampson got an offensive rebound with seconds left and was fouled. If he made both free throws, the Rockets would win. Sampson had not scored a point in the fourth quarter or overtime and was only able to make the first shot, sending the game into double overtime. I've seen many good NBA players choke at the free throw line when they are in the pressure cooker. Sampson was one of those players.

The second OT was a continuation of Olajuwon versus the Sonics. Chambers, X-Man, and Ellis kept matching baskets with Hakeem until the game was tied at 125. With 50 seconds left, Ellis drove baseline only to have his shot blocked by Olajuwon. Dale rebounded his miss and quickly laid the ball in the basket over the outstretched arms of Olajuwon and Sampson.

With less than a minute left in the second overtime, CBS Sports broadcaster Dick Stockton, the play-by-play announcer for the national telecast, said: "Isn't it phenomenal the way this Sonics team with nine new guys including [Continental Basketball Association] refugees, one rookie, and a blend of veterans are showing such poise? The Sonics have no fear."

Dale's layup was the last basket of the game. A Clemon Johnson free throw with five seconds left gave us our final point and a 128–125 win. In all, Chambers and Ellis combined for 73 points, and McMillan dished out 16 dimes. We were exhausted, and the fans were exhausted. The series-clinching victory did not end until after midnight in Seattle.

Dale Ellis called it the happiest moment of his life. "I think we're going to go all the way," he said. "Our team has shown character all year long in coming back from adversity. We did it again tonight. No one expected us to be here, but we're still here."

The next morning, as we boarded our flight to Los Angeles, my ears were still ringing from the roar that had filled the coliseum after that win. It might be the most exciting playoff game I've ever been a part of. Winning a close-out game is always hard. Doing it on your home court in front of a crowd going absolutely wild is extremely special. It's hard to describe just how exhilarating it was to rise from those depths so unexpectedly. Regardless of how we did in the conference finals, I couldn't have imagined a more gratifying and vindicating conclusion to our first season as a team.

Instead of turning out to be the worst team in the NBA, we had a Cinderella season that lit up our hometown with unbridled pride about their once-great team's resurgence in the playoffs. It marked the end of a glum era and the beginning of a new and thrilling chapter in Sonics history.

Western Conference Finals

It's a big deal to make it to the NBA Conference Finals. Four teams have never made it that far: the Memphis Grizzlies, the Minnesota Timberwolves, the New Orleans Pelicans, and the Charlotte Hornets. It took the Los Angeles Clippers 51 years—their entire existence as an NBA franchise—to make it all the way to the conference finals in 2021. The Sacramento Kings have made it just once; the Atlanta Hawks, Brooklyn Nets, and Toronto Raptors, twice. The Washington Wizards last made the NBA Final Four 44 years ago (back when they were the Bullets).

The Sonics had appeared in the Western Conference Finals three times before 1987. The fourth appearance was accomplished with the most inexperienced team and with the youngest president and general manager in the league. The NBA and TV networks had been hoping for a Houston–Los Angeles showdown that year. Two of the league's biggest markets and biggest stars: Olajuwon and the defending conference champs versus the Lakers, which had won three NBA titles since Magic Johnson joined the team in 1979. Instead, they got David versus Goliath. A new-and-improving Sonics squad in the first year of a teardown and rebuild versus the star-studded "Showtime" Lakers.

I'm sure by this point, most people figured that whatever luck had gotten such a scrappy team this far in the playoffs was bound to run out. But we knew it was a lot more than luck going our way. We had *earned* our spot on this national stage. We had worked our tails off for it, digging deep, game after game. We were ready for this.

In a low-scoring Game One for both teams, we trailed by 14 points with 2:36 left in the third period, then barreled back with a 13–2 run, including 11 points by Tom Chambers alone, two of them three-pointers. We closed LA's lead to just three points, then didn't score until almost the sixth minute of the fourth quarter, missing 11 of our first 12 fourth-quarter shots, while the Lakers piled on eight unanswered points. The score was 90–87 when Magic Johnson was called for a dribbling violation. With 38 seconds left, we got the ball and had a chance to tie the game or get within a point, but Chambers missed a 16-footer. We lost 92–87, and I'm sure the LA crowd never expected to be chanting "De-FENSE! De-FENSE!" late in the game. And who would've imagined Lakers coach Pat Riley singing our praises like this:

"The Sonics are going to be a team that's going to constantly be able to come back because of how they play, and we can't rely strictly on our offensive posture to win."

Aside from getting outrebounded 42–29, we held our own in Game Two. After trailing by ten late in the first period, "Fast Eddie" Johnson, a six-foot-two shooting guard, came in and penetrated the Lakers' defense, scoring ten to give us a seven-point advantage. Down 56–55 at the half, some of our most reliable scorers missed shots they would usually make. The Lakers won the battle of the boards, and we lost the game, 112–104. Though it wasn't a thumping, we flew back to Seattle feeling the pressure was on for us to turn things around.

Xavier McDaniel scored a career-high 42 points in Game Three, in front of a Seattle crowd that was ready to blow the roof off the coliseum. Ten of X-Man's points came in the last nine minutes, including a three-pointer—the last shot of the game—that narrowed the Lakers' lead to a single point. X-Man also tied Kareem Abdul-Jabbar with ten rebounds, but he was in no mood to celebrate his performance after the game. The Lakers' championship experience prevailed, and they squeaked out a 122–121 victory.

"It doesn't look good for us," X-Man told the *Seattle Times* after the game. "I guess it's like we're in the hospital in critical condition."

We were so out of gas by Game Four, playing the best team in the league, which had had a week off before playing us in the conference finals. Coming off an exhilarating and exhausting six-game series against the mighty Western Conference champs, we gave it our all until the bitter end, when our sellout crowd of nearly 14,500 fans rose to their feet, cheering "Bernie, Bernie, Bernie!" In the final seconds of the Lakers' 133–102 victory, Magic Johnson walked over to Coach Bernie Bickerstaff, embraced him, and said, "You should be proud."

This playoff run was the spark that lit the fuse in the turnaround of a flailing franchise. It unlocked the Sonics bandwagon, and the whole city was rushing to get back on. Those who had doubted a 30-year-old rookie GM could revive a tired team suddenly had confidence in me. Intense pressure to succeed comes with the first year of a new GM's contract, especially for a GM as young and unproven as I was. Our Cinderella season in 1986–87, capped by an epic playoff run, cemented my reputation as a bold, hardworking risk-taker who got results.

I'll never know for sure, but I probably would've been fired that first year if we'd laid an egg in the first round. Remember, Ackerley had cut my contract from three years to two with the cavalier stroke of a pen. Why wouldn't he send me packing if all my trades that first year had fallen flat? If my vision for a fast-paced, athletic team hadn't borne fruit that first year, what would've stopped an impatient and impulsive owner from giving me my walking papers? If I hadn't gotten a second and third year to continue rebuilding the Sonics, they probably would've fallen deeper and deeper into decline. And the Sonics powerhouse built around Shawn Kemp and Gary Payton might never have come to be. Instead, the 1987 playoffs gave the world an electrifying glimpse at the future of a promising work in progress.

Late one night during the 1987 playoffs, I was driving home after a game, waiting at a red light, when a car full of fans spotted me and started shouting, "Sonics RULE!" their fists pumping as I flashed an ear-to-ear smile. My, how things had changed since my first summer in Seattle, when I couldn't even get the chamber of commerce to help me sell tickets. We played every home game against the Mavericks, Rockets, and Lakers to sold-out crowds. The whole city had Sonics fever. Their team was *back*!

CHAPTER 7

SEAL THE DEAL

ALL BUT THREE MEMBERS OF the Sonics' astoundingly successful 1987 playoff squad came to the team during the flurry of trades I made my first year in Seattle—everyone was new, except Tom Chambers, Xavier McDaniel, and Danny Young. In all, I made seven trades and signed six new players that first year, most of them in the spring and summer before the 1986–87 season started. Every time I made another deal, the coaching staff would say, "Whoa . . . the Liquidator strikes again!" I chuckled and took no offense. I knew what I was doing. This wasn't a going-out-of-business sale. I was building something new, a team with depth, breadth, athleticism, and ambition. A team that could bring Seattle another NBA championship—a goal I unabashedly set for the team to achieve within five years. I'm sure some thought I was being brazenly unrealistic, maybe even arrogant. That wasn't it. I was rebuilding a team, and everything I did, move by move, had our next championship in mind.

The Liquidator didn't last long as a nickname. A host of others came and went—Whiz Kid Whitsitt, Boy Wonder, Barter Bob. The one that stuck, even following me to the Portland Trail Blazers, was Trader

Bob. I've always taken it as a compliment, an acknowledgment that I'm someone who knows how to close deals. I've negotiated countless deals throughout my career. I never kept a running tally but got curious recently and counted up all the trades I made during my 17 years as a general manager in the NBA: 48 in all, not counting the many draft picks and free agents I signed. A lot of GMs go entire seasons without making a single trade.

Every deal has its own unique set of advantages and disadvantages. Some take a few weeks to put together. Some, years. Some are fairly simple. Others involve multiple teams and require maneuvering around complex contractual and salary-cap constraints. Sometimes, you have to rant and rave to get a deal done. Sometimes, it's more effective to play nice, be polite. At times, you have to deal with tight cost constraints that make the prospects of a deal seem dismal. And at times, you're negotiating for someone with so much money, the owners are willing to spend a lot more than you think they should.

The word "negotiate" wields a lot of power, but when you break it down, it's a simple thing, really—a skill everybody uses every day. Say you're meeting a friend for lunch. You want to meet at noon. They want to meet at one. Do you split the difference and make it twelve thirty? Is your reason for favoring noon more compelling than theirs is for one? How much does your time matter to you? In the moment, you might not realize you're thinking through all these questions, but you are. The same is true for most decisions you make every day, and decisions others make that affect you.

Just about everything I did as a GM involved negotiating, not just the multimillion-dollar player contracts that got the most attention. I negotiated with municipalities and landlords, the radio and TV stations that broadcast our games, the vendors that sold food to our fans, the media that covered the teams, and the sponsors who advertised with us. I negotiated with league officials about fining or suspending players; with architects, general contractors, and subcontractors; with investment banks, arbitrators, and season ticket holders. I negotiated ticket prices with our marketing department. I negotiated employment contracts, sometimes dealing directly with employees, sometimes with their agents. A lot of GMs hire agents to negotiate their own contracts. I have and always will do my own because I don't think anybody could do a better job. If I can't do it on my own, I shouldn't be the guy negotiating for my team.

A lot of people ask me what it takes to become a successful negotiator. There's no tried-and-true formula that works every time, no checklist that you can always count on to get the results you want. Strategies and tactics that work in one set of circumstances might fail in another. That said, I *can* share some advice that consistently worked well for me over my many years of negotiating.

1. DO YOUR HOMEWORK.

I overprepare, researching all outside factors: from salary cap and cash ramifications to media pressure and coaches' influence; a player's age, health, and injury history to locker room chemistry; fan and sponsor perceptions; comparable transactions; and more. Most times, I'm lucky if I use 25 percent of what I learn from my negotiation homework. It's not enough to know everything about your side of the negotiation. You need to know the other side's position even better than your own. That way, when you go into the negotiation, you have a firm grasp of where they're coming from before you start talking. You know what's important to them, what's not, where they might give, where they won't budge. Nothing will surprise you.

If I'm preparing to negotiate with someone I don't know very well, I learn everything I can about them. When dealing with player agents, I look at every contract that agent has ever done. Most GMs don't do that, even though they have access to the contracts for every player who's ever signed with an NBA team. All you have to do is ask the league office for a copy. When I'm reading through contracts, I look for patterns. Is the agent willing to negotiate deferred money? What about guarantees? Contracts don't have to be guaranteed. They could be fully or partially guaranteed. Disability protections and countless other items can be considered. A lot of things you can negotiate do not involve money. If you spot patterns, you can go into a negotiation with some concrete ideas of how to get the conversation moving in a productive direction. Sometimes, I go *against* the pattern I uncover.

Even if I'm willing to go there, it might be something I save for later, when it can give me leverage, something to give away when we're close to the finish line, when it feels more valuable to the other side than if I offered it early on.

Take good notes while doing your homework. They'll serve you well—and save you time—as you rehearse what you'll say and how during the actual negotiation. I write my notes out longhand at the beginning because it helps me learn. The first section focuses on background, for both the player and the agent. I like breaking the ice and establishing trust with an agent by having small talk. We might discuss his college or hobbies. Maybe we grew up in the same part of the country or enjoy the same music. The subject doesn't matter, but find something that will make the agent feel comfortable with you before you start negotiating.

The longest section in my notes is about "comps": players with comparable statistics to the one I'm negotiating with. Players with contracts similar to the one I hope to negotiate for my player, I consider good comps. Agents get sick and tired of me comparing their client to this group of players.

Players with statistics similar to my player who earn more money than I am willing to pay, I consider bad comps. If the bad comps outnumber the good comps, I need to develop counterarguments detailing why my player should earn less money. Perhaps the bad comp players' teams won more games or play in bigger markets that generate more revenue. Maybe the bad comp players played in more games or are younger and healthier. If no counterargument exists, I claim the bad comps as outliers that do not reflect current market conditions. Under no circumstances will I negotiate using the bad comps as a baseline.

2. MAP OUT YOUR STRATEGY.

Once you've done your homework and taken good notes and you feel prepared, it's time to outline a strategy that covers the key points you'll make. You can work up a set of talking points to help you feel focused and organized. You can role-play and rehearse, practice quick comebacks and counteroffers. As you rehearse, your notes should evaporate into a condensed outline. When the subject matter becomes second nature, a one-word bullet point outline should suffice, serving only as a reminder to discuss any given topic. If you negotiate over the phone, refer to your outline, check off each point after you make it, and take more notes as you talk.

Many negotiations are done in teams. In these cases, designate one person to take notes and study nonverbal language during negotiating sessions. It's easier to pick up cues from the opposition when you do not have to focus on giving a response. Keep your notes at the table when negotiating, but don't look at them while you're talking. Maintain steady eye contact. Great poker players read their opponents as much as the cards. A person's facial mannerisms can tell you if they are bluffing or confident, nervous or excited, sincere or just throwing ideas against the wall, hoping something sticks.

If you're on a video call or face to face, don't look at your notes while you're talking. Eye contact requires reciprocity, which puts you in charge. It's fine to jot down key points as you negotiate—words you can circle back to later when you write a summary recapping important details of the negotiation. Do this as soon as possible after the meeting ends, while the conversation is fresh in your mind.

No matter what your negotiation strategy is, you must answer an important question right away: Who has the authority to make the final deal? A lot of times, I figure this out as part of my homework. If not, it's one of my first questions in a negotiation. It might seem like a strange question to ask at the beginning, like you're fast-forwarding unnecessarily far, but it's important to know this right from the get-go. Ask nicely, matter-of-factly. Then, if they're smart, they'll ask you the same thing. Usually, the answer is something like "The owner has the final say but has empowered me to negotiate the deal. I know what the parameters are, but I still need to get their final approval." With a clear and shared understanding of what you and your negotiating partner can and can't approve, everyone is less likely to worry about last-second tricks that might be pulled. Negotiations are always fluid situations, so it's OK to keep some aspects of your offer to yourself until close to the end of the process. You might need a little bit of an out, a squeeze to get the deal across the finish line.

3. SET A TIMELINE.

In many cases, it's the league office that sets the timeline, whether it's a trade deadline, draft day, or the beginning of free agency. Sometimes, though, you can create your own deadlines. After negotiating many agreements with me over the years, agents eventually learned that when I set a deadline, it's real.

Xavier McDaniel's agent, David Falk, learned that in 1990, when I set a firm deadline to negotiate a new deal for the Sonics star. X-Man was scheduled to become an unrestricted free agent after the 1990–91 season. We wanted to re-sign him if we could or get something by trading him if we couldn't. We had already lost Tom Chambers to unrestricted free agency, and I was determined not to have the same thing happen with X-Man. When I set the deadline, I told Falk I would trade X-Man if we couldn't agree on a new contract by December 1. True to form, Falk demanded more money than our owner was willing to pay. We did not make a deal by December 1, and David assumed he had all the leverage. He believed I would continue to increase our offer as the season rolled on. He assumed wrong. I made it clear our best offer was on the table, but it fell well short of Falk's demand.

One week later, I traded X-Man to Phoenix for Eddie Johnson, a six-foot-eight forward, and two future first-round picks. The fans and media hated the trade. I took a lot of heat. But like all trades, this one would take time to fairly evaluate. We were 5–10 when we traded X-Man, and we ended the season 41–41. Eddie was a great scorer, unstoppable when he got hot. Trading McDaniel helped Shawn Kemp blossom, and the next three years, we won 47, 55, and 63 games. As good a player as X-Man was, trading him turned out to be a great deal for the Sonics.

They say timing is everything, and it's true for many negotiations. During the 1990–91 season, for example, Sonics owner Barry Ackerley called me one day and told me to cut Dale Ellis. Dale was wrestling with some personal problems that were negatively impacting the team, including substance abuse, domestic violence charges, and a car crash that left him with a collapsed lung and three broken ribs. Cutting him would require us to pay the remainder of his contract and would have been the wrong thing to do for two other reasons. First, if I got Dale into a treatment program, he could get healthy and put his life back on track. Second, by giving Dale the time he needed to get better, we would stand a greater chance of getting a solid player if and when we decided to trade him.

Barry still thought nobody in the NBA would give anything of value for Dale. Nevertheless, he gave me the time I needed to put together a trade. The player I had in mind was Ricky Pierce of the Milwaukee Bucks, a member of the 1991 All-Star team and a two-time NBA Sixth Man of the Year, awarded to the league's best player coming off the bench for his team as a nonstarter. Pierce was having his best season in Milwaukee but was in a contract dispute with the Bucks, which played into my hands. Despite having no management experience, Del Harris was leading the Bucks as both coach *and* general manager. I watched the battle of egos between Milwaukee's coach and star player heat up. Ricky skipped a few practices, demanding a new contract. Del griped about Ricky in the media. With the trade deadline less than a week away, I waited for the Bucks to lose a few games and for Pierce to skip another practice. Then I called Harris and pounced.

"Del," I said, "if you cave to Ricky's demands, every player on your team will want a new contract. A lot of people think you are not qualified to be a GM, so you have to win this battle." I told him a story about legendary Green Bay Packers coach Vince Lombardi, who was also general manager when Jim Ringo came into his office demanding new contract. Ringo felt he deserved a new deal because he was a perennial First Team All-Pro NFL selection. Lombardi knew if he gave Ringo a new contract, other star players on the team would want to renegotiate, too. Vince decided to make a statement that he was in charge. Lombardi called the Eagles and immediately traded Ringo to Philadelphia. The other Packers players saw what happened to their All-Pro teammate and realized the same could happen to them. No other player approached Lombardi for a new contract, and the team won the championship the following season. I told Harris this was his "Lombardi moment." Five days before the trade deadline, Del traded Ricky Pierce, a current NBA All-Star, to the Sonics for Dale Ellis, whose best days in the NBA were already behind him. And timing had everything to do with it.

4. LISTEN WITH FOCUS.

Getting the results you want has less to do with what you say than how you *listen*. And there's a lot more to good, active listening than hearing words. Oftentimes, a person's body language, tone of voice, and overall demeanor reveal more about their position than the words they speak. Inexperienced negotiators can get lost in their own thoughts, thinking about the next thing to say rather than actively listening, a mistake that can lead to missed opportunities. There are so many things that go into reading and hearing what the other side is saying. They might send signals or casually drop a significant change in terms that could impact the negotiation immensely.

I've always been a good listener. As a three-sport athlete in high school and college, I knew the importance of listening to coaches. Their job was to help me become a better player by teaching fundamentals and installing a team system. They also had to make sure I knew the game plan for the upcoming opponent. If you didn't listen, you wouldn't learn. If you didn't learn, you wouldn't play. I listened, I learned, and I played. Unfortunately, some of our most talented players never made it onto the field because they didn't listen well enough to learn the system.

Careful listening played a pivotal role in my negotiations over Gary Payton's contract in 1990, when we signed him as the second overall pick in the NBA draft. Gary had a team of three people representing him: Aaron and Eric Goodwin (a.k.a. the Goodwin brothers) and Don DeJardin. The trio had no other clients at the time. This contract negotiation meant everything to them. I flew to Oakland for the first negotiating session and quickly realized each of them thought they were the lead negotiator. They kept talking over each other and telling me why Gary trusted them so much. As I listened, they kept demanding a contract that averaged $3 million per year. I told them we wanted a six-year contract, but they insisted on a shorter term, allowing Gary to reach free agency sooner. I never made an offer but repeatedly told them $3 million was too high. To their dismay, I said the meeting was a waste of everyone's time, so I was flying back to Seattle. They were shocked and told me to make an offer but to keep in mind, "We will never accept anything lower than $2.5 million per year."

During the weeks of negotiating, Team Payton stood firm on a four-year, $10 million fully guaranteed contract. Just by listening, I moved them from $3 million a year down to $2.5 million a year *without* making a proposal. When an agent tells you they will "never" do something, do not believe it. Eventually, we signed a six-year, $13.5 million contract—an average of $2.25 million per year.

5. ASK SMART QUESTIONS.

I never give the opposition information I don't want them to have. I'm also always amazed at how much useful information the other side is willing to share. All you have to do is ask—in the right way, at the right time.

One day before the NBA trade deadline in 1991, I traded Sonics center Olden Polynice to the Los Angeles Clippers for Benoit Benjamin, who was about to become a free agent and wasn't agreeing to any of the Clippers' offers to renew his contract. After the trade, the pressure was on for me to sign our new starting center. We did not want to lose Benoit to free agency, and we did not want to overpay to keep him.

Longtime boxing promoter Don King was one of Benoit's representatives. When I called him to start talking about a contract for Benoit, King told me, "Team Benjamin is willing to negotiate with Trader Bob. James Casey will speak for us. I'll have him call you." James was a character who loved to talk. He didn't understand the collective bargaining agreement, but I enjoyed his personality.

Before the trade, the Clippers told me Benoit had rejected a five-year contract offer worth $18 million, so I decided to open our negotiations with a five-year, $16 million offer. This was below market but not insulting. James countered with five years, $22 million with a $4 million signing bonus. We went back and forth for weeks. Every proposal from Team Benjamin included a signing bonus. I needed to know why the signing bonus was so important, so I cut to the chase and asked, "What is Benoit going to do with the signing bonus if he gets one?"

To my surprise, James said the bonus would pay for two things: the 4 percent agent commission that he would split with Don King and Rolex watches for each member of Benoit's posse, "his boys." This was the information I needed to close the deal. For some midnegotiation homework, I called up Ben Bridge Jeweler and found out that Benoit had already ordered six Rolex watches valued at $125,000 apiece.

I knew the signing bonus was the most important item for Casey, so I made it the focal point of the negotiations—without letting on to Team Benjamin that this was my strategy. First, I made a move that I knew they wouldn't like. "My owner does not believe in signing bonuses," I said, "so let's take that off the table." Casey countered that the signing bonus was a deal-breaking issue. The possibility of including a signing bonus became the leverage I needed to get Team Benjamin to scale back its demands. When agents are in jeopardy of losing their most important item in a negotiation, they tend to make compromises very quickly.

Within a week, we agreed on a five-year contract worth $16.5 million, which included a signing bonus of nearly $2.2 million. It was no coincidence that, after taxes, the net signing bonus added up to just enough to pay Benoit's agents their commission, plus six Rolex watches.

6. IT'S NOT ALL ABOUT WHAT YOU SAY.

Getting the results you want often has less to do with *what* you say than *how* you say it. And sometimes, saying nothing works even better. Silence is one of my favorite negotiating tactics. Someone can make me an offer, and I might just sit and look at them, not saying a word. After about a minute, most people will start talking again. They could even make a better offer, just because I said nothing.

This is much easier said than done. Usually, the other side will ask if you heard what they said or if something is wrong. This is when you have to be patient. If they do ask, you can say something like "That offer was so far off course, I needed time to make sure I wouldn't say something I'd regret."

Silence worked well for me in one of several trades I made during my first year with the Sonics. A couple of weeks before NBA training camps were set to begin in October 1986, John Nash, then a rookie general manager of the Philadelphia 76ers, called me saying his owner was upset he had not made one deal, while the "guy in Seattle" was making a trade every week. The 76ers owner was pressuring John to make a deal, but John was unable to find a willing trade partner. I told him I was open to any deal that included a first-round pick and that I liked their backup center, Clemon Johnson, from our days together with the Indiana Pacers. I then sang the praises of Tim McCormick and Danny Vranes, two players I was trying to get rid of. John called back the next day and offered me Clemon Johnson for McCormick and Vranes. I told John he had a deal if he would include a first-round pick. John said he would give me a second-round pick in 1987.

I said nothing.

John then nervously talked for five minutes and said he could not give me his first-round pick in 1987.

I said nothing.

John continued talking and eventually asked if I would accept a first-round pick in 1989. I said yes, and we made the deal, giving me an extra pick that I used three years later to draft Shawn Kemp.

7. ALWAYS BE READY TO NEGOTIATE.

When I was negotiating Shawn Kemp's contract, his agent, Dr. Charles Tucker, was based in Michigan, three hours ahead of Seattle. There were a number of times when the phone rang at three or four in the morning. I'd be dead asleep, then jump out of bed to answer the phone. My wife would stir a bit as I tried to sound more awake than I was.

"Hello? . . . No, you didn't wake me. Let's talk."

We'd negotiate for an hour or so, I'd hang up, go to bed to get my last hour of sleep, and my wife would say, "Who are those idiots? Why do you tell them, 'No, you didn't wake me?' Of course he woke you! Tell him to call at a different time."

I never did, though. Tucker had a history of leaving messages in the wee hours of the morning so he could avoid talking. The stall technique could drag out for days and get teams to panic. Many GMs increased their offers close to training camp to prevent the unsigned player from missing practice time. I didn't want to give Tucker the upper hand or for him to think he could hide from me. I was ready to negotiate at any hour of the day.

I don't miss those days. It's a lot easier now because you can fire off a quick email or text without being jolted awake in the middle of the night.

8.   KEEP CALM AND EMPATHIZE.

When negotiations get heated, it almost always works to your advantage if you can hang on to your composure, especially when the other side comes unglued. Back at the start of my career, when I was negotiating my first big contract with Clark Kellogg, after the Indiana Pacers drafted him in 1982, I listened carefully to every word his agent said and showed him that I not only heard what he was saying (or shouting) but I actually *understood* his position.

"I *agree* with you," I said. "Clark is worth more than what I'm offering—a lot closer to what you're asking for than what I have at my disposal. It would be different if I had a big pile of money here and didn't want to give it to you. That's not what's going on here, so let's work together."

I laid out the options: Clark could accept our offer and begin his NBA career with a team where he'd be a star. Or he could sit out an entire year, make nothing from basketball, and reenter the draft the following year, when he might be drafted in a much lower position. Lots of things can happen in a year.

"There's a lot of uncertainty," I said, "but today, we're offering your client the certainty of $1 million over five years, guaranteed. That may not be what you want. But it's all we have. What do you say?"

Ultimately, they accepted our offer, and the deal became the talk of the NBA. Everyone was asking how the hell this what's-his-name Whitsitt kid had managed to sign such a coveted first-round pick for half of what he was worth. It was the first high-profile deal I'd done, and the biggest factor had less to do with my negotiating skills than the cold, hard reality that we didn't have a penny more than we'd offered. That combined with sincerity, determination, and calm persistence got me the result I wanted.

Things worked out pretty well for Clark, too, even if he didn't get as much money as he deserved. He earned a spot on the NBA All-Rookie Team and came in second place for Rookie of the Year, averaging more than 20 points and ten rebounds per game. He played three standout years for the Pacers before blowing out his knee. After his shortened playing career, Clark channeled his talent toward a successful career as a TV basketball analyst. You might recognize him as one of the in-studio analysts for the NCAA Final Four.

9. BE CREATIVE.

The path to a deal can involve twists and turns that feel like roads to nowhere. But if you're willing to look for alternatives, to chart your own course, to find different ways to get where you want to go, you'll find your way. Even when you think you've exhausted every option, there are always others.

A lot of GMs quit pursuing a trade, saying the other team just didn't want the players they were offering up. Or they blame a lack of salary-cap space or any number of constraints. That's not what I do. Sometimes, you have to find nuanced exceptions within the collective bargaining agreement. A great general manager finds every way possible to make a team better.

During my first season with the Portland Trail Blazers, we found and exploited a loophole in the NBA labor agreement to sign free agent journeyman Chris Dudley. Teams only used to be allowed to re-sign their own free agents if they had available salary-cap room. But in 1983, Boston Celtics star Larry Bird became a free agent, and the Celtics had no salary-cap room to re-sign him. The NBA did not want Boston to lose its star, so "Bird Rights" were granted to the Boston Celtics. The NBA then instituted a league-wide rule that allowed teams to re-sign their own free agents for any amount of money to retain them—a rule teams used for years when their prized players' contracts expired. The labor agreement also allowed teams to negotiate an option year into a contract, and for players to negotiate an opt-out year. These were not commonly used provisions. But when players did use the option year, or the opt-out clause, it was usually in the last year of their contract.

Chris Dudley had been a free agent in 1993 (the year before I went to Portland), and the Blazers wanted to sign him. Dudley was offered $3.5 million a year to play in New Jersey. Portland was over the salary cap and could only offer a contract with a starting salary of just under $800,000 a year. How could the Blazers get Chris to sign for

$2.7 million *less* than the Nets were offering in year one? It would take something special. Portland offered him a $10.5 million contract with a first-year salary just under $800,000. The special touch was a unique structure that allowed him the right to opt out *after the first year.* If he opted out, he would be our free agent, and we could then use our Bird Rights, paying him any amount we wanted to keep him.

The NBA rejected the contract, claiming the Blazers had circumvented the salary cap. If player opt-outs were allowed after just one season, the NBA knew player salaries would skyrocket. The Blazers were trying to open Pandora's box, and the NBA wanted to slam it shut. The league took Portland to arbitration and lost. The NBA was furious. The following year, Dudley opted out, and we re-signed him to a six-year, $24 million contract. The NBA nixed the contract again, claiming salary-cap circumvention. I testified against the NBA in New York. It felt very weird because the NBA players' union was on my side. They wholeheartedly supported anything that would let players make more money. We prevailed in arbitration, then in a New Jersey federal appeals court. The one-year opt-out clause became very popular league-wide in acquiring free agents. Eventually, the NBA reworked the labor agreement so players could not opt out until they had completed at least two years of a contract.

That wasn't the only time I used a loophole in the labor agreement to close a deal. After the 1999–2000 season, I was working on a trade that would send Blazers forward Jermaine O'Neal to the Indiana Pacers for Dale Davis, a reliable scorer, a double-digit rebounder, and an "enforcer" on the court. Both teams wanted to make the trade, but salary-cap restrictions prevented the deal from happening because Davis made more than O'Neal—just over the salary-cap rule requiring contracts of players being traded to be within 15 percent of each other. Teams trading players with contracts outside 15 percent of each other could include other players in the trade to balance out the salaries. Unfortunately, the Blazers had no other player contract to add to O'Neal's that would satisfy the "within 15 percent" salary-cap requirement. We were stuck.

Then I had an idea.

Joe Kleine, a seven-foot center, had finished his 15-year NBA career in Portland, playing only 31 minutes over a span of seven games.

He had retired and gone home to Arkansas to open a barbecue restaurant, but he had never submitted official retirement paperwork. Technically, that meant I could include him in the trade. My plan was to sign Joe to a $1.2 million guaranteed contract. (That was the least amount of money a 15-year NBA veteran player could sign for under the collective bargaining agreement.) I could then combine the Kleine and O'Neal contracts to make the trade for Davis.

NBA rules allowed only guaranteed contracts to be aggregated in player trades like this, but the rules said nothing about whether a "guaranteed" player would have to stay on the roster. I proposed that the Pacers waive the requirement for a player to get a physical before being traded, cut him after the trade, and pay Joe $1.2 million. Pacers GM Donnie Walsh agreed to my idea because it was the only way to satisfy salary-cap rules.

When I called Joe Kleine to tell him how I'd involved him in the Jermaine O'Neal–Dale Davis trade, I told him he had just won the lottery without having to buy a ticket. Joe signed the contract, never left Little Rock, Arkansas, the Pacers waived him, and he got $1.2 million for not showing up. Joe told me, "Bob, you've got free barbecue and ribs for life anytime you are in Little Rock, Arkansas." Someday, I plan to make the trip to Arkansas and enjoy a barbecue dinner with Joe.

10. GET TO THE HANDSHAKE.

You need to know how to close a deal, but it can be very challenging. A lot of times things can get pretty aggressive. Sometimes, it's hard to say yes. At a certain point, it starts to become clear that a deal is close to happening or close to falling apart. No matter how long it takes to get to this point, you always want to have the last tweak, to offer something new at just the right moment—like I did when we were trying to get Pittsburgh Steelers linebacker Chad Brown to sign with the Seahawks when he became a free agent after the 1996 season. Seahawks GM Randy Mueller and coach Dennis Erickson thought Chad was the best free agent available but that we stood no chance of getting him. They planned to wait until the top free agents signed, then try to get a lower-priced, lesser player.

"Those days are over," I said. "We've got to start thinking like winners. If Brown is who we want, let's make that happen!" I told them to get a meeting with Brown—*in Seattle*—the first day of free agency. "Tell him the two of you will be picking him up in Pittsburgh on Paul Allen's private jet. Invite his wife and anyone else he wants to join him."

I asked for an analysis of linebacker salaries and what they expected Chad could get in the free agent market. Randy guessed around $3.5 million per year. I also asked who the second-best linebacker in free agency was, behind Chad Brown. Randy's answer: Micheal Barrow of the Houston Texans. I told Randy to schedule a meeting with Micheal Barrow in Seattle on the *second day* of free agency.

Randy and I discussed how we would convince Chad to sign with the Seahawks. I felt it was important to sell Chad and his wife on the commitment to winning under Paul Allen. But it was equally important that the Browns see what Seattle had to offer. The plan was to bring Chad to town, show him the practice facility in suburban Kirkland, then tour the city. Randy and Dennis would entertain the Browns and make sure they had a grand time. Then everyone would come back to Kirkland and discuss a contract.

I briefly met Chad and his wife when they returned to Seahawks headquarters. Randy was handling the negotiations. After a few hours, he came to my office to give me an update, saying the meeting went well. Chad said he would get back to us after his visit to the Broncos the next day. I asked about the contract terms. Randy said he'd told Chad and his agent we "could probably pay around $3.5 million per year" and they had seemed pleased with the offer. I knew we were being used as a stalking horse. Chad planned to take our offer and leverage it to get a better deal in Denver. Chad had played college football in Colorado. He loved the area and had a chance to play "at home" with a good team. I had previously discussed this possible scenario with Paul and was ready to be the closer. Randy and Dennis laid the groundwork, but now it was time for some creativity. It was get-to-the-handshake time.

I went down to the conference room, where Chad and his wife were waiting, and told them how much we wanted them to join our team. It was Valentine's Day. I put a check for $7 million on the table, looked at Chad and Kristin Brown, and said, "Happy Valentine's Day!"

I let the moment sink in.

"This is a signing bonus," I said. "Your total contract will be $24 million for six years. Our offer expires as soon as you leave this building. You are the number one priority for the Seahawks, but we have scheduled a meeting with Micheal Barrow tomorrow. We will leave you alone to talk, and hope you take our offer."

Chad Brown did not leave our office until he had signed the six-year contract. Randy's quote in the paper the next day: "This was the best signing we've ever had."

It was a classic negotiation where money ruled the day. Chad had earned $350,000 his last season in Pittsburgh. I thought a $7 million check on Valentine's Day would close the deal. I was right.

11. KNOW WHEN TO WALK AWAY.

Sometimes, no matter how hard you try, you just can't make a deal. You might think it's worth chasing, but in all likelihood, you'll be wasting your time. You need to know when to walk away.

In 1993, I went as far as I could trying to get Dennis Rodman to come play in Seattle. He was in the prime of his career, leading the league in rebounding and earning First Team All-Defense honors five years in a row with the Detroit Pistons. "The Worm" would be the perfect basketball complement to put the Sonics over the top. We had won 55 games in 1992–93, advancing to the Western Conference Finals and losing in seven games to the Phoenix Suns and an unstoppable Charles Barkley.

After that season, our coaching staff urged me to find another star player to help us compete against Barkley and Karl Malone of the Utah Jazz. I knew Detroit was willing to trade Rodman because of his infamous off-court antics. During the 1992–93 season, the Pistons suspended Rodman for three games for refusing to go on a road trip. Later that season, Rodman was found in the parking lot of the Palace in Auburn Hills, asleep in a truck with a loaded gun and reeking of alcohol.

After a lot of negotiating with Detroit, I was able to strike a deal for Rodman without giving up any of our rotation players. The basketball fit was perfect, but the off-court behavior very troublesome. Before agreeing to the trade, I demanded permission to talk with Rodman.

The Pistons honored my request. I called Rodman and left a message for him to call me. An hour later, I got a phone call from someone on an airplane. It was Dennis. We had a fascinating talk for the next two hours. The first half of the conversation was all basketball. Dennis knew the players in the league inside out and dissected our roster perfectly. He knew our players' tendencies as well as any coach. It made sense that Dennis had such a savant-like understanding of the game. He was the best defensive player in the NBA.

The second half of our conversation centered around his desire *not* to play in Seattle. Dennis rattled off a host of personal reasons why the Pacific Northwest was not the right place for him. Seattle was too far away from his daughter, who lived in Oklahoma. The drizzly gray winters would be too depressing. Rodman spoke respectfully and convincingly, with sound reasoning. I honored Dennis's wishes and walked away from the deal because he did not want to be a Sonic. I valued our team chemistry too much to risk adding Rodman to the roster. I felt good about the "non-move." We won a league-best 63 games the following year.

One last thing about walking away: Never do it as a negotiating bluff. The ploy is rarely successful, and you will lose credibility for future negotiations. A good negotiator always discusses BATNA (best alternative to a negotiated agreement) with a client before walking away. As bad as a negotiation feels, the end result may still be better than walking away from a deal.

12. STUDY YOUR MISTAKES.

You can learn a lot from negotiations that don't go well, so take some time to analyze what didn't go your way and why. Was it something you did? Or didn't do? If you could have a do-over, what would you do differently? Seize mistakes as valuable opportunities to sharpen your skills, change things up, and become a more effective negotiator.

One of my most humbling mistakes was getting screwed out of the third year of what was supposed to be my initial contract with the Sonics. I had already left the Sacramento Kings, sold my house down there, moved to Seattle, and had no reason to doubt that Sonics owner Barry Ackerley would honor the handshake commitment he had made to give me a three-year contract. The Sonics were in such terrible shape, as a team and as a business, that I had jumped in and gotten to work right away. I didn't feel the need to demand we sign on the dotted lines before diving in to turn things around. Little did I know it would take weeks of persistent prodding to get Barry to sit down and make my employment official.

As exasperating as the experience was, it taught me several important lessons that have served me well in virtually every negotiation since:

1. You can't always trust a handshake.
2. Get everything in writing.
3. Use clear language.
4. Read carefully before signing.
5. Sign on those dotted lines.

When it came time to negotiate my second contract, I wasn't going to let history repeat itself with a signing-day surprise. Barry and I sat down during the All-Star break in February 1988, months before my initial contract was set to expire. We agreed to terms on a new five-year contract that would begin in late summer, at the start of the 1988–89 season. I knew I wanted to get the new contract signed before the 1988 playoffs started. A bad playoff performance by the Sonics might cause Ackerley to renege on our agreement. I also knew I did not want to sign the contract in his corporate office, like we had with my first contract. We needed to sign the agreement somewhere he would not feel emboldened to change or delete agreed-upon terms.

I hired a lawyer to draft a contract reflecting the terms we had agreed to. The agreement was very simple, but the language was binding for both parties. This "memorandum of agreement" was so straightforward, Ackerley would not need his lawyer to review it. Any layperson could understand it. I kept the contract in my briefcase, waiting for the right time and place to ask Barry to sign.

The Los Angeles Lakers were coming to Seattle on March 1, 1988, to play the Sonics. The coliseum was sold out, and the city was excited to watch us play the defending NBA champions who had beaten us in the Western Conference Finals the previous year. The "Showtime"

Lakers, led by future Hall of Famers Magic Johnson, Kareem Abdul-Jabbar, and James Worthy, were riding a ten-game winning streak and had won 17 of their previous 18. They had the best record in the NBA at 45–9, which made our 114–100 victory that much sweeter. It was a thrilling game, with balanced scoring from Dale Ellis (26), X-Man (24), and Tom Chambers (22). Barry and his wife, Ginger, could hardly contain their excitement as they watched us beat the Lakers.

With about two minutes left in the game, I turned to Ginger and said, "Do you think Barry would have time after the game to sign my new contract? Both of us have been very busy, and we would like to get this done."

"We have no plans after the game, so of course that would be fine," she said.

Ginger then turned to Barry and told him of the postgame plan. After I made my rounds in the locker room and the crowd had cleared out of the arena, Barry, Ginger, and I sat in the stands. Barry and I reviewed my simple contract. He was unlikely to start making changes, since Ginger knew we had agreed to terms. We'd just beat the best team in the NBA. Both of us signed the contract on the exact terms we had agreed to.

I'm not sure if I had more leverage than Barry at that moment, but without question, I was negotiating from a stronger position than I had the first time around. In the end, the Sonics would pay me far more in the first year of my second contract than I would have earned in the third year of my first contract. Go figure.

CHAPTER 8

THE GLOVE

ALL GREAT NBA BASKETBALL TEAMS need at least two stars. Michael Jordan didn't win a playoff series until Scottie Pippen joined the Chicago Bulls. Shaq didn't win a championship until he teamed up with Kobe in Los Angeles. LeBron went ringless until he joined Dwayne Wade in Miami.

I could tell Shawn Kemp was developing into one of the Sonics' stars. The second one we needed entered the NBA draft the summer after Reign Man's rookie year. A lot of times, the general manager, the coach, the coaching staff, and the scouts have different ideas about which players they want to draft. For us, though, that year, it was unanimous: All-American Oregon State point guard Gary Payton was our guy. The draft didn't have many other great players that year, and we weren't the only ones who wanted Payton. *Sports Illustrated* named him Player of the Year, calling him "the coolest, edgiest and most trash-talkin' player, the slickest defender, the deadliest passer, the cockiest leader—in short, the best college basketball player in America."

The Sonics had finished the 1989–90 season with 41 wins and 41 losses, same as the Houston Rockets. The NBA used a predetermined tiebreak procedure to send one of us to the playoffs and the other to the draft lottery. Houston had a better record in the Western Conference, so they went to the playoffs and we stayed home—the only time during my eight seasons with the Sonics that we missed the playoffs.

On one level, it was a low point. On another, it gave us a golden opportunity. If we lucked out in the NBA lottery, which all teams that don't make the playoffs enter, we might get one of the top picks. We *did* get lucky and ended up picking second. But we had no guarantee that the team ahead of us wouldn't pick Payton first. In fact, I knew the New Jersey Nets had their sights set on Gary, too. And so, I got to work behind the scenes. In the week leading up to the draft, I spent a lot of time on the phone with the Nets. I had to make the case that Derrick Coleman, a power forward from Syracuse, would be the best player out of the draft. I needed to talk them into liking Coleman enough to choose him over Payton, all without letting on that I was playing puppet master behind the scenes.

Nets GM Willis Reed pressed me on why I wanted Payton rather than Coleman, who was ranked number one. "I *love* Coleman, but I don't *need* him," I said. "I've already got a Coleman; his name is Shawn Kemp. You guys need a Shawn Kemp; and if you pick Derrick Coleman, you'll get him!" I also reminded Willis he'd drafted an excellent point guard, Mookie Blaylock, in the 1989 draft. It made no sense for the Nets to draft point guards in consecutive drafts.

I could tell it would take more than a good argument to get New Jersey to agree to take Coleman. I would need to offer something valuable in return for their guarantee, so I reached out to the two teams behind us in the draft: Denver (picking third) and Orlando (picking fourth). I knew neither of them wanted Coleman. In Denver's case, it was because he didn't play the position they wanted. Orlando didn't think he had enough of the good-guy image they wanted for Disney World's hometown. I tried to bluff both Denver and Orlando, saying Coleman might be available when it was their turn to pick—and that it would look bad if they didn't pick such a highly ranked player. I said I could guarantee he would already be gone by the time they picked. I would just need something in return, say an extra second-round pick.

Denver didn't blink. Nuggets coach Doug Moe told me nicely he planned to take Chris Jackson, a guard from LSU. Doug thought Jackson's abilities to run an offense, score, and shoot with range were exactly what the Nuggets needed. That left me with Orlando. I knew they felt serious pressure to get one of the top draft picks that year. They needed a pure shooter and had their sights set on Georgia Tech's Dennis Scott. This six-foot-eight small forward was the type of young player who could breathe life into a team that had just finished a dismal 18–64 season. I also knew they had qualms about off-the-court issues with Coleman. He had pending criminal mischief and harassment charges for allegedly punching multiple people in fights while at Syracuse. They had brought about ten draft prospects to Orlando to interview for their selection, each time holding a news conference about it. They did not interview Coleman.

"It's going to look terrible if you have a chance to take Coleman and you don't," I said. Then came my pitch, the one that would give me the leverage needed with New Jersey the next time I tried to convince them to take Coleman. "Give me two second-round draft picks," I told Orlando GM Pat Williams, "and I'll guarantee Coleman won't be there when it's your turn so you won't have this PR problem."

It wasn't a sure thing that New Jersey would pick Coleman. But I had a pretty good feeling I could convince the Nets to take him as long as I could offer them something in return. Say, an extra second-round pick. Orlando agreed and gave me the two second-round picks I had requested. I promptly offered one of them to New Jersey, which they accepted in exchange for their guarantee to select Coleman, ensuring Gary Payton would be available as the number two pick in the first round. And that's how we got Gary Payton—plus that extra second-round pick from Orlando.

This was a major negotiation—two of them—that I spent the better part of a week working on day and night. Nobody agrees to anything until the last second, so both deals were finalized on draft day. All this behind-the-scenes maneuvering took an enormous amount of work, savvy, and skill. And yet it doesn't really go down in Sonics history. No one even wrote about it. It was just "New Jersey picks Derrick Coleman at number one, and the Sonics take Gary Payton at number two." If I hadn't put in all that work to make sure we could get Gary, the Sonics juggernaut of the mid-1990s might never have come to be. In fact, I'm fairly certain it wouldn't have. Gary Payton was *that* important an addition to the team we were rebuilding. The Sonics' second star.

The boos I got for announcing Shawn as one of our first-round picks in 1989 rang as loud as the "Payton, Payton, Payton!" cheers fans chanted at the Sonics' draft party in 1990. It was no secret that Gary was destined for NBA greatness. He had finished his four-year college playing career as the leading scorer in Oregon State history, with 2,172 points. He also ranked second in the NCAA for all-time assists (938) and third in steals (321).

Gary was cocky, a nonstop chatterbox, trash-talker extraordinaire. His motor was fantastic, and the engine was his mouth. In a radio interview the day I drafted him, he boasted, "Players like me and Magic Johnson don't come around very often."

I remember thinking, *Oh, geez . . . I guess I need to go talk to my rookie.*

"I love your game and don't want you to change your personality," I said. "But your name does not belong in the same sentence with Magic Johnson *yet*, and that kind of talk will not earn you the respect of veterans."

I reminded Gary that Magic had won *five* NBA championships, *three* league MVP awards, and had been selected to the All-Star team *ten* times. He'd won the NCAA championship his final year at Michigan State, defeating Larry Bird and Indiana State.

This was the first of many "NBA moments" I had with Gary. We had a great relationship. He was always very respectful toward me, and I quickly learned that it was more important for me to manage other players so Gary could be Gary. A lot of guys have bravado, and you don't want to take that away from them. It's part of what makes them great players. They need it for their confidence. Sometimes, it's an insecurity thing. Sometimes, it's a motivating tool. Sometimes, it's a technique to distract their opponents. Sometimes, it's all those things.

Gary's bravado was so true to his core, he really *did* believe he could play with Magic Johnson and other NBA greats. He believed he was as good as those guys. I didn't want to take that away. I wanted to build on it.

Shawn was different. He kept his self-confidence in check as a rookie. He knew he had a lot to learn and needed to work hard to earn his playing time. The Reign Man let his play do the talking.

Different as they were from one another, Shawn and Gary hit it off on the court. They played together seamlessly. In their first scrimmage during training camp, Gary made a perfectly timed alley-oop to Shawn, one of his seven assists in a "Green and Gold" game played in front of 3,800 fans. After the game, Shawn raved about his new teammate, who had missed most of the first week of training camp while we sorted out the details of his $13.5 million, six-year contract.

"Hey, this is the first time I met this guy, and he was getting me the ball all night like he'd been here all week," Shawn told the *Seattle Post-Intelligencer*.

Gary agreed. "I felt like I'd been playing with these guys a long time."

Shawn and Gary developed a chemistry on the court and a friendship away from basketball. In time, they realized the team was being built around them. Some players don't want that pressure, others do. Shawn and Gary were up for the challenge and did not disappoint. Our full-court fast-break style of play fit their skill sets perfectly. Every game, fans could count on seeing an amazing Payton-to-Kemp highlight dunk. A Payton steal leading to a Kemp dunk became commonplace in Seattle.

Gary was good right away, but it took him about three years to become "the Glove." (He chose the nickname himself—he wanted one for marketing purposes—after a cousin told him it looked like he was holding a baseball in a glove when he was "holding" the player he was guarding.)

Everyone remembers Gary's mouth and his tenacious defense. What people don't talk about is his toughness and durability. I remember many nights when trainer Frank Furtado would tell me, "Gary's back is causing him too much pain. He can't play tonight." I would then go see Gary, and he would tell me, "I'm playing." Payton missed only seven games out of the 1,086 games he played over his 13.5 years with the Sonics.

A lot of guys didn't like Payton, though. He couldn't shoot the ball. He talked too much. He was brash and cocky. But nobody questioned Gary's defensive talent or his competitiveness, most of all Nate McMillan, who gave him by far the warmest welcome of any teammate. That says something, considering that Gary would be taking Nate's spot as starting point guard. Out of respect, I pulled Nate aside and said, "If you feel this isn't right for you, I will quietly work on a trade so you can go to a team where you could be a starter." But he insisted he was right where he wanted to be.

"Look," Nate said, "I still want to be a starter. I want to compete for it. I love this team. I love Seattle. And I don't want to be traded."

Nate remained a core player on a team that did a remarkably good job pressuring opponents from one end of the court to the other. Athletic players like Gary, Shawn, Nate, and Derrick McKey were able to guard multiple positions. Our trapping and switching defensive schemes allowed us to lead the league in steals.

Gary had testy relationships with some of his teammates, especially veteran players like Ricky Pierce and Eddie Johnson, who thought rookies had no business being as loudmouthed as Gary was. When I'd try to talk to them and get them to ease up a bit, they'd say, "Bob, rather than tell us to tolerate the guy, why don't you tell him to shut the fuck up!"

I'd do a little of both. "Gary, can you take it down a decibel? And, guys, can you put in some earplugs or something? As irritating as he is to you sometimes, think about how irritating he is to opponents."

Ricky "Deuces" Pierce was in his 13th NBA season when we played the Denver Nuggets in the first round of the 1994 playoffs. His role as a small forward was to come off the bench and score. He was very efficient, averaging about 15 points a game in just 20 minutes of playing time. Payton's job as point guard was to distribute the ball to the right people and make sure the offense ran smoothly.

Right before halftime of our second game against Denver, Pierce and Payton got into an argument on the bench. As we went to the locker room with a 50–37 lead, things heated up. Ricky was mad that he wasn't getting enough shots, and he thought Payton was shooting the ball too much. These flare-ups happened a lot because Gary's lack of diplomacy usually turned constructive criticism into a contentious argument. The two players had to be separated in the locker room because neither would back down. With testosterone and adrenaline flowing, the players threatened to bring guns to the locker room the following day. Thankfully, we won the game 97–87, and after I talked to each player, they calmed down.

But the tension never went away. Gary Payton led our team in shot attempts during the regular season and playoffs, going for 15 in Game One and 16 in Game Two. With the Pierce-Payton cloud still hovering, Gary Payton overreacted to Pierce and attempted only six shots in Game Three. We lost the game and the series because we could not recapture the team chemistry that had fueled our league-best 63-win season.

When others wished Gary would just shut up, I viewed his nonstop chatter as a sign that everything was OK with him. One of the rare times he gave off an oddly quiet vibe, I pulled him aside to see if something was wrong. It was All-Star Weekend in Denver, and I thought he might be sick or something. Clearly rattled, he told me he'd been robbed at gunpoint while down in Oakland visiting friends and family during the break right before All-Star Weekend. It had happened in his neighborhood, making the incident all the more disturbing. We had a good talk and I told him he was no longer "one of the boys" when he went home. He was a rich guy wearing expensive bling. He thought he could go out and that everyone would want to kiss the ring. No, they wanted to *take* the ring. I suggested he consider moving his permanent residence to a city where less trouble would find him. Eventually, he took the advice and made his off-season home in Las Vegas.

There are lots of opinions out there about what's better for an NBA team: two stars or three. My take: It's not an either-or thing. Both can work, and both can fail.

Michael Jordan and Scottie Pippen won championships for the Bulls, Shaq and Kobe for the Lakers, while Karl Malone and John Stockton fell short with the Jazz, along with the Suns' Devin Booker and Chris Paul. Shawn Kemp and Gary Payton came as close as any Sonics team besides the 1979 champions to winning a title in 1996, but ultimately, they landed in the category of ringless dynamic duos.

As for three-star teams, Magic Johnson, Kareem Abdul-Jabbar, and James Worthy shined for the LA "Showtime" Lakers, winning three titles together in the 1980s. It was a decade many consider the best in NBA history, defined by the epic rivalry between the Lakers and Celtics, anchored by the three-star powerhouse of Larry Bird, Kevin McHale, and Robert Parish, who clinched three championships for Boston together. Other three-star championship teams: the Miami Heat (LeBron James, Dwayne Wade, Chris Bosh), the Detroit Pistons

(Isiah Thomas, Joe Dumars, Dennis Rodman), and the San Antonio Spurs (Tim Duncan, Tony Parker, Manu Ginóbili).

Some three-star teams got close but never won a championship: Hakeem Olajuwon, Charles Barkley, and Scottie Pippen of the Houston Rockets; and Charles Barkley (again!), Kevin Johnson, and Dan Majerle of the Phoenix Suns.

Regardless of how many superstars a team has, the key to success is having a strong roster that supplements the stars. That's what made the early to mid-1990s Sonics such a spectacular team.

The core of our roster was made up of veteran players. Each would have been a solid starter on *any* NBA team, and each could play multiple positions. Having interchangeable players gave the coach the flexibility to use many different lineup combinations and play a "switching" defense.

At six foot nine, Michael Cage was a 230-pound chiseled specimen. He was a gifted rebounder averaging 10.5 a game for the Sonics. One season, he led the league in rebounding, grabbing 13 a night. We played Michael at center and power forward.

Sam Perkins was fundamentally very sound. He learned the game with Michael Jordan, playing in North Carolina for Coach Dean Smith. "Big Smooth" averaged 11 points and four rebounds a game, and played center and power forward. Sam could really stretch the floor, shooting an amazing 38 percent from three-point range. Nate McMillan was our floor general, a two-time NBA All-Defensive selection who could defend both guards and small forwards. "Mac 10" led the NBA in steals during the 1993–94 season.

Detlef Schrempf could do anything he wanted at the offensive end of the court. Depending on opposing defenses, Detlef could play small forward, big forward, or shooting guard. He was a three-time All-Star and selected Sixth Man of the Year twice.

The core group was athletic, versatile, and talented—a defensive juggernaut. But their biggest strength was basketball IQ. It was easy to make in-game adjustments because of their basketball smarts. These guys played the game with purpose and selflessness. They all wanted to win—and there's no doubt in my mind that Gary Payton was the engine that propelled the Sonics' meteoric rise in the mid-1990s.

Gary earned NBA All-Defensive Team honors nine times and NBA

Defensive Player of the Year in 1996. Many consider him the greatest Sonic of all time and one of the best point guards in NBA history. He was inducted into the Basketball Hall of Fame in 2013. And in 2021, he was named to the NBA's 75th Anniversary Team as one of the greatest basketball players of all time.

TRADER BOB'S TOP 25 NBA PLAYERS OF ALL TIME

You might wonder why Gary Payton doesn't appear on my list of the top 25 NBA players of all time—rankings I started compiling during my NBA career and update every year. It's an inherently subjective exercise. There is no consensus, nor should there be. My rankings are based on multiple factors. I place the most weight on the following criteria:

1. **Winning.** A "greatest player" should have been the best player on a championship team. Winning is a team achievement, so it must be balanced with individual performance. Some of the greatest players played on teams with other Hall of Famers, while some were teamed with mediocre supporting casts.
2. **MVP.** A "greatest player" should have dominated the league and earned an NBA MVP award sometime during their career.
3. **Longevity.** A "greatest player" must have a significant body of work. I consider ten years (approximately 800 games played) a requirement. In addition, I place value on three individual milestones that only happen if the player has played enough games.
    *   **25,000 career points**
    *   **10,000 career rebounds**
    *   **10,000 career assists**

4. **All-Star/All-Defensive.** A "greatest player" should be a perennial selection on NBA All-Star and All-Defensive teams.

To make the top ten in my rankings, a player must have **all three** of the following achievements (versus **at least two** to qualify for 11–25):

1. **Play on a championship team.**
2. **Be selected as the NBA's Most Valuable Player.**
3. **Achieve a significant individual milestone.**

I study analytical models and discuss the "best ever" with people who have been close to the NBA for decades. I have seen most of the greatest NBA players play in person, which factors into my rankings. To make the list, players need to have dominated during the era in which they played. It's impossible to make head-to-head comparisons among players from different eras. Playing conditions, training techniques and facilities, salaries and benefits, and rules have changed dramatically over the years.

With all this in mind, and more (trust me, I spend a *lot* of time considering these rankings), here is the latest edition of Trader Bob's Top 25 NBA Players of All Time, finalized after the 2021–22 season:

1. **Kareem Abdul-Jabbar**
2. **Wilt Chamberlain**
3. **Michael Jordan**
4. **LeBron James***
5. **Oscar Robertson**
6. **Bill Russell**
7. **Larry Bird**
8. **Magic Johnson**
9. **Hakeem Olajuwon**

10. **Kobe Bryant**
11. **Jerry West**
12. **Shaquille O'Neal**
13. **Moses Malone**
14. **Steph Curry***
15. **Bob Pettit**
16. **Rick Barry**
17. **Elgin Baylor**
18. **Elvin Hayes**
19. **Tim Duncan**
20. **Karl Malone**
21. **John Havlicek**
22. **Kevin Durant***
23. **Julius Erving**
24. **Kevin Garnett**
25. **Dirk Nowitzki**

Still active as this book went to press.

Many players who are rightfully considered some of the greatest of all time are not on this list. Some of them used to be until rising stars took their place. Others are unquestionably talented but fall short. They still deserve an honorable mention. The same is true for rising stars.

Honorable Mentions

- **Charles Barkley**
- **Walt Bellamy**
- **Clyde Drexler**
- **Allen Iverson**
- **Sam Jones**
- **Pete Maravich**
- **George Mikan**

- **Gary Payton**
- **Scottie Pippen**
- **David Robinson**
- **John Stockton**
- **Isiah Thomas**

Rising Stars

- **Giannis Antetokounmpo**
- **Luka Dončić**
- **Joel Embiid**
- **Nikola Jokić**
- **Kawhi Leonard**

CHAPTER 9

THE RIGHT COACH

COACHES CAN MAKE OR BREAK a team. GMs usually hire them, and when they do, it's one of the most important decisions they'll make. I had no say in my first two coaches in Seattle.

Bernie Bickerstaff came to Seattle after 12 years as assistant coach of the Washington Bullets. He was hungry for the opportunity to step up as head coach. I liked Bernie a lot. He had good energy, and we worked well together. It was probably a little scary for him at first, having a 30-year-old guy come in and take over as president and general manager. The Sonics had finished their first season under his leadership with the same 31–51 record, the second worst in the league for the second year in a row. I could tell Bernie was on board with the up-tempo system I planned to put in place.

Bernie and I both had risen up the ranks by working hard, showing up every day eager to learn and contribute. We both cared less about our egos than whatever we could do to help the team get better. Bernie loved the role of underdog and was very much a "team" guy. We communicated well. We had each other's backs. Anytime I made a decision, he would be on board and do all he could to make it work. He was one of the few coaches I've worked with that had a good eye for talent.

He was a big believer in our 1986 second-round pick, Nate McMillan. He also embraced my decision to draft Shawn Kemp and did a good job mentoring and developing the 19-year-old NBA newbie during his rookie year. He allowed Bob Kloppenburg to teach and coach the defense, appreciating that Kloppy was more experienced and a defensive guru.

I've always respected what a hard job coaching is. Sometimes, you're a teacher, sometimes, a counselor. Sometimes, your job is to motivate. Sometimes, it's to cool down hot tempers. You have to earn the trust and respect of your players, individually and as a team. In my early 20s, I thought I might coach for a living (as a side gig while teaching high school) if I didn't get into graduate school. And in a lot of ways, the work I did in the front offices of NBA and NFL franchises included aspects of coaching. We spent a lot of time team building, collaborating, teaching, motivating, and sharing in organizational successes and failures. I also spent a good bit of my time "coaching the coaches."

One time, I even subbed in as an assistant coach when Bernie had to be rushed to the hospital with a bleeding ulcer. It was March 10, 1989, at the start of a road trip in Milwaukee. That same day, Assistant Coach Bob Kloppenburg had such a severe arthritis flare-up that he couldn't get out of bed. Another assistant, Gary Wortman, was on a road trip scouting and was unable to join the team until we got to Chicago the next day. That left Tom Newell, a relatively inexperienced assistant coach known for his tendency to be verbose.

"You can't let Tom coach," Bernie insisted when I visited him in the hospital. "The guys won't listen to him."

It would've humiliated Tom if I hadn't let him coach, so I compromised. He would be head coach, and I'd be his assistant. I urged him to keep his pregame talk short and sweet. I planned to tell the guys, "Our top two coaches are sick, but they'll be OK. Let's keep it simple, play hard, and have some fun. The best thing we can do for Bernie and Kloppy is to try to get a win. You guys know what to do," then turn it over to Tom.

"Great," Tom told me, "but I want to do just a little bit of Xs and Os when you're done."

"Sure, Tom," I said. "Thirty seconds. Just tell them, 'This guy does this. This guy does that. Let's rebound, let's go get 'em!' Then we're out of there."

About 30 minutes before game time, I gathered the team in the locker room and told them what was up. "So, guys, we're going to need you to help out a little bit more tonight because Tom's going to be the head coach, and I'm going to fill the role of assistant coach. Obviously, we're understaffed, so we'll keep it simple. Let's just go play hard and have some fun. Tom, do you have a point or two you'd like to add?"

Tom went to the blackboard and started drawing, talking with his back to the guys. I slid to the back of the room to see who, if anyone, listened. No one did. He went on for ten minutes, his back to the guys the whole time, oblivious that no one was paying attention.

At one point, Nate McMillan gave me a look, pointing to the clock as if to say, *We needed to get out on the court for warm-ups five minutes ago!*

So I jumped in. "OK, Tom, we got it. Let's all break on three . . . one, two, three!"

Tom was still talking as guys ran out of the locker room.

I decided to have a little fun during my unexpected stint on the bench. Early on in the game, I went out of my way to give referee Jack Madden some grief about a foul he had called. "Jack," I yelled, "that was a *terrible* call!"

As he ran past our bench, he flashed me a smile. "Enjoy the game, Bob. You're on the bench until it's over."

I could mouth off all I wanted, and nothing I said (or shouted) would get me ejected from the game. I didn't say another word to the officiating crew the rest of the game.

Today, NBA teams usually have several assistant coaches on the bench and another five or six immediately behind the bench. I'm not sure why they have so many, but we could have used another one or two that night. It was stressful to be that shorthanded.

We lost the game, but not miserably: 102–90. Tom tried, but it was a classic case of a coach who compensates for his inexperience by rattling off everything he knows about the game. A good coach knows a lot but will give the team just a little bit of direction—nothing complicated.

Tom's dad, Pete, was a coaching legend and a mentor to Bernie.

Our video coordinator Paul Woolpert's dad, Phil, coached Bernie in college at the University of San Diego. Kip Motta's dad, Dick, hired Bernie as an assistant coach at Washington. Some of these "favor" hires were qualified for their jobs. Some were not. Either way, Bernie felt strongly that he "owed" their fathers.

Bernie loved the game, but the stress that came with soaring expectations of a winning team took a toll on his health. A couple of months before the start of his final season with the Sonics, he talked me into hiring K. C. Jones as an assistant coach. They had a tight friendship and deep mutual respect, having worked together for the Washington Bullets, where Bernie served as an assistant coach under K. C. from 1973 to 1976. Bernie stayed in Washington as an assistant for 12 years, until he got his first head coaching job with the Sonics.

By the end of the 1989–90 season, Bernie retired as coach but remained an important part of the team, moving to the front office as vice president of basketball. Not long after, the Denver Nuggets hired him as president and general manager. (Maybe I did too good of a job as a front-office mentor!) Bernie led Denver's front office for seven years, also coaching the team from 1994 (the year the Nuggets eliminated us in the first round of the postseason) to 1996.

Bernie's retirement opened a door for me—or so I had thought. Then Barry tied my hands. He insisted that we promote K. C. Jones from assistant to head coach.

Barry waxed starry eyed when he explained why K. C. Jones would be our next coach. Barry had seen K. C. play college ball with Bill Russell at the University of San Francisco in the 1950s.

"Well, Barry, that was a long time ago," I said. "What's that got to do with what I'm talking about? If he were still any good, he'd be coaching in Boston!" Instead, the Celtics had sidelined him from head coach to a front-office job as vice president of basketball operations the year before. Barry went on and on about K. C.'s star power, how a basketball legend could surely channel his multiple years of experience in the NBA Finals to give the Sonics the boost they needed to win another championship.

"K. C. Jones is no longer a head coach," I countered. "He's past his prime. He was a great head coach in his day, and he can be an assistant because he's a fatherly figure to the players and a confidant for Bernie, but he can't be our head coach."

But all Barry could talk about was how he had seen K. C. play in college.

I kept pushing back. "Barry, I'm telling you he's not the guy we want. I love him, and I'm happy if he stays on as an assistant. If he had any head coach left in him, he'd still be the head coach of the Boston Celtics."

Barry's mind was made up. "Bob, I'm hiring K. C. Jones."

So, in May 1990, we hired K. C. Jones, signing him to a five-year contract for about $2.5 million. K. C. was thrilled. And I kept quiet about my reservations. One thing K. C. had going for him: everyone on the team knew him. And they respected him. He had won eight NBA championships as a player, another as an assistant coach, and two more as a head coach, when his teams were packed with All-Stars and future Hall of Famers: Larry Bird, Kevin McHale, Robert Parish, Dennis Johnson, and Danny Ainge. During his last two years as head coach in Boston, he had five future Hall of Famers but didn't get to the finals.

We all wanted K. C. to succeed as head coach, and I hoped he would prove my doubts wrong. But soon enough, signs indicated things weren't working out. He wasn't a great communicator. He seemed out of his element. He couldn't draw up a play in a huddle. He'd call time out and couldn't figure out what the players should do. Players told me he didn't know their names. He had no experience dealing with difficult personalities, like the two players who got into an infamous brawl that spilled out onto the street in front of Sonics headquarters.

It happened one afternoon in late November 1990, not long after K. C. called me to say he'd canceled practice after Dale Ellis and Xavier McDaniel had gotten into a vicious fight. At one point, Dale had broken off the handle of a broom and gone after X-Man, wielding it like a spear. It had taken several teammates to break them up.

"I don't know what to do," K. C. said, still shaking 20 minutes after he had ended practice. "I've got two players who want to kill each other."

I called both players individually and had them come to my office, scheduling the meetings an hour apart so they wouldn't cross paths. Dale came first, and I laid out the consequences if anything like that happened again. "If you guys even look cross at each other, you're both suspended for five games without pay," I said.

I walked Dale out of my office, on the second floor of Sonics headquarters, and to the elevator.

K. C. and I were talking in my office, waiting for X-Man, who was supposed to show up 20 minutes later, when an executive vice president I had just hired leaned into my office with a deer-in-the-headlights look. "I'm sorry," Kathy Scanlon said, "but there are these two really big guys fighting out on Queen Anne Avenue. I think they're your players." She wasn't sure who they were because it was one of her first days on the job.

K. C. and I rushed down to the first floor and saw X-Man and Dale going at it in the middle of Queen Anne Avenue. I knew Xavier was bigger and stronger, so I told K. C., "You go to Dale. I'll grab Xavier."

I grabbed X-Man while wearing a suit and tie and got my arms around him to lock him up. If you were to bet who would win a fight between Xavier and any other tough guy in the league, it would be X-Man 100 times out of 100. At six foot seven and almost 220 pounds, he stood four inches taller than me and outweighed me by 20 pounds. I was still working out a lot and lifting weights back then, so I was pretty strong. He just flexed and broke my grip on him. If Xavier had decided to redirect his wrath toward me, he could've done some serious damage. Easily. Lucky for me, he didn't take any of his rage out on me. By the time it was over, my shirt was ripped, my tie yanked to the side, there was blood all over me, and K. C. was walking Dale down the street. Dale must have known he stood no chance in a fight with his furious teammate.

After K. C. and I separated Dale and Xavier, I walked Xavier inside. I soon learned that Dale had thrown the first punch, clocking Xavier in the face as X-Man was walking into the elevator—holding a baby in his arms! Xavier had handed the baby to a woman in the lobby, then gone after Dale. I wound up suspending Dale for five games for the fight he'd instigated minutes after I'd told him I would suspend them both if they did so much as look at each other sideways. X-Man hadn't even gotten the chance to hear what I expected of him, so he didn't miss any playing time. This was one of many times in my career when I had to roll with a situation I never would have expected.

During K. C.'s first season (1990–91), we squeaked into the playoffs with a 41-41 record, then lost to the Portland Trail Blazers in the first round. The mediocrity continued the following season. We had won 18 and lost 18 when Barry gave me the go-ahead to fire the guy he'd fought so hard to hire.

One of the hardest things to do in any business is to fire somebody, especially when it's a guy as nice as K. C. Jones. I didn't sleep very well the night before. When I called K. C. into the office, he almost finished my sentence when I started to break the news to him. He wasn't surprised at all. He didn't object or convey any hard feelings. A minute or two into the meeting, he very politely reminded me that he still had about three and a half years left on his contract. I had already discussed this with Barry and assured K. C. that we would pay him for the remainder of his contract. Once we got that squared away, he asked if I could help him find a box to pack up his office.

A couple of weeks later, K. C. called to let me know his paycheck hadn't arrived. True to form, Barry had decided not to pay him. I couldn't believe it. And yet I *could*. That was how Barry operated. He had no qualms about going back on his word.

"You signed him, Barry," I said. "You gave him a five-year contract. You paid him more than you had to. And now you're refusing to pay him. You can't *do* that!"

Ultimately, I got NBA commissioner David Stern involved, who put heat on Barry to do the right thing. Then, I finally had the chance I'd been waiting for to hire the right coach.

When I first called George Karl about our opening for head coach, he thought I was somebody playing a prank on him. Everyone else in the NBA had written him off as too hotheaded. He burned bridges like they were kindling, trash-talking owners, general managers, his own players, anyone who did or said anything that challenged his view on how the game should be played. He was passionate about basketball— still is—so passionate it often got him in trouble. He'd get kicked out of games for going ballistic on refs. He would light into his players if he thought they were slacking. He once tore a player's locker apart after losing a close game and getting swept out of the playoffs. Back during his playing days with the San Antonio Spurs, he'd thrown some of the first punches in an infamous brawl that had emptied the benches in a game with the New Jersey Nets.

George started his pro basketball career by turning down the New York Knicks, who had picked him in the fourth round of the 1973 NBA draft. He went to the ABA's San Antonio Spurs instead. He spent three years as the Spurs' backup point guard, where his aggression on defense and the way he dove for loose balls earned him the nickname Kamikaze Kid. He rarely played after the Spurs joined the NBA, retired as a player in 1978, then joined the Spurs' coaching staff for a couple of seasons before taking his first job as head coach with the Montana Golden Nuggets in the Continental Basketball Association (CBA). I love how he describes the CBA in his memoir, *Furious George*. "Think AA or AAA minor league baseball. *Bull Durham* stuff—a lot of bus travel, bad food, cheap hotels, no money."

George coached the Golden Nuggets to the CBA Finals in 1981 and 1983. Then the franchise folded, and he returned to the NBA for a stint as director of player acquisition for the Cleveland Cavaliers. He then became head coach in 1984. During his first year, he led the Cavs to the playoffs for the first time in six seasons, but the success didn't last. He got fired after a 25–42 start the following season, then made his way to the Golden State Warriors. During his first year as head coach, he took the team to the 1987 playoffs for the first time in ten years. The future of the franchise was looking bright, until three of his top players got traded away to save money, a fourth entered alcohol treatment, and injuries hobbled others. The Warriors had a 16–48 record by the time George was fired.

That's where his story gets really interesting. He went back to the *minors*, taking an enormous pay cut to replace Phil Jackson as head coach of the CBA Albany Patroons. (Phil had just taken a job as an assistant coach for the Chicago Bulls.) He spent the next four years bouncing back and forth between Albany and Madrid, where he was when I called him about coaching the Sonics.

At first, I asked if he would consider being an assistant coach. He didn't realize this was a test, and he passed. I wanted a coach who was hungry, infectiously passionate about the game, and willing to develop the young stars I had drafted. For the next three and a half years, we

Shawn Kemp reverse dunks on Phoenix Suns players Danny Ainge and Oliver Miller during the 1993 NBA Conference Finals. AP photo/Gary Stewart.

Fred Brown and Bob Whitsitt at a press conference announcing the Sonics' decision to retire Brown's number on November 6, 1986. Grant H. Haller/MOHAI, Seattle Post-Intelligencer *Collection.*

Kareem Abdul-Jabbar shoots a sky hook over Xavier McDaniel in the Sonics' 1988–89 regular season finale. The Lakers won the game despite X-Man's 39-point performance. AP photo/ Reed Saxon.

In 1985, Bob Whitsitt sold the Sacramento Kings' arena naming-rights sponsorship to ARCO. This first-of-a-kind title sponsorship became a game changer in sports marketing. Rocky Widner/NBAE via Getty Images.

Sonics owners Barry and Ginger Ackerley sitting courtside with Bob Whitsitt at a Sonics home game. Kurt Smith/MOHAI, Seattle Post-Intelligencer Collection.

Bob Whitsitt's first draft pick as Sonics president and general manager, Nate McMillan, being guarded by Phoenix Suns All-Star Kevin Johnson. AP photo/Gary Stewart.

Sonics guard Dale Ellis initiating a step-back jumper against Indiana Pacers Hall of Famer Reggie Miller. AP photo/Gary Stewart.

Bob Whitsitt announcing the Sonics' 1990 first-round draft selection—future Hall of Famer Gary Payton. Gilbert Arias/MOHAI, Seattle Post-Intelligencer *Collection.*

Bob Whitsitt at a press conference, announcing K. C. Jones as the Sonics' head coach and Bernie Bickerstaff as vice president of basketball operations. AP photo/Gary Stewart.

Gary Payton, George Karl, and Detlef Schrempf having fun prior to a Sonics NBA preseason game in Berlin, Germany. AP photo/Jan Bauer.

*Gary Payton and Bob Whitsitt in Utah after a 1992 Sonics playoff-game loss to the Jazz. Rod Mar/*Seattle Times.

Benoit Benjamin, agent James Casey, and Ricky Pierce join Bob Whitsitt at a press conference to announce both players signed contract extensions with the Sonics. Mike Urban/MOHAI, Seattle Post-Intelligencer *Collection.*

The Sonics' Sam Perkins, rising up for a jumper. AP photo/Elaine Thompson.

Bob Whitsitt and P. J. Carlesimo at a 1999 Blazers press conference. Gary Settle/Seattle Times.

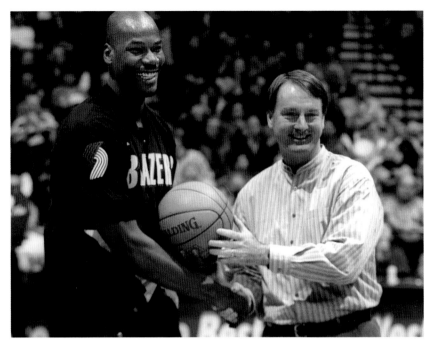

Bob Whitsitt presents Cliff Robinson with the game ball after Robinson scored his 10,000th point as a Portland Trail Blazer against the New Jersey Nets on March 4, 1997. Joel Davis/ Oregonian.

Two Hall of Famers, Portland Trail Blazer Arvydas Sabonis and Karl Malone of the Jazz, in a classic matchup. Brent Wojahn/ Oregonian.

Bob Whitsitt, Paul Allen, and Bill Gates enjoying a Blazers playoff game courtside. AP photo/ Jack Smith.

The Blazers' Rasheed Wallace letting off steam with a thunder dunk. AP photo/Jack Smith.

After being selected by Bob Whitsitt with the 17th pick in the 1996 draft, Trail Blazer Jermaine O'Neal became a six-time NBA All-Star. Layne Murdoch/NBAE via Getty Images.

Blazers coach Mike Dunleavy with point guard Damon Stoudamire. AP photo/Douglas C. Pizac.

Scottie Pippen and Blazers president and general manager Bob Whitsitt at a press conference announcing Pippen's arrival to Portland after a six-player trade with the Houston Rockets in October 1999. Dan Levine/AFP via Getty Images.

Blazers head coach Maurice Cheeks assists a national anthem singer who forgot the words. Jon Ferrey/Getty Images.

Seattle Seahawks owner Ken Behring attempted to move the NFL team to Los Angeles. Mike Urban/MOHAI, Seattle Post-Intelligencer *Collection.*

Bob Whitsitt signs the purchase and sale agreement for Paul Allen's acquisition of the Seattle Seahawks on July 1, 1997. King County executive Ron Sims and Washington governor Gary Locke are applauding the signing. Photo by Rob Sorbo.

Mike Holmgren preparing to coach his first Seahawks preseason home game against the Buffalo Bills on August 14, 1999. AP photo/Lauren McFalls.

After months of negotiations, the Kingdome was imploded on March 26, 2000, paving the way for a new outdoor Seahawks football stadium. The implosion took only 17 seconds. Ellen M. Banner/Seattle Times.

Bob Whitsitt gives the media a tour of the new Seahawks stadium in May 2002, just three months before final completion. AP photo/Elaine Thompson.

Bob Whitsitt and Paul Allen sit in a suite at the new Seahawks stadium on July 17, 2002. AP photo/Elaine Thompson.

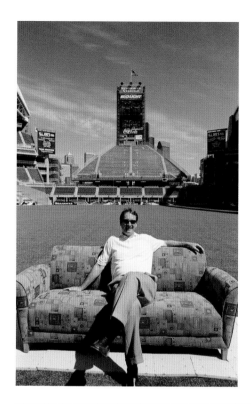

Bob Whitsitt relaxing on a couch during the grand opening of the new Seahawks football stadium in 2002. Melina Mara/MOHAI, Seattle Post-Intelligencer *Collection.*

Law student Bob Whitsitt preparing for graduation in 2021 with his grandsons Liam, Clancy, and Dylan. Courtesy of Bob Whitsitt.

Bob met his wife, Jan, in 1984, when she was vice president of broadcasting and marketing for the Sonics. Courtesy of Bob Whitsitt.

Shawn Kemp and Bob Whitsitt at the LA Clippers vs. Portland Trail Blazers NBA preseason game in Seattle on October 3, 2022. Courtesy of Bob Whitsitt.

would be paying the remainder of K. C.'s contract in addition to our new head coach's salary, so I had to make sure I got this hire right.

I loved the fact that George had gone to the CBA *after* coaching in the NBA. Not only do you have to put up with small crowds, little towns, cold weather, and bad gyms, but you have to be flexible because, any day, your best player(s) could be called up to the NBA to fill in for someone who was injured. CBA coaches learn how to adapt, how to coach with the players they have in the moment. They know how to switch up their game plans, run different plays that are better suited for the active roster. George was innovative. In a league where big men often dominated, he would play "small ball," initiating offense from the forward position and sending a guard to post up near the basket. Usually, the opposing coach would try to match George's smaller lineup by substituting big men for guards, with little success.

I didn't seriously consider any candidates other than George. I interviewed a number of experienced coaches, but they were all stale cookie cutters, retreads, same old, same old. I wanted someone who would work hard and coach to the strengths of our versatile players. Not all coaches do that. A lot of them take shortcuts and run the same system they have always run. They get their big payday, and that's all they care about. George was different. He worked hard. Every day. And clearly, he wasn't just coaching for the money. He was coaching because that was all he wanted to do.

I had to work hard to talk Barry Ackerley into letting me hire George. At first, Barry and his wife, Ginger, both said no. They wanted someone well known, like Mike Fratello, a TV commentator who called games alongside Marv Albert after coaching the Atlanta Hawks and New York Knicks. They asked me who in the NBA could vouch for George, and I told the truth: no one. I had called 20 or so coaches and GMs, and everyone I'd talked to had rather pointedly urged me not to hire George. I listened to everything they had to say and didn't disagree with a lot of their criticism. His volatile, loudmouthed temper would be a liability—especially when he drank, which wasn't a rare occurrence. They said he liked to leak information to the media, which made it hard to make trades. Of all the people I talked to—many of them friends with George—only one person had a neutral opinion of him. Chicago Bulls GM Jerry Krause told me he would never hire

George but he would never tell me not to. All those criticisms were valid, but so was my hunch that George would give everything he had to the Sonics and that he had the passion and the energy to lead the team to another NBA championship.

At one point, during the last of several conversations we had about George, Barry asked me, "Bob, do you think all those people in the NBA, me and Ginger, everyone who thinks this guy's no good . . . do you think we're all *wrong*?"

"I'm not saying you're wrong," I replied. "I'm just telling you I believe this is the right guy, at the right time, for this situation, working with *me*. And I believe *we* can take this team to the next level. This is the guy *I* want to hire."

We were sitting at Barry's house at Hunts Point. I wasn't letting up, and finally, Barry looked at Ginger and said, "I hired K. C. over Bob's wishes, so we should probably let him make this decision. He's heard us loud and clear. If this one doesn't work out, he's gone."

The more I talked with George, the more excitement he exuded, and not just about joining the Sonics. I could tell he was eager to work with *me*. He was known for clashing with his previous GMs, blaming losses on bad trades and draft picks. Talking to me, though, he made it clear he liked the team I had built, loaded with talent, guys who could play multiple positions. We could extend the court defensively with full-court, three-quarter, and half-court traps. We had enough depth, we could bring in fresh players whenever we wanted. Nate McMillan had moved from point guard to small forward when Gary Payton came in, so Nate could play three positions. Gary could play two. Shawn Kemp and Michael Cage could each play two positions. Derrick McKey could play *five* positions. We could keep mixing and matching, and with the right coaching, we would find a combination on the court every single night, every single possession, where the Sonics had the advantage.

George knew I was taking a big risk on him. He knew my job was on the line. And he could tell I was sincere when I said I would do everything I could to help him succeed. My job depended on it. He didn't flinch when I said I planned to manage him more closely than he'd ever been managed before. I would make sure he kept his ego in check. Same with his temper. I didn't expect him to not go ballistic on refs ever again. But it couldn't happen as often as it had back with

Cleveland and Golden State. Sometimes, when a coach receives a technical and gets thrown out of a game, it can light a fire under a team in a good way. Every now and then, when I sensed the team was running low on motivation, I'd pull George aside before the game and suggest it might be a good night to let loose. George always smiled and got excited when I suggested the tactic.

I would often spend a few minutes with him after games, especially ones that didn't go our way, to help him calm down and dial in the remarks he would make in the postgame news conference. Most coaches don't want their GMs talking to them immediately after a game. George and I had a different relationship. He trusted me. And I trusted him. I respected his passion for the game, the high energy he brought to every practice, every game, every conversation about the game, the team, and how to keep improving. Players need that high energy from a coach. We all need it sometimes. If you're running a race, and you're tired, and suddenly someone leans in, all fired up, and gives you that pep talk you need to keep going—that's the kind of coach and person George was.

Sometimes, a great coach and a great player don't get along. I spent a lot of time smoothing out the friction between George Karl and Gary Payton—not an easy job, but one I knew had to be done for the team to have a chance at a championship. George also had issues with Benoit Benjamin, a talented center we got from the Clippers in a trade that sent Olden Polynice, a decent but limited player, to LA. Benoit did better in Seattle than in LA, but he had a lax, happy-go-lucky way about him, when the thing George wanted most out of his players was hard work and hustle.

There were some tense moments when it looked like George was about to implode with frustration, so I said, "George, I agree with you, but here's what I'll do. I'll find a way to trade Benoit. This won't be an easy deal because we've signed him to a new long-term contract. He's a big-money guy, and this is where we've got to work together. If you start bashing him and ripping him in the media, I can't move him. So I want you to love him, embrace him, kiss him, or at least not bash him. And I'm telling you, I will get him traded before the season's over. I'll get us a hell of a deal, but you just coach and stay on that page, and let me do my thing."

I made good on my word with one of the best deals of my career: I convinced Lakers GM Jerry West to give me Sam Perkins for Benoit Benjamin and the rights to Doug Christie. Sam was a great player, who could play both forward and center. Sam's long arms made him an effective shot blocker and a good anchor for our team defense. He was fundamentally smart and a very good three-point shooter. He could take bigger players outside away from the paint with his perimeter shooting. He could also dominate smaller players in the post. He was the "final piece" we needed for a championship-caliber team.

I thought George might ask me to marry him after I made that trade. He was so happy. He couldn't stand it. . . . He loved Sam Perkins for many reasons. Just like George, "Big Smooth" had played college ball at North Carolina for Dean Smith. Sam had played for the Tar Heels when they won the NCAA championship in 1983. He was a smart ballplayer, a true professional, a huge part of the Sonics' success for many years, and a fan favorite.

The Sonics had a tremendous season in 1993–94. With our league-best 63 wins, we were heavily favored to win the championship. We went into the playoffs feeling like this was the year we would finally bring another championship home to Seattle. I was named NBA Executive of the Year. We sold out every game.

Our first-round opponent was not an easy matchup for us, primarily because of their seven-foot-two dominant defensive center, Dikembe Mutombo. Every time we drove into the paint, Mount Mutombo stood in the way. Just the threat of blocking a shot forced our players to alter another half dozen shots a game. We won the first two games in the best-of-five series at home, then lost the next two in Denver. The series clincher was played in Seattle and was a hell of a basketball game. It went into overtime. Mutombo played spectacularly, and we lost 98–94.

Losing in the first round of the playoffs was not part of our game plan. The day after the Game Five loss, Ackerley called me into his office. He was livid. He'd thought we would win the title. He couldn't stop criticizing George Karl and insisted I fire him immediately. I tried to calm him down by saying we all felt terrible. I told him the best thing we could do was take a week off to let our emotions cool down before we started making any basketball decisions. He wanted no part of waiting. I told him I was traveling east for the week with my family to attend my wife's college reunion at Yale. I tried to get him to understand there was no urgency and that whatever we decided to do could be done in a week. He finally agreed to stand down and continue our discussions when I got back.

The next day, when I was on an airplane flying to the East Coast, Ackerley held a press conference announcing that I had resigned. His quick temper had gotten the best of him (again), and he broke his promise to not make any decisions until I returned.

I spent most of my "vacation" out east returning calls to the media, telling them that I had *not* resigned. Ackerley had his lawyer call to tell me not to return to my office when I got back to Seattle. I asked if I was fired. He said no, so I went to my office when I got home. It was time for intense draft preparation, which meant many meetings with coaches and scouts.

My second day back in the office, I was greeted with a surprise. Ackerley had sent my assistant, Sarah Furtado, on an indefinite paid leave. He had also cleaned out my office. I had no phone, no fax machine, no furniture . . . nothing. He refused to fire me; he would've had to pay the remaining two years on my contract. And he refused to let me work. The coaches, players, and front office were all in shock.

NBA commissioner David Stern called me during this standoff period. He told me Ackerley was a loose cannon but he was the owner. He also told me some owners did stupid things. I had known David for a long time. I had started working in the NBA while he was still a lawyer at a prestigious corporate, sports, and entertainment law firm in New York. David told me to work out a deal with Ackerley and become a free agent. He assured me I would have a choice of jobs. Some owners were already calling him, inquiring about my availability. This all happened less than two weeks after I had been named NBA Executive of the Year.

Ackerley did not want me running the upcoming Sonics draft, and he did not want me running another team's draft. With the help of Commissioner Stern, we negotiated a settlement. Ackerley would pay me through June, but I could not work in the NBA until after the draft. Afterward, he would pay me part of the remaining years of my contract, provided I pay him $500,000 if I took another NBA job.

This was a bittersweet time for me. I truly believed we would win at least one title during the next four years. We had the best record and a team in its prime. We also had a lottery pick in the upcoming draft and salary-cap room to be used for a free agent or a trade. We were in great shape. I knew we could use the first-round loss as a motivating tool and come back the next season hungry and determined.

On the other hand, it is hard to put your soul into an organization when the owner does not want you around. I've always respected the fact that owners have the right to do as they see fit. Ackerley wanted someone fired, so I decided to take the fall. If I left, George could remain in Seattle to finish the championship quest. The Sonics needed George Karl to stay on as coach more than they needed me to continue as president and general manager.

As painful as it was to me, personally and professionally, I knew I was making the right move. I didn't tell George the full story about how and why I left. If he'd known how much Barry had wanted him gone, it would've pounded his ego and flooded him with self-doubt. He's not the guy you want looking over his shoulder. You want him looking straight ahead, ready for battle. In one of our last conversations before I left, I told him it was a good time to negotiate a contract extension. Despite our early exit from playoffs, he still had those 63 wins as leverage.

George Karl coached another four seasons in Seattle, winning more games than any other coach in franchise history. Two seasons after I left, the Sonics made it to the NBA Finals, losing to Michael Jordan and the Chicago Bulls. Shawn Kemp was fantastic throughout the series, averaging 23 points and ten rebounds. Payton averaged 18 points, six rebounds, and seven assists. It was great to see the two stars I had drafted play so well on the biggest basketball stage in the world. Unfortunately, George waited until the Bulls had a three-to-zero series lead before letting Gary Payton guard Jordan. With the Glove guarding MJ, the Sonics won Games Four and Five before losing the series in Game Six.

It was the closest George got to winning a championship. After Seattle, he coached the Milwaukee Bucks, the Denver Nuggets, and the Sacramento Kings. During his 27 years of NBA coaching, he amassed 1,175 regular-season wins and 22 playoff appearances, ranking him the sixth-winningest coach in NBA history. At his 2022 induction into the Basketball Hall of Fame, he joked that to this day, he still has no idea why I hired him when everyone else in the league had written him off. Maybe someday he'll understand that I knew exactly what I was doing and how glad I am that I gave him that second chance.

TRADER BOB'S TOP TEN NBA COACHES OF ALL TIME

Just like my list of all-time best players, I keep an updated list of the best coaches in NBA history. My rankings are based partly on stats and analytics. A coach should have at least 500 wins to be eligible. The list is also based on how well I think these coaches implemented basketball systems that utilized their players' strengths. I looked at adaptability, creativity, and how well they maximized the rosters they had to coach.

1. **Phil Jackson** (1155–485) .704 win percentage, 11 NBA championships
2. **Red Auerbach** (938–479) .662 win percentage, 9 championships
3. **Pat Riley** (1210–694) .636 win percentage, 5 championships
4. **Gregg Popovich*** (1344–701) .657 win percentage, 5 championships
5. **Larry Brown** (1098–904) .548 win percentage, 1 championship
6. **Jerry Sloan** (1221–803) .603 win percentage
7. **George Karl** (1175–824) .587 win percentage
8. **Don Nelson** (1335–1063) .557 win percentage
9. **Steve Kerr*** (429–200) .682 win percentage, 4 championships
10. **Erik Spoelstra*** (660–453) .593 win percentage, 2 championships

*Still coaching as this book went to press.

Honorable Mentions

- **Rick Adelman** (1042–749) .581 win percentage
- **Red Holzman** (696–603) .536 win percentage, 2 championships
- **Jack Ramsay** (864–783) .525 win percentage, 1 championship
- **Rudy Tomjanovich** (527–416) .559 win percentage, 2 championships
- **Lenny Wilkens** (1332–1155) .525 win percentage, 1 championship

Rising Stars

- **Tyronn Lue** (225–149) .602 win percentage, 1 championship
- **Nick Nurse** (186–122) .604 win percentage, 1 championship
- **Monty Williams** (322–299) .519 win percentage

CHAPTER 10

PAUL ALLEN CALLS

IT TOOK SEVERAL FRAUGHT AND frustrating weeks for my departure from the Sonics to become official. After eight exhilarating years of rebuilding a team from train wreck to title contender, I wrestled with some fierce emotions as I declined to comment on all kinds of speculation about the hotly disputed terms of my exit.

In the late spring and early summer of 1994, about a dozen or so teams called me, wanting to know if I was interested in being their GM—the Philadelphia 76ers, the Toronto Raptors, the Los Angeles Clippers, and others. But I only seriously considered the two teams closest to Seattle, where my family and I wanted to stay.

As an expansion team just getting off the ground, the Vancouver Grizzlies would require a lot of heavy lifting, much more than I could do without living there full time. Grizzlies owner John McCaw, a Seattle telecom billionaire, offered to let me manage the team from Seattle, but I declined. I would never take a job and put in anything less than the full effort I knew would be necessary to do it well.

When Trail Blazers owner Paul Allen called, he also offered to let me keep my family in Seattle and commute to and work in Portland. The Blazers were an "old" team in decline, with the second-highest payroll in the NBA, way over the salary cap. It needed to be broken up and rebuilt—a lot like the Sonics did in 1986.

The front office was a whirling dervish of dysfunction, riddled with turf wars. Geoff Petrie, a popular GM who had played for the Blazers in the 1970s and led them to two finals appearances in the early 1990s, had just quit. He'd been feuding with Brad Greenberg, vice president of basketball operations, who had clashed with the team's longtime and beloved head coach, Rick Adelman. Brad would later clash with me, too, because he wanted the Blazers GM job himself. Then there was Marshall Glickman, son of Blazers founder Harry Glickman, who ran the business side of the franchise; no one liked him.

I had only talked to Paul Allen one time before he called me about the GM job in Portland. He had reached out during my first year or so in Seattle to gauge Barry Ackerley's interest in selling the Sonics. Barry had rebuffed him, and in 1988, Microsoft's elusive cofounder had bought the Trail Blazers. He was 35 at the time, just a few years older than me.

My interview took place at Paul's sprawling estate on Mercer Island. As soon as we started talking, it became clear he wasn't very social and was quite awkward interpersonally. The first thing he wanted to know was if I was talking with John McCaw about the Vancouver Grizzlies job. I told him we'd had several good meetings and that I was joining John for lunch on his boat at Shilshole Marina on Puget Sound later that day. I manufactured some small talk to make our meeting a little more comfortable before we started talking basketball. Paul kept asking me how I made so many great trades and draft selections. I kept my answers vague but specific enough to show him I knew what I was doing. Paul loved our Sonics squad. He wanted to know if I could build another fast-paced, athletic team that played with excitement and flair. I said I could but told him no two teams were ever the same.

I told him there are two ways to build a great team. The easiest way is to tear the team down by trading any players who have value to other teams, accumulating as many first-round picks as possible. Miss the playoffs for five years, then you qualify for the draft lottery, which guarantees you five high draft picks. Have a low payroll with lots of salary-cap room. Around the five-year mark, sign a couple of good free agents to complement the drafted players, and the team should be very good—if you draft well.

The second way is much more difficult. Remain competitive and rebuild while staying in the playoffs every year. This requires a general manager who knows how to play NBA chess instead of checkers. My checkers-versus-chess analogy really piqued Paul's interest. A chess master trades for players nobody else in the NBA wants—players who might have character or work ethic issues, injuries, or too many years on his contract. You can acquire undesirable players like this without giving up much, then you've got to put in the work, give them the guidance they need to improve, and they'll not only make a positive impact on your team, they'll become attractive to other teams someday. The risk is obvious. If undesirable players don't pan out, you're stuck with them. If they *do* improve, you'll trade them when the time is right for an even better and more reliable player.

Paul asked me for an example, and I told him how I had traded Olden Polynice—a backup center with very little trade value—for Benoit Benjamin, a center known for being lazy and unreliable, who had never led his LA Clippers to the playoffs. With a lot of effort, we had squeezed some good years out of Benoit. As soon as we had created some market value, I'd traded him to the Lakers for a much better player: Sam Perkins, who became a star on the mid-1990s Sonics team that came close (so close!) to winning Seattle's second NBA championship in 1996.

The NBA has very few chess masters because a high-risk trade is the easiest way to lose a job. When the first part of the chess move doesn't pan out, the GM responsible for the deal often gets fired. The personal risk outweighs the possible upside for the organization. Paul asked me if I could rebuild the Blazers without missing the playoffs. I said it would be very difficult but that I believed I could do it.

I could tell Paul had the necessary passion and commitment to make the bold moves that would transform the Blazers. He wasn't afraid to ruffle feathers. Not long before he hired me, he had pissed off Portland by firing Rick Adelman as head coach—just days after Geoff Petrie had resigned as GM. Brad Greenberg filled in as interim GM and talked Paul into replacing Adelman with P. J. Carlesimo, paying him $1.5 million a year for five years—a lot of money for an NBA coach back then. P. J. had coached at Seton Hall University for more than a decade but had no NBA experience. He needed some coaching himself to fully grasp key differences between NCAA and NBA rules and how to coach professionals versus college students.

Paul knew that hiring a head coach is one of the most important jobs a GM does. While I was interviewing, he admitted, "Geez, I'm kind of doing this backwards. I've already hired the coach and paid him a lot of money. I've got an old team that we should've broken up a year ago. . . . Oh, and I need to tell you—I think I promised Clyde Drexler another contract extension like I did last year because he talked me into it. But under no circumstances am I giving him more money. And you've got to be the guy to get me out of that."

A fan favorite who had played his entire career in Portland at that point, Clyde Drexler had convinced Paul to add another year and a lot more money to his contract—twice. First, at the end of the 1992–93 season, he got a raise from $1.6 million a year (what he would earn in 1994–95) to $10 million (what he would earn in 1995–96). That was the first of two extra years he got Paul to agree to add to his contract, each at $10 million.

Having to trade away Drexler right off the bat subjected me to some of the same fan hatred I had dealt with during my first year at the Sonics, when Jack Sikma—the only remaining member of Seattle's 1979 championship team—demanded to be traded. Portland fans and the media were already seething that their team's Seattle owner had not only just hired another Seattle guy to be the Blazers' GM—but the guy who had *just* left the Sonics? They welcomed me about as warmly as a fox would be greeted at the door of a henhouse.

To this day, Clyde "the Glide" Drexler ranks as one of the best Blazers of all time, right up there with Bill Walton, the superstar center of Portland's 1977 NBA championship team, and Damian Lillard. Clyde was the Blazers' all-time leader in scoring, assists, steals, and rebounds. I also had to get rid of three other veterans—Jerome Kersey, Terry Porter, and Buck Williams—all members of the teams that had gone to the finals in 1990 and 1992. There was no question it was time for them all to go. The Blazers needed new blood.

Rebuilding the team would be a big job in and of itself. And there was more. Construction of a new arena was underway, and Paul wanted me not only to help him wrap that up but to make sure we continued to make the playoffs.

"We're going from a 12,000-seat arena to one with 21,000 seats," he said. "If we stop making the playoffs, we won't be able to sell tickets for the other 9,000 seats."

It would be a lot to oversee the completion of Portland's Rose Garden while rebuilding a team and making the playoffs, all in the same year. I had faced similarly daunting odds when I'd set out to turn around the Sonics. I had started out with a lousy team, with no salary-cap space, no draft pick, and had built them into a championship-caliber powerhouse with not only the best record in the NBA but an abundance of salary-cap space *and* a lottery pick because of a trade I'd made the year before. So I took the job in Portland, signing a six-year contract that included an opt-out clause allowing me to leave after three years if I wanted to.

During my first week on the job, Clyde Drexler came running into my office, griping that he was underpaid and needed a new deal. Paul wanted him gone. And at first, Clyde wanted to go to a bad team, thinking he could command more money. I saw things differently. I wanted to trade him to a team where he could be the difference maker and win a championship.

"Clyde, believe me," I said. "All you care about is money right now, but when it's all over, you'll be happy you won a championship somewhere."

As the season unfolded and Clyde got increasingly antsy, I decided to pursue a trade that would be painful for me but great for Clyde— and great for the team I'd just left. I offered to trade him to the Sonics for Kendall Gill and a first-round draft pick. Both players were athletic shooting guards, but Kendall was six years younger than Clyde. The age difference mattered in my rebuild strategy; Gill would still be in his prime when our team became ready to win a championship.

To this day, I'm confident that deal would have won the Sonics the championship in 1995. Michael Jordan wasn't playing in the NBA that year; he was chasing his dream of playing professional baseball with the Chicago White Sox. Clyde Drexler was just the player the Sonics needed to win their second championship. Clyde was a big guard, six foot seven, and athletic. He had played for the gold-medal-winning Dream Team in the 1992 Olympics. He'd played in the NBA Finals, so he was playoff tested. George Karl wanted Clyde, and Clyde wanted to play in Seattle. George would have found creative ways to put Clyde's talents to use. Paul, however, had serious misgivings about the idea of trading Drexler to the Blazers' chief rival only to have him win a championship for the city Portland fans hated.

"As hard as it would be for you and me, Paul, I think it's a fair deal for Portland, and it's a great deal for Clyde," I said. "We need to trade Clyde. And I'd like to give him a chance to win a championship. He's earned it."

"OK," Paul relented. "If you really believe we should do it, I'm OK with it."

So I called up Sonics GM Wally Walker and said, "Merry Christmas, Wally. I'm going to give you a championship!" I outlined the deal, and Wally seemed to agree it would be a terrific move for the Sonics. Then he went radio silent.

George and Clyde both kept impatiently asking me when the deal would close. "They've got to want to do the deal," I said, wondering what could possibly be getting in the way.

When Wally finally got back to me, he said he was not comfortable taking any deal involving me to Barry Ackerley. "Barry's going to automatically assume if we're trading with you that you'll get the better end of the deal," Wally said.

"Look, Wally," I countered. "If anybody should have a problem with this deal, it's me. I'm trading our best player to the Sonics, to an owner who didn't exactly treat me very well after all the good work I did for him. Portland won't be happy losing their best player to Seattle, especially if you wind up winning the championship. This deal will make it look like you fleeced me. You're going to be a hero. It's a no-brainer."

Nothing I said would change his mind. "I just can't take that one upstairs," Wally said. "The answer is no."

Seattle was the number one seed, and even though it was now my job to rebuild a team that could take the Sonics down, I would've loved to see George and the incredibly talented team I had assembled win a championship. Instead, I wound up trading Clyde (along with small forward Tracy Murray) midseason to the defending champion

Houston Rockets, who went on to win their second consecutive NBA championship, sweeping the Miami Heat. In addition to his ring, Clyde got a good deal that included a contract extension for two more years at $5.5 million per season. In return, Portland got a first-round draft pick and Otis Thorpe, a power forward and center who was a good player but too old for the rebuild; we traded him to Detroit the following season for a first-round draft pick. We also got the rights to 1993 second-round draft pick Marcelo Nicola, a versatile power forward playing in Europe at the time. We had the option to use Nicola in future trades or eventually bring him on to our roster. He wound up playing the rest of his career in Europe.

Paul made it clear from the get-go that he wanted me to build a winning team without worrying about player-image problems. "We've got to be willing to bring in bad boys," he said. "I think you can manage the bad boys, Bob."

Some "bad boys" on the team had caused a high-profile stir the year before I got there. In early 1993, four Blazers were accused of sexually assaulting two teenage girls in Salt Lake City while on a road trip. The incident shined a disgraceful spotlight on the team, straining relationships among players, management, the community, and the league, which continued investigating the incident even after prosecutors declined to file criminal charges.

This was well before people started calling us the "Jail Blazers," suggesting I was deliberately ignoring the checkered pasts of players I added to the roster. That was the prevailing perception. In reality, I carefully considered each player's strengths and weaknesses, the assets they'd bring to the team, the liabilities that might get them in trouble, and everything in between. Ultimately, a GM's job is to assemble the kind of team the franchise owner wants. Paul wanted young, raw, explosive talent and was not only *willing* to take risks on players with "bad boy" reputations but *welcomed* it.

When young players come into the league, they're usually not very mature. Getting flung into fame and fortune is a hard adjustment. They've got a big pile of money, and bad things tend to find them if they're not careful, because bad things find money. And when things go sideways off-court, players don't generally run into your office and say, "Hey, boss. I'm struggling."

Putting in the time to know your players, to build trust, is key so they'll be honest with you if and when their problems get in the way of them playing their best. Over the years, I've helped players work through a host of personal and professional challenges, from marital strife and substance abuse to money problems and conflicts with coaches and teammates. On road trips, I would always invite a player to join me for a one-on-one breakfast or lunch. Everyone on the team would get their chance. We'd talk about life, our families, how they felt about the team, all kinds of stuff, a lot of it beyond the realm of basketball. I always appreciated getting to know them not just as athletes but as people. I believed in every athlete I brought to my teams, even those typecast as "bad boys." I did what I could to help them avoid the pitfalls that might prevent them from playing their best basketball.

One of the most frustrating challenges those first few years had less to do with off-court antics than our coach. When I was first hired, Paul gave me the go-ahead to fire P. J. Carlesimo if I wanted to, but that would've made the organization look stupid. So I did my best to work with P. J., discussing NBA rules, the NBA game, and how to deal with players.

During his 12 years of coaching at Seton Hall, the Pirates had won the regional championship in 1989, when the National Association of Basketball Coaches named Carlesimo Coach of the Year. Being a good coach in the NCAA does not mean you're prepared to coach NBA basketball, which has different rules. For example, you can save precious game time in the NBA by calling a time-out and advancing the ball to half court. We lost a few close games because of this type of game mismanagement. P. J. liked to blow a whistle. He always had one around his neck, and he blew it a lot. He also made a big deal of guys not having their practice jerseys tucked in. That kind of discipline might work in the NCAA. Not in the NBA. Pros find that stuff irritating and insulting.

Players stormed into my office, complaining that P. J. didn't know the game, didn't know how to make adjustments. I'd try talking to P. J. so he could make more headway gaining players' respect, but he'd tell me, "Bob, you've got a great history, a great track record. I know you've done a great job, but let me be clear: Paul Allen hired *me*. Paul Allen paid *me* about five times what I needed to take this job. Paul Allen guaranteed me a five-year contract, so why would I change anything? I'm just going to be me because that's what he bought. Me."

P. J.'s on-court behavior stood in complete contrast to his true personality. Away from basketball, he was one of the kindest people I'd ever met. I tried to get P. J. to think of our relationship this way: "You're the movie director. The players are the actors, and we're going to let you direct the movie, but think of me as the producer. I'm your boss. I'm in charge of everything—the actors, the director, the budget—and I report directly to the studio. So we're still going to let you be you, but we need to do certain things to the script to make it work. And I'm here to help you make it work."

P. J. never saw things that way.

We made it to the playoffs at the end of the 1994–95 season, facing the Phoenix Suns in the first round. Good coaches will watch closely and nimbly jump at opportunities to change things up, sometimes to surprise the other team, sometimes to adjust defensive strategy based on the other team's surprises. P. J. made no adjustments of any kind. Phoenix swept us in three games. Nevertheless, I still felt he deserved more than one season to prove he could coach in the NBA.

Plus, I had other personnel problems to deal with. Brad Greenberg, who had filled in as interim general manager before I got hired, felt the GM job should've gone to him. At one point, Paul suggested I fire Brad, but I convinced Paul to keep him on staff so I could work with him, developing him into capable GM material. I even talked Paul into letting me give him a bonus for the extra effort he'd put in as interim GM.

So I met with Brad and said, "Look, the fact that you don't have my job isn't because of me. You had two months, and Paul watched you and decided he didn't want to hire you. Now you can either get on board, be a part of what we're doing, learn, have some success, and maybe someday become a general manager, or you can piss and moan and second-guess like you've been doing the last couple of years, and if that's the case, you won't be around too long."

That was when I handed him a check for $100,000, a good-faith gesture for the work he'd done above and beyond his job title. Most guys would have jumped across the table and kissed me, but Brad barely said thank you, and I thought, *Oh geez, this is not good.* Brad stayed with the team my first season, then kept doing the same things he'd done before

I arrived—undermining the GM, backstabbing everyone, and making end runs to the owner to make himself look good. Paul was fed up with Brad's antics and insisted I fire him. About a year later, the Philadelphia 76ers hired him as GM for the 1996–97 season. I could have submarined him when they called me for a reference, but I chose to help Brad land the job. The 76ers fired him after only one season.

I made fewer trades my first season in Portland compared with my first season in Seattle, in part because the deals I did make were more complicated, like finally getting Arvydas Sabonis into a Blazers uniform. Portland had drafted the seven-foot-three Lithuanian center in 1986, back in the days before the fall of the Soviet Union, when players would be forced to stay in their homeland while they were still in their prime. (Some young athletes from the USSR risked their lives and defected to play in other countries, such as three of the NHL Detroit Red Wings' "Russian Five.")

Sabonis played for the Olympic gold-medal-winning Soviet basketball team in 1988, then in Europe for several seasons. He was playing for Real Madrid, one of the top teams in Europe, in 1994–95. Toward the end of that season, I flew to Spain to scout prospects and watch Sabonis play. He dominated on both offense and defense, averaging 23 points and 13 rebounds per game. He shot 63 percent from the field, 78 percent from the free throw line, and 34 percent from three-point range. Despite a history of multiple injuries, he was playing 35 minutes per game.

Before visiting Sabonis, I had spent two months "negotiating" with his agent Herb Rudoy. I wanted Sabonis on the Blazers' roster at the start of the 1995–96 season. Herb told me the Blazers had said the same thing every year since 1987 and that nothing ever happened. "Arvydas has lost all interest in Portland because they have never made him a priority," Rudoy said.

I made sure this time would be different. After watching Sabonis play for a week, I had no doubt about his ability to play in the NBA. I spent some time with Sabonis and his wife, Ingrida, an intelligent woman who was very supportive of her husband. The former Miss Lithuania told me she was encouraging Arvydas to join us in Portland. She did not want the best basketball player in Europe to have regrets about not playing in the NBA.

After the usual basketball discussion including our roster, coaches, owner, and facilities, I described the Pacific Northwest to the Sabonis family. To my surprise, the seven-foot-three, 300-pound "Sabas" loved to fish. The more we discussed catching salmon and fly-fishing for trout, the more excited he got about the Northwest. Another passion we connected on was the Sabonis Basketball Academy in Lithuania, which Arvydas had developed for young basketball players to refine their skills. He felt an obligation to help future generations earn basketball scholarships in college or perhaps earn a living playing professionally. He asked me if the Blazers could make a financial contribution to the school. I told him we would be happy to help raise funds, participate in clinics, or write a check, provided we complied with NBA salary-cap rules. (The academy still exists. Located in Kaunas, Lithuania, Sabonio Krepšinio Mokykla has four basketball courts, a weightlifting room, a cafeteria, a lounge, nine locker rooms, 13 full-time coaches, and serves about 700 kids each year.)

Near the end of my week with Sabonis, we went out to dinner with a group of his friends. As I was reaching for the check, his giant hand grabbed my arm, and with a booming voice, he said, "No!" He took the check, said I was his guest, and insisted on paying. To this day, he's the only professional athlete who has ever bought me a meal.

Another amusing thing about Arvydas: He usually had one of his agents, Arturo Ortega, around to act as an interpreter. Sometimes, he would talk to me fluently in English, and other times he might shrug and ask Arturo to interpret. I didn't get this at first. As our relationship developed and we earned each other's trust, I learned the real secret. Arvydas was fluent in Lithuanian, Polish, Spanish, Russian, and English. He didn't like the intensity of the global media spotlight that shined on him during his stardom in Europe, which was one reason he chose to play for the Blazers. While in Portland, the media rarely asked him more than one or two simple questions because he could get away with giving them a quizzical shrug as if he didn't understand what they were asking. Whenever I saw Sabas use this trick, I would look at him and smile. He knew exactly what they were asking.

Arvydas would become a cornerstone of our rebuild. He was fundamentally sound and a great passer from the high or low post. It took our players a while to realize how much fun he was to play with. Pass the ball to Sabonis, cut to the basket, and he would get you the ball back for a layup or easy shot. He threw "bowling ball" bounce passes, behind-the-back passes, lobs, baseball passes, over-the-head passes, and others I don't know how to describe. His passes were accurate and always made with the style of a showman. When Sabas got the ball on the block, he had an unstoppable hook shot. But the big man also shot a good percentage from three-point range. Unlike other NBA centers who were bricklayers from the free throw line, Sabas was deadly from the charity stripe. Arvydas was fun to watch because he could do it all.

The rebuild was starting to come together, but problems with P. J. Carlesimo persisted. Veteran point guard Rod Strickland repeatedly mouthed off about it to the media, saying things like "I don't like him. You can print that!" I was constantly trying to help P. J. smooth things over with Strickland, but P. J. was too set in his ways. He felt players had to adjust to him because he was the coach. I tried to explain that coaches are not the same authoritarian figures in the NBA as they are in college. In the NBA, coaches have to communicate, collaborate, and motivate.

Less than two days before the trade deadline in February 1996, Rod demanded a trade because he couldn't stand P. J. I did not make a deal, because I was unwilling to trade Rod for less than equal value. After the trade deadline passed, Rod went AWOL, so I suspended him indefinitely. A magician at driving to the basket and making shots in the paint, he averaged 19 points and almost ten assists per game. As one of our best players, he was making $2.3 million a year, so each game he missed cost him about $28,000 in lost salary. It took me about two weeks (and Rod losing $168,000) to convince him to be professional, get back on the court, and play the rest of the season for P. J.

The animosity between Carlesimo and Strickland weighed heavily on the team. No one was having fun. The vibe on the court and in the locker room prickled with tension, nonstop pins and needles. Everyone was waiting for the next blowup between the two.

We finished 1995–96 with 44 wins and 38 losses, the same as the season before. We made it to the playoffs, and while we lost in the first round again, we did not get swept. We gave the Utah Jazz a run for their money, losing the series three to two. We lost the first two games in Utah but then held serve in Portland, winning Game Three 94–91 and Game Four 98–90. Then Utah destroyed us in Game Five 102–64. It felt like a number of players had quit because they didn't want P. J. to get credit for winning a playoff series—impossible to prove, but stranger things have happened in the NBA.

Rod Strickland and P. J. Carlesimo obviously could not coexist for another season. I was committed to trading Rod but adamant about getting a star player in return. The Washington Bullets had three very talented big forwards—Juwan Howard, Chris Webber, and Rasheed Wallace—but they lacked a pure point guard who could get the ball to the talented frontcourt players. Rasheed Wallace, a six-foot-eleven power forward center out of the University of North Carolina, was one of the top draft picks in 1995, fourth overall. He had played two years in college with Dean Smith's Tar Heels, along with teammate Jerry Stackhouse, who had also entered the NBA draft in 1995, selected third by the Philadelphia 76ers—one pick ahead of Rasheed, who had gone to the Washington Bullets for his rookie season.

I tried to trade up in the 1995 draft to acquire Kevin Garnett or Rasheed Wallace. I was not able to acquire a top-five pick to make that happen but felt I might be able to get Wallace during the summer of 1996. Rasheed had a perfect NBA physique. He was long, quick, athletic, an excellent shooter, and a good passer and rebounder, and he could block shots. His foot speed and lateral quickness allowed him to defend multiple positions. And he could also run the floor. If there were an Olympics for men over six foot nine inches tall, Rasheed would win the gold medal in the 100-meter dash. He was an unselfish player, and his teammates loved him.

I started negotiating a trade with the Washington Bullets before the draft. The discussions centered around Strickland for Wallace. The entire league thought I had to "get rid" of Strickland because of his well-publicized feud with our coach. Washington tried to use our player-coach dysfunction to force me to include our 1996 first-round pick in the deal.

During the 1996 draft, I was focused on acquiring a hot-shot high school player everybody was talking about: Kobe Bryant. I knew the Lakers had a deal with Charlotte to trade Vlade Divac for the Hornets' 13th pick. They were taking Kobe at number 13. We owned the 17th pick. I almost acquired the eighth pick from New Jersey for Rod

Strickland. I planned to draft Kobe with number eight and another high school player, Jermaine O'Neal, at number 17. Both players would be projects and take time to develop, but Kobe would be NBA-ready much sooner than Jermaine.

I couldn't get the eighth pick, so the Lakers ended up with Kobe at number 13. I drafted Jermaine at number 17. He was a six-foot-eleven big forward center. Although he was very young and slender, he loved basketball and wanted to become a great player. The two NBA skills he possessed from day one: the abilities to rebound and to block shots.

It was important to create an environment for Jermaine where he could develop and mature. I hired his former high school coach, George Glymph, to join our staff in Portland. George could mentor Jermaine and be available to help his transition from South Carolina to Portland. I had no guarantee Jermaine would make it in the NBA, but I felt his upside was much greater than other players' available for our pick. Over time, Jermaine proved me right.

Three weeks after the draft, I revisited the Strickland-Wallace discussions with Washington. They finally understood I wouldn't give them a first-round pick, and negotiations got serious. We agreed to a deal sending Rod Strickland and Harvey Grant to the Bullets for Rasheed Wallace and Mitchell Butler.

Rasheed was an immediate starter and key player on our team. Despite being only 22 years old, he had a very good season, averaging 17 points, seven rebounds, and one blocked shot per game. Jermaine played in only 45 games, but he did enough good on the floor to confirm I had made the right selection. Jermaine was still more project than polished, but Rasheed was already "prime time." Rasheed's age, skill level, and versatility would make him as important to rebuilding the Blazers as Kemp had been to the Sonics.

Another key addition to the team that summer: Isaiah "J. R." Rider, who had played his first three years in the NBA with Minnesota. He led the Timberwolves in scoring in 1995–96, averaging almost 20 points per game. He also led the team in off-court troubles: marijuana possession (small amounts, like most players in the NBA who get caught with pot), gambling in public (whatever that is), possession of illegal cell phones. About a month before we traded for him, he was arrested in connection with an alleged rape but never criminally charged. For all these reasons and more, the Timberwolves were itching to get rid of J. R. Where they saw deal-breaking distractions, I saw untamed immaturity that could be reined in with guidance and discipline. And I knew that he was far more valuable than what we were trading for him: James Robinson (an undersized off-guard who lacked point guard skills), Bill Curley (who simply lacked enough talent to play in the NBA), and a future first-round pick.

At six foot five and 215 pounds, J. R. was built like a football player. He used to tell me he wanted to try out for the Seahawks as a defensive back and how awesome he would be. He was strong and explosive, a great finisher in fast breaks. His biggest strength on the court was taking weaker players down low in the paint and posting them up. He had a good jump shot with easy three-point range. On the day he was drafted, he famously predicted he would win the NBA Slam Dunk Contest his rookie year, and he did.

For all his gifts as an athlete, he was a complicated piece of work, a smooth talker, and a brazen bullshitter. Teammates loved him, but the same could not be said of the coaches. He would play big in big games because he wasn't scared of the moment. He could show fierce mental strength in high-pressure situations and also snap without warning. I assigned different staff members to go to his house to ensure he got to practice on time so coaches couldn't complain about his tardiness.

A lot of people questioned my judgment in trading for such a high-maintenance player. Publicly, I assured critics that we would expect J. R.—like all players—to conform to a code of conduct and commit to being a good role model in our community. And we played up the prospect that coming to a winning organization would bring out the best in J. R., compared with constantly losing in Minnesota. Privately, I had a feeling he would become the foundation of a masterful chess move.

CHAPTER 11

SAVING THE SEAHAWKS

IT ALWAYS AMAZES ME HOW many people forget that Seattle almost lost the Seahawks. Or never knew in the first place. It's hard to imagine the Pacific Northwest's one and only NFL franchise skipping town for Southern California. But it almost happened. And I'm the guy who worked my butt off for months to make sure it didn't.

It was 1996, my second year as president and GM of the Blazers. Ken Behring, a real estate developer who had bought the Seahawks from the Nordstrom family almost a decade earlier, hated the Kingdome. He wanted a new stadium, and it wasn't happening, so one day, he announced he was moving the team to Anaheim. He ordered the closure of the team's Kirkland headquarters and brought in moving vans to haul away office equipment. Players started doing off-season workouts in an old Los Angeles Rams building in Anaheim.

It was a big deal. There was a huge outcry. Fans were so upset they lined up in front of the moving vans to try to keep them from leaving. The fans weren't about to let their home team that had been there for 20 or so years be swept out of town just like that. The protest didn't last long. The moving trucks managed to make their way past the blockade of fans and drove to Anaheim. King County sued, and the NFL threatened to fine Behring half a million dollars a day until he moved the team back to Seattle. Business leaders and politicians wanted Paul Allen to buy the team, but they couldn't get to him, so they got to me and asked if *I* could get to him.

"You're Paul's right-hand man," they said. "Would you see if he's interested?"

I talked to Paul, and he had no interest. Not even a little. And yet I had a feeling I could get him to change his mind. In addition to my job as president and GM of the Trail Blazers, Paul put me in charge of several of his other Portland business interests: the 12,000-seat Veterans Memorial Coliseum (the Blazers' original home), the 20,000-seat Rose Garden Arena (where they moved in the 1995–96 season), an airport advertising company, and a Red Lion Hotel, among others. I would talk to Paul every day. We discussed all kinds of things. I was probably the only one working for him who wasn't a yes-man. I knew that he usually started at "No" and that he needed two things to make a final decision: time and compelling arguments. I had persuaded him to change his mind before, and I felt I owed it to Seattle to make every effort to move him to "Yes" for the Seahawks.

"Paul, come on. This is our community," I said. "We can't let this happen."

I outlined all the reasons the Seahawks were worth keeping in Seattle: They were an important part of the community—a major league city and high-tech innovation hub for global corporations like Microsoft, Boeing, Starbucks, and Costco. This wasn't just about a football team. Fans across Washington and beyond—Alaska, Oregon, Idaho, even parts of Utah and Hawaii—considered the Seahawks "their" NFL team. A generation of Washingtonians, including Paul and his dad, had grown up watching the Seahawks. Families and entire communities bond over sports, passing their devotion to their teams from one generation to the next. California already had three NFL teams. Seattle didn't just deserve to keep the Seahawks; the city *needed* the Seahawks. And Paul was one of only a few people in the community who had the means to buy the team and keep it in Seattle.

He listened to everything I had to say. We spent a week or so discussing the Seahawks. It wasn't an easy sell. I asked NFL commissioner Paul Tagliabue and executive vice president Roger Goodell to come to Seattle to have dinner with Paul and me. The league officials helped convince Paul that they would change the rule to allow him to own both the Trail Blazers and the Seahawks. (The cross-ownership rule, at the time, barred NFL team owners from owning pro sports teams outside their football team's market; the league didn't want NFL owners competing with each other for the same sports dollar in any given market.)

I wanted Paul to have confidence that buying the Seahawks would be a good investment. The NFL was not nearly as popular then as it is today, so I told the league officials they needed to convince Paul that the NFL was moving professional football in a profitable direction. As he grew more open to the idea, Paul asked me what the Seahawks would be worth five years after he bought it. He was concerned that if he paid $250 million for the team, the value would drop five years later. I told him I was confident the team would be worth $500 million or more. Eventually—and rather reluctantly—he said, "OK. Under the right conditions, I would *consider* buying them."

"Well, what are the right conditions?" I asked.

First off, the Kingdome had to go. The "Concrete Cupcake" and its hulking roof—the largest of its kind in the world at the time (more than seven acres!)—were starting to show troubling signs of age. In 1994, several Kingdome ceiling tiles had collapsed, forcing the Seahawks to play five games at UW's Husky Stadium. If Paul was going to have anything to do with the Seahawks, the team needed a new stadium. No more indoor football. No more blue Astroturf. "I only want football that's played outdoors," he said.

As the cofounder of Microsoft, Paul Allen was the third-richest man on the planet at the time, but he wouldn't singlehandedly bankroll the construction of an NFL stadium. "I've got to get the community to pay for the bulk of the new stadium's cost with public money," Paul said.

Getting the public to pony up tax dollars for an NFL stadium not only to appease a billionaire who refused to pay for the whole thing himself but also to make him even wealthier? Pulling that off would not be easy.

I started meeting with local politicians and the business community. Ken Behring had tried to get King County officials to rezone a massive amount of land he had purchased east of Bellevue for residential and commercial development, where he wanted a new football stadium for the Seahawks. He also wanted public money to build it. His demands were ignored. The Seahawks were terrible on the field, and fans blamed Behring for mismanaging the team. Seattle saw Ken as a Californian—not part of, nor truly invested in, the local community.

Everyone I met with said they could meet Paul's terms. "Tell Paul to buy the team, and we will build him a new outdoor stadium." They liked the idea of a hometown billionaire owning Seattle's NFL team. We discussed various user-generated taxes that could fund a new stadium *and* retire the Kingdome's remaining debt. Ideas included hotel and motel taxes, taxes on sports merchandise sold in Washington, ticket taxes, deferred business and occupation taxes, a gas tax, and many more. There were no bad ideas. Politicians kept telling me they could secure public funding for a new stadium. The business community said they would buy stadium suites and sponsorships. The NFL once again assured me they would change their cross-ownership rules, allowing Paul to own both the Portland Trail Blazers *and* the Seattle Seahawks.

After a couple of months of nonstop efforts to make this deal come through, it felt like we were getting somewhere, building great momentum. Then I'll never forget Easter Sunday 1996, when I got a call from Paul. He was leaving for Japan in the morning and planned to be there for a week. I'd just finished doing an Easter egg hunt with our kids. It was one of the few afternoons where I could actually enjoy some family time, but instead, I was on the phone with Paul for a couple of hours. He told me his PR person would be faxing a press release to my house, that I would have a press conference the following day to announce that he was withdrawing his bid to buy the Seahawks.

It was not a negotiation. He was done. He was out. I'd have to do the press conference while he was out of the country. Then, all the dust could settle before he came back.

When the press release came through, I could hardly believe my eyes. It was a single page with a matter-of-fact headline declaring that Paul Allen was no longer a candidate to purchase the Seahawks. In a few short paragraphs, he thanked the community for allowing him to be part of the discussions on keeping the Seahawks in Seattle. He noted what a challenge it was to own a professional sports team and how seriously he took his ownership responsibilities for the Portland Trail Blazers. He did not want to shortchange his commitment to the NBA. His business and philanthropic commitments left far too little time for him to take on an endeavor like owning an NFL team. He thanked me as well as then King County executive Gary Locke (elected Washington's governor later that year) and Seahawks fans for their passion and efforts.

This came as a complete shock. He gave me no forewarning. Not even a hint. I asked him why he was out. And he rattled off several reasons.

"One, I don't think I really want to own a team in my home city because now, when I'm in Seattle, people leave me alone. It's easy. If I owned the Seahawks, they'd have a stronger opinion of me. I'd hear my name on the radio more. It's harder to stay under the radar when I own a professional sports team in my own city.

"Number two, my mom's health isn't so good right now. I don't want to have new businesses coming online that might need my attention in case my mom gets more ill.

"Number three and probably the biggest reason. You're telling me that the politicians will give public money to help me build this new stadium after I buy the team. But I'm pretty sure that once I buy it, they'll say, 'Oops. Can't do it. Gee, you do it by yourself, Paul. You're one of the richest guys in the world.' And so, suddenly, I'll own the team and because I'm the big billionaire, they won't help me. I'll have to spend all my own money. I want the community to do its part before I consider doing mine."

Too many people had put in too much hard work to figure out a way forward. I couldn't let this energized effort to save the Seahawks fizzle, not like this, over the phone, on the sidelines of my family's Easter Sunday celebration.

"We've worked very hard to figure out a way forward. Many people in the community have put in a lot of effort to keep the Seahawks in Seattle. Look, Paul," I said, "I think we can buy the team from Ken Behring. I've worked with the NFL. I've been negotiating with Ken

Behring. I've been negotiating with the county executive, the mayor, politicians, business leaders. We've got so much momentum on this thing. I just think it would be devastating to lose it at this point."

He paused for a moment, then said, "Well, that's my decision. I'm sorry."

His voice held an almost apologetic quality. He knew how much work I had poured into this effort on top of all I was doing to run the Trail Blazers. Then I had an epiphany.

What if I could get Ken to sell it to us for no more than $250 million—$50 million less than he'd been asking—and we got an option to buy it at a date in the future? During the option period, the community would put together the public funding package that would be guaranteed if Paul Allen bought the team. That way, the public money for the stadium would be guaranteed *before* Paul committed to buying the team.

"Well, that's an interesting idea," he said, "but you've got no chance of that happening."

"Well," I replied, "I'm the guy who's been working with all these different factions. I have a feel for it, and I think I might be able to figure something out. Can I have the week while you're in Japan to work on this?"

He agreed to give me the week. "When I get back in one week, if you haven't gotten that option deal done, we'll just change the date of the press release, and you'll have a press conference and say I'm out."

"That's fine because nobody knows you're out anyway," I said. "What's one more week?"

It didn't matter that it was Easter Sunday. I had no time to waste. I immediately called Ken Behring.

"Ken, Paul's out," I said. "We've got to get creative here. I've got some ideas, but we have a deadline of one week, or you're on your own."

Ken sounded caught off guard. "What are you talking about? Is this part of a negotiation?"

I told him exactly what Paul had told me. After I laid out Paul's reasons for withdrawing from the process, Ken agreed to meet with me. The next day, I flew down to Northern California, a place called Blackhawk, where Ken lived. I spent the next few days with him.

What I told Ken was this: "Ken, the NFL doesn't want you to move to LA because you haven't gone through the relocation process properly. They'll resist you moving. You may not get the team to LA because you'll have the NFL fighting you, and you will have lawsuits all over the place. Why don't we do this? You give us an option to buy the team. We'll agree on a price. We'll pay some of the money up front. Give us a long enough period to work on this. If we don't exercise the option, you'll keep some of the money that we gave you as nonrefundable.

"We will work on building a new outdoor stadium in Seattle, which includes public money. If we don't pick up the option, that means we can't get the public-participation part of the stadium deal done. You'll be able to go to the NFL and say, 'Look, if Paul Allen, a local son and billionaire, couldn't get the public to help him build a stadium, they're sure as hell never going to help the California guy build a stadium in Seattle. Paul Allen was going to buy the team, but he couldn't figure out how to get it done. Therefore, you have to let me move to LA.'"

We spent the better part of three days talking. Ken took me to his car museum. He gave me a tour of Blackhawk. We had lunch at his house. We built trust in one another, and it felt like we were working together, both focused on a win-win solution.

"Ken, we will get the NFL to agree that if we can't figure it out, nobody can, and you'll be allowed to leave. Also, if you do get to go to Los Angeles with the league's blessing and without all the lawsuits, your franchise would be more valuable the day you get there. But if you don't go through this process, you're not going to get there." I told him it would take two years to make this happen. "I need two years, Ken. A two-year option."

"I'll give you six months," he said.

Ken wanted us to make a decision during the 1996 season so he would have plenty of time to move the team before the 1997 season. After days of back-and-forth, I got Ken to loosen his position. I explained we needed the 1996 season as well as the 1997 draft and free-agency period to improve the team and evaluate the business operations. The community needed to see our commitment to fielding a winning team. Ken listened, and we finally settled on 14 months. The purchase price I negotiated: $180 million—$70 million under the ceiling Paul had given me (which Ken never knew, of course).

We had to give Ken a $20 million nonrefundable deposit toward the $180 million. Ken would get that money for allowing us to tie up the team for 14 months. During the 14-month option period, we were granted "comanagement" rights of the Seahawks. I became copresident with Ken's son, David. Every financial decision that was made at the Seahawks had to be agreed upon by both the Behring camp and the Paul Allen camp. I also attended every NFL owners meeting during this period. Besides learning the inner workings of the NFL, I used these meetings to build relationships with owners, to get the league officials on my side about changing its cross-ownership rules for Paul to become an owner. I needed allies in the NFL ownership ranks.

Paul insisted on one more condition before accepting the option to buy the Seahawks. He would only go through with the purchase if I agreed to step up and lead the organization as president. Running the Blazers and Rose Garden Arena in Portland kept me busy enough. I tried to make the case that it would be more efficient and effective to have a different person as president of the Seahawks, but he held his ground adamantly.

"If you don't agree to run both teams, I will not buy the Seahawks," Paul said. Very few of Paul's employees reported directly to him. I was one of them. He had earned a reputation for being introverted and uncomfortable dealing with people, but he had a history with me. We shared a passion for NBA basketball. We talked about personal issues, things you would only discuss with your closest friends and trusted family members. He did not want to have to put in all the work it would require to get comfortable with a new person. I accepted the position, knowing that running both teams would require a nonstop commitment. The job I signed up for—without asking for, or getting, another dime for all the hard work it would take—basically required that I conduct the orchestra while writing the music. It seemed like an impossible feat. And as you know now, it came perilously close to *not* happening—more than once.

Paul eventually signed the option agreement with Ken, then we had to convince the politicians and the community that it made sense to implode the Kingdome so a new outdoor stadium could be built. We were met with huge resistance because the publicly owned stadium still had about $200 million of debt and was a functional facility—good enough to host the NCAA Division I Men's Final Four basketball tournament in the spring of 1995. We negotiated hard and persistently with the politicians. We needed King County's political support and a public financial package that would win over state legislators in Olympia. As we built support, the home, boat, and auto shows lobbied heavily against us. They had a sweetheart rental deal for the popular trade shows they hosted at the Kingdome. Many other groups, including the neighborhood south of downtown (SoDo), voiced fierce opposition to financing a football stadium with public dollars, especially when a man as rich as Paul insisted on it. We had to find a way to convert the opposition into partners.

After months of brainstorming and lobbying, we came up with a winning idea. Instead of a football-only stadium, we would design a world-class football *and* soccer stadium, with an attached exhibition center, which would serve as a much better space for trade shows than the Kingdome. The soccer community became instant champions of our project. We also agreed to create a $10 million mitigation fund to address the impacts a new stadium would have on the Pioneer Square and International District neighborhoods—things like parking and transportation, public safety and clean-up initiatives, business assistance and affordable housing.

The public financing would come from user-generated revenue, not the general fund. The public funding portion would be capped at $300 million. The largest amount—$127 million—would come from the Washington State Lottery. Other sources of public funding would include a county sales tax, a hotel and motel tax, and parking and admissions taxes. Our final budget came out to $430 million—$360 million for the stadium, $44 million for the exhibition center, and $26 million for a parking garage. We agreed to give 20 percent of all exhibition center revenue to a state education fund. The Seahawks would retain stadium naming-rights revenue to pay for facility improvements and capital projects.

The Washington legislature finally agreed to our proposed funding package for the stadium and exhibition center—with one *big* condition. The proposal had to go to a statewide vote. The taxpayers had to approve our public-private partnership.

I spent the months leading up to the vote pitching the proposal at town halls, editorial boards, community groups, and to the media in every major and minor city across the state of Washington. It became a full-time job on top of my real full-time job as Blazers president and GM. One night, I went head to head in a debate with the opposition's hired gun, environmental and consumer rights advocate Ralph Nader. The debate took place in Vancouver, Washington, just across the Columbia River from Portland. This was Blazer country, and it took about 15 minutes of my pitch to get the crowd riled up, in a good way. Ralph, by contrast, came across as unprepared. There were valid arguments against the referendum I was urging everyone to support. I had studied them in detail so I would be ready to respond with compelling counterarguments. But I never got a chance to tear apart a good argument. Ralph didn't make any. He had a weak grasp of the issues. It seemed pretty clear that he was only there because someone had written him a check.

Many former Seahawks players, community leaders, and fans helped in our statewide lobbying efforts. They knew the Seahawks' future in Seattle depended on our success, and they came out in droves to do their part. Convincing a majority of Washington voters to approve the stadium financing proposal was a Herculean task with huge consequences. We hired a public affairs firm led by Bob Gogerty to run our campaign. They were pessimistic and brutally honest about our chances of getting the referendum passed. Even though we had a lot of fervent support, taxpayers had a serious case of "stadium fatigue." The Seattle Mariners had gone through a similar process for a new baseball stadium just one year before.

In 1995, King County voters had rejected the Mariners' bid to finance a new ballpark with public money. After the Mariners' owners threatened to sell the team, Washington governor Mike Lowry called the state legislature into special session, and lawmakers put together a package that authorized King County to use taxes from restaurant and tavern meals and car rentals. Taxpayers sued, lost, and the Mariners started playing in their new ballpark four years later.

It's important to remember that the Seahawks were a pretty lousy team at this point. They had missed the playoffs for eight consecutive years. The Seahawks couldn't sell out the Kingdome, so why did the team need a larger, more expensive stadium? Imploding the Kingdome also meant Seattle could no longer host major events. Plus,

Washingtonians east of the Cascade Mountains often bristled when asked to vote for taxes supporting projects benefiting city-slicker Seattle. We had to hope that Spokane, Yakima, the Tri-Cities, and communities in Central and Eastern Washington had enough die-hard Seahawks fans to vote yes. We knew it would be extremely difficult to win this statewide vote on June 17, 1997—two months after the NFL draft.

The Seahawks had the third and sixth picks in the first round of the 1997 draft. It was a real opportunity to improve the team. Ken Behring did not want to pay the salaries of two high draft picks and told his son, Seahawks president David Behring, to trade the picks for less expensive players and cash. David presented the plan to me. I said we needed to discuss it in more detail. I asked him to set up a meeting with the director of player personnel. The football personnel department was very excited about the prospect of drafting Shawn Springs, a defensive back from Ohio State, and Walter Jones, an offensive tackle from Florida State. To sign both players, the team would have to guarantee about $25 million in salaries.

I tried to convince Ken Behring to keep both draft picks. He said we could draft Springs and Jones, but only if Paul Allen would pay the $25 million in guaranteed salaries if he did not buy the team. Ken knew our statewide vote was a couple of months away and that the polling was not weighing in our favor. Paul knew very little about football. But he loved to look at basketball player highlights, so I told the personnel department to make me highlight tapes of Springs and Jones. As the NBA playoffs approached, Paul and I talked about the Blazers every day.

About a week before the NFL draft, I went to Paul's house on Mercer Island to watch the Blazers play the Spurs in San Antonio. I brought the Springs and Jones tapes, knowing Paul wanted an update on the upcoming NFL draft. After the game, Paul was in a good mood. We'd won easily against the Spurs. Rasheed Wallace had led our team in scoring with 19 points. Arvydas Sabonis had added 18 points and 12 rebounds.

I quickly shifted our focus to the Seahawks, the upcoming NFL draft, and how the third and sixth picks in the first round opened an excellent opportunity to improve the team substantially. I told Paul about Ken Behring's financial reluctance to keep the first-round picks. We watched the player-highlight tapes, and Paul got excited watching Springs make interception after interception. He didn't know what to think about Jones, because an offensive tackle never gets to touch the ball. I lobbied Paul to allow the Seahawks to keep the two high first-round picks and pay the guaranteed $25 million in salaries, even if he didn't buy the team. I urged him to agree to Ken's demand.

"Paul, you're never going to have to pay the $25 million to Ken Behring because you're going to buy the team," I said. "We're going to win the statewide vote and get this done. You'll regret it if you didn't draft one of the best offensive tackles ever to play the game."

He agreed the Seahawks needed Springs and Jones. I signed documents the day of the draft, obligating Paul to pay Behring $25 million if he did not buy the Seahawks. We drafted Shawn Springs third and Walter Jones sixth. "Big Walter" would eventually be inducted into the Pro Football Hall of Fame.

Our option to purchase the Seahawks expired at the end of June 1997. The statewide vote—Referendum 48—was scheduled for June 17. We had no backup plan. If the voters rejected the referendum, the Seahawks would move to Los Angeles. My NBA teams had played in many big playoff games. Each was incredibly stressful. But the pressure of an NBA playoff game paled in comparison to what was at stake with this vote. *Seattle would lose its NFL team if we lost!*

We campaigned full tilt until the polls closed the day of the vote. We knew it would be close. Paul rented Union Station in downtown Seattle for a party to celebrate with all the volunteers who had worked so hard to save the team. Win or lose, those people dedicated their working lives to saving the Seahawks, and we wanted to thank them. Referendum 48 was trailing when early ballots were counted. The atmosphere felt grim. Finally, sometime between 10:00 and 11:00 p.m., the votes shifted our way, and people started getting excited. When all the votes were counted, Referendum 48 passed with a razor-thin 51 percent of the vote. Of 1.6 million ballots cast, yes votes outnumbered noes by less than 37,000. It was hard to believe we had won the right to celebrate. Paul grabbed his guitar, joined his band onstage, and began jamming with a giant smile on his face.

On June 30, 1997, Governor Gary Locke and other local politicians joined me at Seahawks headquarters in Kirkland. The media packed into the conference room to watch me sign the purchase and sale agreement on behalf of Paul Allen. Paul was the new owner of the Seahawks, and the future of the team in Seattle was safe.

It took a year and a half of structural analysis, site investigation, and other planning to determine the best way to demolish the Kingdome. Ultimately, the experts hired by our stadium management company (First and Goal Inc., of which I served as president) narrowed the options down to one: implosion. At 8:32 a.m. on March 26, 2000, after four and a half months of designing the demolition, gutting the building, placing each explosive charge at its precisely engineered spot, the Kingdome's 125,000 tons of concrete and 443 tons of structural steel came cascading down in just 17 seconds. The cost, excluding insurance: $9 million.

The Seahawks played at the UW's Husky Stadium for the next two years until the new 67,000-seat stadium opened a little over two years later, on July 20, 2002. We got it built on time and on budget, with more than one-third of the new facility built with materials from the Kingdome. In all, 97 percent of the Kingdome was processed or recycled. Not bad for an old concrete cupcake.

For what it's worth, I would never recommend taking on as much as I did during my double-duty days running both the Trail Blazers and the Seahawks. It was too much, yet I felt a deep sense of obligation to the community to do all I could to keep the Seahawks in Seattle. I'll always be grateful that Paul gave me one last chance to negotiate with Ken Behring. And I'll always be glad that the press release Paul called me about on Easter Sunday never saw the light of day.

CHAPTER 12

RIP CITY REVIVAL

GREAT COACHES ADJUST TO THE talent they have. They'll change up their playbook to get the most out of their team. I don't think I've ever seen a coach do a better job at this than Pat Riley, who led Magic Johnson, Kareem Abdul-Jabbar, and the "Showtime" Lakers to four NBA championships in the 1980s. They would run. They were fast. They played up-tempo. Riley played to their strengths and made an incredibly talented group of players even better than the sum of their parts. Years later, as coach of the New York Knicks, Riley adjusted his system to fit Patrick Ewing and a much slower-paced team that walked the ball up the floor and ground out the shot clock in low-scoring games. He didn't win a championship in New York, but the Knicks played really good basketball when he was there in the early and mid-1990s.

P. J. Carlesimo was a good coach, and I kept hoping he would make some adjustments to get more out of the team I was rebuilding. But by my third year, he made it clear he would keep coaching the way he had always coached—reminding me over and over that Paul had hired *him* to coach. He didn't push back unprofessionally. He just felt strongly that he was coaching the right way, and he wouldn't budge.

He had a group of incredibly athletic players, and he wasn't tapping into their athletic skills. He would never extend the floor defensively. He wouldn't have the guys pick up opposing players full court. He wasn't into trapping. There are many ways to cover a pick-and-roll, but he used only two. He had no interest in learning more. If we couldn't cover a pick-and-roll, which was three-quarters of basketball plays back then, we were in trouble.

Rasheed Wallace could guard multiple positions on the floor. He had great lateral quickness, even at six foot eleven, with a giant wingspan. Instead of having him fight over every pick, it would've been more effective to have him switch and smother because he could cover the smaller guys. But P. J. wouldn't coach him that way. He didn't motivate and communicate well with his players. Players usually collaborate with their coaches, sharing their views on what will work on the court. If a player believes he can effectively play a certain way, the coach doesn't have to worry about the rest of the team buying into his strategy. P. J. wouldn't listen to their suggestions. He stuck to his authoritarian, whistle-blowing ways. He was holding us back.

We finished the 1996–97 season 49–33, five wins better than the previous two seasons. The rebuild was starting to come together. We made it to the playoffs, and once again lost in the first round. It was time for P. J. to go.

He wasn't surprised when I called him to my office and fired him. It wasn't a fun thing to do, but he took the news professionally. No hard feelings. "You've been true to your word, Bob," he said. "You've told me many times this would happen if I didn't make changes."

Worse things can happen to a coach than getting fired with two years left on their contract, getting paid $3 million not to work. Of all the people I've had the privilege to work with over the course of my career, P. J. was by far one of the nicest and most gracious. I've always thought that if he could've done more to parlay his personality into his coaching style, he would've been a much more effective coach.

On his way out, I encouraged P. J. to take a couple of years off, to work on television, watch the games from a different lens. He'd be more attractive as a potential coach after a year or two. Ironically, the coach he replaced in Portland—Rick Adelman—had just gotten his walking papers from the Golden State Warriors. I urged P. J. not to go for the job. The roster wouldn't work for him, especially Latrell Sprewell, who made Rod Strickland (the former Blazer who had such a toxic relationship with P. J. that I had to trade him away) look like he was sitting in the front church pew.

True to form, P. J. went his own way and took the Warriors' coaching position. His first several months on the job, P. J. rode Sprewell hard in practice. Then, one day, Sprewell finally snapped. P. J. yelled at him in practice, saying he needed to pass the ball more sharply. Things got ugly fast. Sprewell reached out and choked P. J. so hard, it took several teammates to pull him off. The incident left P. J.'s neck scratched and bruised. Sprewell got ejected from practice. He showered and allegedly came back and punched P. J. A flurry of discipline and legal activity ensued. Eventually, the NBA suspended Sprewell for the remainder of that season.

I felt really bad for P. J. Nobody deserved to be treated like that. To make matters worse, the Warriors fired him midway into his second season. Their record at that point: a dismal 27–50. When P. J. took the Golden State job, the Trail Blazers no longer had to pay him the remaining $3 million left on his contract. I couldn't help wishing that he had heeded my advice.

The search for a new coach came at a time when I had my hands fuller than ever, juggling my many duties as Trail Blazers president and GM, running several of Paul's business interests in Portland, and leading the charge to save the Seahawks. The Blazers' 1996–97 season ended on April 24, a 95–77 loss to the Lakers in Game Four in the first round of the playoffs. The very next day, Referendum 48 passed in the Washington State Legislature, then came the campaign to win statewide voter support to pony up tax dollars for a new NFL and Major League Soccer stadium. As I ran point on this campaign, the future of the Seahawks franchise felt like a ton of bricks sitting squarely on my shoulders—right as I needed to find a new coach for the Blazers. Not many were available at the time. We wanted a seasoned NBA coach. My first choice was Phil "Flip" Saunders, who had just led the Minnesota Timberwolves to the playoffs for the first time in his first full year as head coach. I really liked Flip, but ultimately, he decided he wanted to stay in the Midwest, where he and his family had deep roots. The only other candidate I seriously considered was the one I wound up hiring.

Mike Dunleavy had coached the Lakers to the finals in his first year as head coach in Los Angeles, beating the Blazers to win the 1991 Western Conference championship. He had a lot of NBA experience, first as a player. Drafted 99th overall in 1976, he played his first season in Philadelphia alongside future Hall of Famer Julius "Dr. J" Erving, when the 76ers lost in the finals to—wouldn't you know it—the Trail Blazers. A six-foot-three guard, he played for the Sixers for a few years, followed by stints with the Houston Rockets, the San Antonio Spurs, and the Milwaukee Bucks. He started his coaching career in Milwaukee in 1988, first as an assistant, before leaving to replace Pat Riley as the Lakers' head coach in 1990. He returned to the Bucks in 1992, serving as both head coach and vice president of basketball operations, missing the playoffs for four years straight. He had basically failed upward to a nominal position as GM.

Mike was a shameless self-promoter, though he knew he wasn't the hottest commodity at that moment in time. No one had touched him for about a year after he was fired as coach. He played up his success in LA and explained away his unimpressive performance in Milwaukee as the result of the players' failure to execute his concepts. He also claimed Bucks owner Herb Kohl wasn't patient enough. As I saw it, he did poorly when he tried to coach *and* pick all his players; his Milwaukee teams had gone 107–221 under his watch and hadn't made the playoffs once. But during his two years in LA, under Jerry West—the legendary player turned coach turned GM—Mike's win–loss record was 101–63; they made the playoffs both years. I felt confident that with the right person (me) in charge of bringing in the right players, Dunleavy could do a great job as coach. Even though he was never a star, I knew players would respect him, as they generally do respect coaches who have done what they do.

Under normal circumstances, making a coaching change would become a GM's main project for the year, the biggest thing they would focus on. But there I was, dead center in the most critical and difficult period of the campaign to save the Seahawks. I had an entire organization of Seahawks employees (a couple hundred people) who were all two months away from losing their jobs if we didn't pull this thing off. I had a lot of help, but nobody was the more public face of it than me. Paul was ultimately the man with the checkbook, but I was the one out there living and dying it on a day-to-day basis.

If you add all that up, I had no time to run a complete beauty pageant for the Blazers' new head coach. Any day I might've been locked in a room, interviewing coach candidates, I would've been missing a day to get those votes we needed to save Seattle's NFL franchise. I can't describe the intensity of the pressure I felt as the leader of that do-or-die campaign.

When I first came to Portland, the Blazers had the second-highest payroll in the NBA, way over the salary cap. By the summer of my third year, I had created enough room *under* the salary cap to acquire a sought-after All-Star-caliber free agent. Power forward Brian Grant was exercising the opt-out clause after his third year with the Sacramento Kings, who had picked him eighth overall in the lottery of the 1994 draft. Not only did we get Grant, but we got him for less ($56 million over seven years) than the Cleveland Cavaliers were offering ($63 million) because we, too, included an opt-out clause after the third year in his contract.

Fans loved "the Rosta Monsta" instantly—his trademark locs, his work ethic, how he gave every ounce of energy on every play. He was a power player, not graceful, but at six foot nine, he could play like a seven-footer. He would set picks, get offensive rebounds, and kick them out to our best shooters. He was one of the most tenacious rebounders I've ever seen. He would tip the ball, tip the ball, tip the ball, then get the ball, drawing raucous cheers from the crowd. He played a significant role in getting us to the Western Conference Finals two out of his three seasons with the Blazers.

Brian made positive contributions to the Blazers, both on and off the court. He formed a foundation, supported local nonprofits with generous donations, and made frequent appearances in the community, visiting kids in hospitals and youth at the Blazers Boys and Girls Club. Toward the end of his second season in Portland, he won the J. Walter Kennedy Citizenship Award—a prestigious honor the NBA gives out once a year to a player, coach, or staff member who shows outstanding service and dedication to the community.

With a strong addition to the roster and a new coach, the 1997–98 season felt like the beginning of a promising new chapter in the Blazers rebuild. Dunleavy's coaching style worked well with the players. He was much more mellow than P. J. He let his assistants do a lot of the coaching and teaching, which meant players were more likely to pay attention to him when he did have the floor. Players always give a new coach a bit of a grace period. They don't want to be perceived as a problem. It finally felt like I had the right coach.

Partway through the season, another solid piece of the rebuild puzzle fell into place in a multiplayer trade that brought Damon Stoudamire to Portland. The 1996 Rookie of the Year no longer wanted to play in Toronto, which had drafted him. Playing in Portland would be a homecoming for Stoudamire. He'd won two Oregon State high school championships at Wilson High, where he had averaged 26 points and nine assists per game. It's hard to be really good in the NBA when you're only five foot ten, but "Mighty Mouse" was a strong outside shooter, good in transition, and deadly at the free throw line. Damon loved the game. He was a real gym rat and would spend extra time in the gym working on his game. Teammates liked him and respected his grit and competitiveness.

With a new coaching staff, a new system, and two new key members of the team, we finished the 1997–98 season 46–36, three wins fewer than the prior season. Some might have viewed it as a tiny step backward. I had a more patient perspective and saw the long arc of the Blazers' turnaround bending toward a championship.

Another roster addition before the summer of 1998 would bend that arc even more. I had tried to figure out a way to get Bonzi Wells before, during, and after the 1998 draft, but Detroit had picked him in the lottery, 11th overall. The Pistons were having salary-cap management issues, and just prior to training camp in 1998, I talked them into trading me Bonzi for a lottery-protected first-round pick in 1999. Bonzi was a big, physical guard, great at going down in the paint and posting up. He had an amazingly quick first step. When he was out on the wing, he could get around a defender and score deceptively fast. He was also a ferociously effective defender and a reliable outside shooter. His shot wasn't pretty, but it went in.

Bonzi had a good sense of humor and a big smile. He always

greeted me the same way: "Hey, what's up, Big Money?"—a nickname he gave me the day he signed his first NBA contract in my office.

I could hardly wait to see how Bonzi fit in with the team. Then I *had* to wait. A long time.

The third lockout in NBA history began on July 1, 1998, and dragged on for months. During the work stoppage, teams could not hold practices or meetings or make any player transactions. A few times during the lockout, I fielded calls from NBA commissioner David Stern and other league officials who wanted me to float this or that idea past one of my former players, Buck Williams, who had just completed his term as president of the players' union and was one of the top negotiators on the union's bargaining team. I had a nice relationship with Buck. He was a reasonable guy, and we had some good conversations about sticking points in the contract negotiations. As usual, the biggest issue centered around money. The league wanted to lower the players' percentage of shared revenue. Players wanted higher minimum salaries and longer contracts. Sometimes, a third-party voice can help ease tensions and find common ground. When I talked to Buck, it sounded like both sides were closer to a deal than they realized. They just weren't really listening to each other. I suggested each party focus on the optics most important to their constituents, then help each other claim a win.

It was the closest the NBA has ever come to shutting out a whole season. We'd had summertime lockouts before. Business would shut down for a few months, but we'd get the labor agreement done, start the season by October, and play 82 games. Some players were convinced there wouldn't be a season, so they didn't work out. At all. NBA owners and the players' union finally did reach an agreement on January 6, 1999. Training would be shortened to just 12 days, starting on January 21, the same day that free agents could be signed. The regular season opened on February 5 and featured 50 games in 90 nights.

J. R. Rider led the Blazers in scoring during the lockout-shortened season, with just under 14 points per game. About three months in, he was on fire in a home game against the Lakers, scoring 16 points in just 21 minutes (Kobe Bryant scored 20 in almost twice as many minutes). J. R. drained six straight baskets, including a three-pointer, plus seven rebounds and three assists, before the game turned into a 113–86 blowout. But J. R. wasn't there to celebrate the win. With about 20 minutes left in the game, he did something I've never seen any other NBA player do: he left the game after a fan heckled him for missing a shot. I could hardly believe what I was seeing when he beckoned his girlfriend down from the stands and just walked off the court, still wearing his uniform.

I followed him to the parking garage and said, "Come on, J. R. . . . what do you think you're doing?" I reminded him that part of being a professional athlete is being able to tune out catcalls, focus on his job, and play the game. I told him I'd suspend him if he left the building. He didn't care. He said the fan was "bullshit" and drove away. The two-game suspension cost him a lot of money, around $120,000. He made a weak effort to try to get me to rescind it. But I stood my ground. It didn't matter that he was one of our best players. Guys need to be disciplined. They need to know there are boundaries. They need to know you'll work for them, that they need to work for you, and that they're not above the team. Ultimately, I think J. R. respected my follow-through. It's how I got the most out of him during his three years with the Blazers. His whole career, he had been catered to and pampered because he was such a good player. Rules never applied to him until he got to Portland.

We finished the lockout-shortened season with 35 wins and 15 losses, good enough to clinch the Pacific Division title. We swept the Phoenix Suns in the first round, advancing to the second round for the first time in seven years. Next, we eliminated the Utah Jazz in six games. The Jazz were always a tough out. They had three really good players and executed the best half-court offense in the NBA. Karl Malone (a.k.a. "the Mailman" because he always delivered in the post) averaged 20 points, 11 rebounds, and 5 assists in the series. John Stockton, one of the best point guards and passers of all time, also played a terrific series, as did Jeff Hornacek, one of the league's top free throw and three-point shooters. We knew Utah would not beat themselves, and they didn't. It took great team balance and consistency to win four times in that series. Rider was our leading scorer, averaging 19 points, followed by Grant with 13, Wallace with 12, and Sabonis with 11. Sabonis and Grant handled the glass, each averaging ten boards a game.

We faced a tough opponent in the Western Conference Finals: Tim Duncan's San Antonio Spurs, who had swept us and the Lakers back to back on the road during the regular season. They swept us again before winning the NBA championship.

Making it to the Final Four in 1999 marked a turning point for the Blazers. We were climbing out of the rut from our first-round playoff losses, emerging as a powerful team packed with young talent, and we were just getting started.

Mike Dunleavy won Coach of the Year in 1999, but behind the scenes, friction between Dunleavy and our youngest player was causing them both serious problems. Jermaine O'Neal was having a rough time adjusting from his status as South Carolina's Mr. Basketball and one of the hottest high school players in the country to just one of the guys busting butt to earn every minute of playing time—and he wasn't getting much. One night, Jermaine played a big role in a win against the Sonics, with 20 points and ten rebounds. Then, the next night, Dunleavy didn't play him one second in a home game. No explanation.

Jermaine would often come to my office in tears, complaining about how little he was playing. At times, he doubted whether he'd made the right decision to go straight from high school to the NBA, like fellow South Carolinian Kevin Garnett had done the year before. Jermaine had been just 18 years old when he'd played his first game as a pro, making him the youngest ever to play in the league—a record he held for almost a decade until the slightly younger 18-year-old Andrew Bynum played his first game with the Los Angeles Lakers in 2005.

Jermaine embraced our team work ethic. He put a lot of extra time in with assistant coaches working on his post moves and jump shot. He loved to play basketball, and it showed. Our strength coach, Bobby Medina, made it his mission to beef up Jermaine's lean frame. His teammates liked to tease him when he flexed and posed in the mirror during weight training sessions. His skinny body was transforming into muscle, and he loved the new look.

It was time to have a talk with Dunleavy. "Look, Mike," I said, "you need to play Jermaine five minutes in the first half of every game. If he plays well, give him at least five minutes in the second half—or as much as you want. But at least five minutes each half. If you ever feel that playing him five minutes in the first half cost us the game, come see me. No problem."

Mike agreed to do it but would never follow through, which infuriated Paul Allen. Paul questioned whether I'd been clear enough, so we had a meeting—Paul, Mike, and me—I restated the minimum five minutes Jermaine was supposed to get each half. Once again, Mike said he'd do it. But it made no difference. Jermaine kept warming the bench. Mike's issues with Jermaine had a more specific origin story. Once, during a road trip in Phoenix, Mike called me to his hotel room, livid. He wanted me to fire George Glymph (Jermaine's former coach and now a scout and mentor to the young player) right there, on the spot.

"Mike, George doesn't even report to you," I said, puzzled. "Why would I fire him?"

Mike claimed that he'd overheard a conversation—with his ear up against the wall of his hotel room—in the room next door. "Mike Dunleavy doesn't know what he's doing as a coach," he claimed George had said. "You should be playing more."

I had to ask, "Mike, first of all, what are you doing with your ear up against the wall in a hotel room on the day of a game?"

He had no answer.

"Second of all, I've never put my ear up against the wall in a hotel room to listen. But if I did, I probably couldn't hear exactly what was being said in the other room. Maybe you didn't quite hear it clearly."

He insisted he'd heard them crystal clear, so I went and talked to George. I could tell by the look on his face that he'd never said what Mike was accusing him of saying. He was adamant that he was supportive of Mike. He and I went to Mike and assured him that whatever he thought he'd heard wasn't true. Mike listened to George but didn't believe him.

As Jermaine's three-year contract ended in 1999, Paul Allen wanted me to re-sign him at all costs.

"Paul, it's going to be tough," I leveled with him. "The kid hates Mike Dunleavy, and Mike Dunleavy hates him." Paul wanted me to fire Dunleavy, but I pushed back.

When we'd hired Mike, he had agreed to give Jermaine a chance to develop into a starter, so I told him he needed to come to a meeting with me and Jermaine in South Carolina. "Mike, you need to tell this kid he's going to play 10 or 15 minutes a game most of the time, if he earns the minutes. He wants to be in Portland. He loves the fans."

Mike joined us for one day in Jermaine's hometown of Columbia, South Carolina, and as I pitched Jermaine on the advantages of staying in Portland, I turned to Mike and said, "Hey, Coach. Why don't you explain to Jermaine how you see his role next year?"

"Well, Jermaine," Mike said, "I'm pretty sure about two-thirds of the games will be matchups such that I could probably get you about 10 or 12 minutes. If you're playing really well. But no guarantees."

Then he left. I couldn't believe it. And at the same time, I wasn't surprised.

Jermaine looked me in the eye and said, "Bob, I don't think the guy wants me. I don't think he's going to play me. I could sign with 15 other teams right now for more money than you're offering me. But you drafted me, and I feel a loyalty to you. . . . If I come back, and he screws me again this year, will you commit to trading me after the season's over? Because my career will be going nowhere fast if I have to sit on the bench."

I told him that was fair. It was the only way he would re-sign with the Blazers as a free agent. I hoped I wouldn't have to make good on my promise to trade him.

That off-season, I made multiple trades that added strength and depth to the team. Three years after Minnesota couldn't get rid of Isaiah Rider fast enough, I played up his stellar performance in the Western Conference Finals and talked Atlanta into a trade that sent J. R. to the Hawks for one of their best players, Steve Smith. Steve was a few years older than J. R., still a high-scoring shooting guard. He was also such a positive force in the Atlanta community. He'd won the NBA's 1997–98 J. Walter Kennedy Citizenship Award. When Steve joined the Blazers, he became the third member of our team who had received this prestigious honor that the NBA gives to just one player, coach, or staff member once a year. Chris Dudley won it in 1995–96, and Brian Grant in 1998–99.

You won't find many headlines about these guys' good deeds.

The same is true for the Points of Light Foundation 1999 Award for Excellence in Corporate Community Service; the Trail Blazers are the first and only professional sports franchise to win the award, given to companies that have strong employee volunteer programs targeting serious social problems. These honors didn't exactly align with the "Jail Blazers" narrative that the media could not get enough of writing about.

Trading J. R. Rider for Steve Smith was my ultimate master chess move. I took a player no one wanted, invested in his development, got his best basketball out of him, then traded him for a quintessential good guy who was one of Atlanta's most popular players.

Another strong 1999 off-season roster addition was Detlef Schrempf. I knew him well from his time at the Sonics, who had just released him. I signed him to Portland the same day, confident he would fit in seamlessly. Det was close to the end of his career, but at six foot ten, he had the versatility and skills to play multiple positions. He was like a Swiss Army knife—he could do a little bit of everything. Det could start or come off the bench and was our insurance policy if a player got injured. At this stage in his career, Detlef was a little more effective in a half-court offense than running in transition. Half-court execution is extremely important in playoff basketball when the game slows down and teams get fewer possessions.

The biggest deal of all was a blockbuster trade I pulled off against the tallest of odds. It took some seriously deft negotiating to get Scottie Pippen to come play in Portland, a much smaller market than where he had been playing. Scottie wanted out of Houston. The Rockets had a decent strike-shortened season in 1999, finishing 31–19. But their three future Hall of Famers—Hakeem Olajuwon, Charles Barkley, and Scottie Pippen—could not find chemistry. Pippen and Barkley did not get along. I think Scottie felt like he was the third fiddle in an orchestra when he was accustomed to being a well-respected wingman to Michael Jordan. Scottie demanded a trade after only one season in Houston. Because he had a no-trade clause in his contract, the Rockets could only trade him to a team he wanted to play for. That team was the Lakers, where he could reunite with Phil Jackson, who had coached him to six championships in Chicago. Scottie and his wife, Larsa, an aspiring actress, loved the warm weather and big city lights of Hollywood. Phil wanted Scottie, too, but it wouldn't be an easy trade. Pippen's contract would be difficult to fit into any team's salary cap.

Shaquille O'Neal was making $17.1 million a year. Kobe Bryant was making $9 million. Together, their salaries made up almost half the Lakers $55 million payroll. Shaq and Kobe were off limits, so any trade would have to include Lakers role players who made much less than Pippen's $14.8 million salary. The Lakers were trying hard to come up with a combination of players and draft picks that the Rockets would find acceptable and that fit within the salary cap, but they kept coming up short. I thought they might try to find a third team to engineer a three-way deal, but that was never part of their thinking.

When Scottie caught wind that I was in the hunt, trying to get him, his agent, Jimmy Sexton, called me and said, "Don't try to get him. He won't play for you. He doesn't want to go to Portland."

I asked Houston for permission to talk to Scottie. When I reached him, he echoed the same sentiments. "I'm not going to Portland. It's a small town. The sun never shines there. It rains all the time. My wife hates it there. I don't want to be there. We want to be in Los Angeles. I'll never go to Portland."

I had to paint a picture that made Portland seem not just viable but a *better* choice than Los Angeles. I played up Shaq's and Kobe's stardom and told him he deserved more than being a team's third-best player. In Portland, Scottie would be the undisputed leader. We had a much better and deeper roster than the Lakers, and our style of play fit Pippen's skill set perfectly—long, athletic, versatile players who could cover multiple positions. We had a deep bench, allowing us to keep our starters fresh for the playoffs. I knew Pip liked to work out in Chicago's practice facility *before* practice. So I played up the Blazers' $7 million state-of-the-art practice facility, which I had led the charge to build in suburban Portland two years earlier. It had two full courts, whirlpools, cold baths, a large weight and training room, spacious training and medical treatment areas, huge locker rooms, and much more. Players could come and go 24-7.

The Blazers didn't even have their own place to practice when I got to Portland; they would practice in the gyms at a Jewish community center and Lewis and Clark College. Practice times changed constantly. The Blazers were not a priority. There was no ability for players to get extra court time for individual work.

Now we practiced in style, which definitely appealed to Pippen. We traveled in style, too, flying to games in our own custom-fitted 757 jet, compliments of Paul Allen. Players loved being treated as royalty, and NBA players definitely knew about the pro-player environment we had created in Portland. Lastly, Scottie's legacy would be legendary if he won "his own championship" without Michael Jordan or Phil Jackson.

I talked about my track record, how I had built the Sonics team that had narrowly lost the 1996 championship to the Bulls a couple of years after I left. In Portland, I had torn apart an old team that was playing terribly, rebuilt it, got it under the salary cap, and we'd made it to the Western Conference Finals that year; the Lakers hadn't.

Scottie went from a hard no to telling Houston he would consider either the Lakers or Portland. Once I got in the game with Houston, my job was to figure out what the Lakers could offer, understand the salary-cap constraints from every angle, and really know where they could and could not go to get what they wanted.

I knew every contract of every player in the NBA, what every team's salary cap was to the penny, like every team should know. I knew what it would take to make trades. There was a lot of cat-and-mouse negotiating and timing. I didn't have a lot of leverage, so I set out to create it however I could. At one point, I said, "Houston, here's my offer. If you don't take it in six hours, I'm out. And when I'm out, I'm going to make sure the Lakers and the whole world know we're not after Scottie Pippen anymore, so you either take a really good deal with me now, or you risk not getting any deal done. Then your owner will be upset that you'll have to pay Scottie Pippen all this money while your team is heading into free fall."

It was one of the most complex deals I had ever made for a player. I traded six players for Pippen (Stacey Augmon, Kelvin Cato, Walt Williams, Brian Shaw, Ed Gray, and Carlos Rogers) and inherited the remaining $66 million on the five-year contract he had signed with the Houston Rockets the year before.

In the news conference about the trade, Scottie said, "This team is far more talented than probably any team that's been assembled in the league."

Scottie took the team to the next level. He was a great leader with an excellent work ethic. He would come to practice early, do his own workouts in the weight room. He stayed after practice to work on his shot and his game. He was very engaged, helping the coaches game-plan. He had a ton of experience. He'd been around the league a long time. Everyone respected his six championships. He taught our guys how to be more professional, to go the extra mile. We finished the 1999–2000 season with the second-best record in the NBA: 59–23. For the second year in a row, we advanced to the Western Conference Finals, eliminating the Minnesota Timberwolves three to one in the first round, the Utah Jazz four to one in the second, followed by a showdown with Shaq, Kobe, and the Lakers in the conference championship. It was a thrilling seven-game battle, ending in a gutshot of a loss, 89–84.

To this day, I'm convinced that was the best NBA team that didn't win a championship. Portland had the better team, stacked with talent. Los Angeles had the better coach. Phil Jackson knew how to manage superstars and how to motivate the role players. He had a way of making opposing coaches play "his game" instead of playing "their game." By contrast, Mike Dunleavy made strategic errors that played an outsized role in our losses in Games One, Three, and Four—first agreeing, then refusing to make certain adjustments that assistant coaches, Paul, and I felt would work better in the playoffs than our matchup strategy in the regular season. The assistant coaches wanted him to play Bonzi Wells more. At six foot six, Bonzi could more effectively guard Kobe (also six foot six), but Dunleavy insisted on playing Damon Stoudamire, who had a hard time defending Kobe because he was so much shorter (five foot ten). When we trailed the series three to one, Mike started using Bonzi, as he had originally agreed to before the series started. We won the next two games and were leading Game Seven in LA by 13 points at the start of the fourth quarter.

The NBA officiating crew (Dick Bavetta, Hugh Evans, and Steve Javie) awarded the Lakers 37 free throws and only 16 for us. That was an unbelievable disparity and the basis for a conspiracy theory. But we still should have won the game and the series. We missed 12 straight shots in the fourth quarter. It was a "team choke." The shots were all good looks and taken by the players we wanted shooting the ball—Rasheed Wallace, Scottie Pippen, Steve Smith, Bonzi Wells, and Brian Grant. Unfortunately, Arvydas Sabonis and Detlef Schrempf did not attempt any shots in the fourth quarter. As a team, we only shot 22 percent the final 12 minutes—with an NBA championship on the line.

From a fan's perspective, it was one of the most exciting games ever. From a general manager's perspective, I've got an ulcer scar that will never go away. It was my championship that just rolled out on me. Shaq and Kobe went on to win the first of their three consecutive championships.

Once again, Paul wanted to fire Dunleavy. We agreed his coaching mistakes early on in the series had arguably cost us the championship. But once again, I pushed back. I've always erred on the side of loyalty with my coaches. I respect what a hard job they have. I talked Paul into giving Mike another year. In hindsight, I shouldn't have.

CHAPTER 13

TOO MUCH

I HAD TO MAKE SOME PAINFUL changes to the roster in the 2000 off-season. One of them was such a bad idea, I tried as hard as I could to talk Paul Allen out of it. Brian Grant had become a free agent and was demanding a seven-year, $86 million contract. Paul wouldn't sign him for anything more than four years. Grant was struggling with a host of nagging injuries—a bad back, a sprained shoulder, an upper-leg stress fracture—that were causing him so much pain, he was playing fewer and fewer minutes or sitting out games entirely. Paul insisted I find a trade so we would get "something" for Grant. I made the case for letting Grant go for "nothing," but Paul didn't want to give away an asset that valuable without getting something in return.

I looked around and couldn't find a lot I would get for Grant. One of the only possibilities was a power forward for the Cleveland Cavaliers: Shawn Kemp. It might sound like a full-circle moment in a storybook narrative, but it was anything but. During the NBA lockout, Shawn had gained a lot of weight. He had fallen woefully out of shape. He was struggling with substance abuse. He was not Reign Man anymore. Paul didn't care.

I wanted to make sure the coach was on board, so I had Dunleavy fly to Las Vegas, where Shawn was living off-season, and watch him work out. In short order, Dunleavy sent Paul an email saying Shawn would work great as a backup center.

It wasn't easy to put a positive spin on a deal I made with great reluctance. Why trade for an overweight player with a huge contract ($71 million) and an attitude that had rubbed a lot of people the wrong way? "He's done everything a guy can do in the NBA but win a championship," I told the *Los Angeles Times*. "He's hungry for it."

As I was working on the Grant-for-Kemp deal, it became clear it was time to make good on a promise I had made Jermaine O'Neal back when we'd re-signed him. No matter how well he did in practice or in games, Dunleavy kept Jermaine relegated to the bench, playing him only eight minutes per game in the 1999–2000 season. I had hoped it wouldn't come to this, but I had to honor my agreement with Jermaine that if he didn't get the playing time he deserved, I'd trade him to a team where he could become a star.

Looking back, this was another opportunity to get rid of Dunleavy instead of trading away a player bursting with potential. But at the time, I didn't see it that way. Once again, I made the case for keeping Dunleavy. "Look," I told Paul, "even though Mike's screwing our player, we're still doing well enough in the big picture. I think Mike deserves to keep coaching. But I do need to trade Jermaine. The only way I got him signed again was to promise I'd trade him after a year if it wasn't working out. Mike will never play Jermaine, and Jermaine's not going to develop here."

Dunleavy had his sights set on Dale Davis, a veteran with the Eastern Conference champion Indiana Pacers. I felt terrible trading away a young player with so much potential, but we were well positioned to make another run for the NBA title, so I supported the coach and traded O'Neal for Davis. I'm sure some GMs would've had no problem telling Jermaine, "Too bad. We've got you for three more years." But when I make a commitment, I always honor it. I lived up to my end of the deal, as disappointing as it was. Jermaine wound up doing a great job with the Pacers, and he finally got the playing time he deserved. During his first seven years in Indiana, he played an average of 35 minutes per game, scoring 19 points, 10 rebounds, and 2 blocked shots. He made the All-Star team six times. All he'd needed in

Portland was the playing time that Dunleavy had refused to give him. I've always wished he could've risen to stardom with the Blazers, as I knew he could. And I'll always be glad I drafted him.

The Blazers had issues in the 2000–01 season. And the biggest one was Shawn Kemp's erratic behavior. He was often late for practices and planes. He worked hard out on the court but was not losing weight. Off the court, he was hanging out with a tough crowd that clearly had a bad influence on him. We did not want them around the team. The locker room knew Shawn was having personal problems, and it affected the team atmosphere. I met with players individually to express my concerns about a teammate they liked a lot. They offered to help me help Shawn in any way they could.

Meanwhile, Dunleavy blamed everybody except himself for our struggles. In one interview, he claimed he'd had no idea we were trading Brian Grant for Shawn Kemp until his son had heard the news on the radio. The players knew Mike was lying and only looking out for himself. Once again, Paul called me in disbelief.

"Do you think Mike has amnesia and forgot he told me he *wanted* Kemp?" Paul asked.

"No," I replied. "This is Mike trying to make himself look as good as possible."

Dunleavy had issues with multiple players. Some would ignore him when he called an offensive play, when he signaled for a time-out, or when he called on them to foul an opponent to stop the clock. They would walk away before he'd finished talking to them. Pippen called me at home repeatedly that season, saying Dunleavy didn't know what he was doing and that he had lost the team. He said none of the players had confidence in him. Everyone had tuned him out. At one point, after several consecutive losses, Damon Stoudamire told the *Miami Herald*, "We're losing, so there's going to be frustration. It's going to keep building if we keep losing. I haven't seen anyone smile on the court for five weeks, any high-fives. It has become like a job for us. We have to start having fun."

This team had an abundance of talent. Some said too much talent. Coach Dunleavy would talk reporters' ears off about how his job felt like a losing battle with too many stars all clamoring for more playing time than there were game minutes to distribute. The *Oregonian* once ran a story headlined, "The Toughest Coaching Job in the NBA."

When Paul Allen caught wind of it, he called me up in disbelief.

"I know," I said. "It's unbelievable."

Teams are snapshots in time, always evolving. Moaning and groaning about "too much" talent is like walking up to an unfinished painting, looking at it for a second, and complaining that it has too much blue. That might be true at that moment, but the artist has more work to do. Other colors are coming, and it's going to be beautiful.

Of course, when Dunleavy had coached in Milwaukee, he'd blamed the Bucks' struggles on not having *enough* good players. That's a legitimate issue. It's why teams get torn down and rebuilt. And as you're rebuilding—a process that takes years—you'd rather have more All-Star-caliber players than not enough. I'm not saying you want to *end up* with 12 future Hall of Famers on your roster. Even if that were possible (which it's not because of salary cap), your job when you have "too much" talent is to figure out which of your eight or nine top players fit well together, then trade the ones who aren't in the rotation. You'll get something valuable for them because they'll be hot commodities.

Good coaches get the most out of their players by implementing a system that maximizes their skills, getting them fired up to play their best basketball, giving it their all every second they're out on the floor, then using the right opportunities to rotate in reinforcements. Mike was a good coach, but he always seemed more focused on himself than the team as a whole, as if he saw his players as disgruntled divas who all thought they deserved to be costars of the *Mike Dunleavy Show* instead of what he needed them to be: dutiful members of the supporting cast.

Though I don't believe Mike had "the toughest coaching job in the NBA," I will concede that we had some hot heads on this team, and hot heads are hard to coach. Rasheed Wallace, for example, set a league record in 1999–2000 by getting 38 technical fouls. The next year, he broke his own single-season record by getting 41 technicals in 80 games. Rasheed had a notoriously quick temper, and once you get a reputation for technical fouls, refs are quicker to call them.

I'll never forget the time Rasheed got a technical for looking at

NBA official Ron Garretson the wrong way—literally. Another time, he tossed the ball toward a ref after the official made a questionable call. Sheed claimed he was just giving the ball to the ref. Another official on the floor saw it differently, came running from the other end of the court, called Sheed for a "tech," then ejected him for mouthing off about it. After the game, Rasheed spotted the ref who threw him out of the game, Tim Donaghy, and got in one more dig. The ensuing altercation made a bad situation worse for Rasheed. The NBA suspended him for seven games and fined him about $1.3 million. (Years later, Tim Donaghy served 15 months in prison after pleading guilty to federal charges in a gambling scandal, admitting to taking thousands of dollars from a professional gambler for inside tips on games and other misdeeds.)

Rasheed's wealth of technical fouls led to a rule change that virtually assures his record will never be broken. Since 2006, NBA players automatically get suspended for one game without pay after receiving 16 technical fouls. After that point, players receive the same suspension for each additional technical foul. Rasheed eased up later on in his career, but by the time he retired, he ranked third in NBA history with 317 technicals, behind Charles Barkley (329) and Karl Malone (332). Though it's not a statistic players brag about, the list of the league's ten most prolific technical foulers includes some of the best ballers of all time: Gary Payton ranks fourth (250), Dennis Rodman fifth (212), Russell Westbrook sixth (172), Kevin Garnett seventh (172), Kobe Bryant eighth (166), Shaquille O'Neal ninth (150), and Jermaine O'Neal tenth (146).

Technical fouls aren't necessarily a bad thing. They can motivate individual players and ignite the whole team. The other team might make one free throw, but that extra point often pales in comparison to the jolt of energy that fires up a team rallying around the teammate who got the technical. That said, there was no justification for Rasheed getting a "T" every other game.

There was a lot more to Rasheed than his hot temper. He was a smart guy and fiercely loyal to his teammates. Because he was one of our best players, the media always wanted to talk to him after games. But he didn't want to talk to *them*. He didn't like how they rarely asked him about basketball and how they typecast him and most of his teammates as "Jail Blazers." Over and over, the NBA fined him for refusing to talk to the media.

One time, I called him into my office and said, "Sheed, this is a lose-lose. You just got fined another $30,000. We just got fined $30,000, and the league is threatening to suspend you." Then I offered him some advice. "Look, just because you're interviewed at a postgame press conference doesn't mean you have to answer every single question. You certainly don't have to answer it the way they're hoping you will. *You* can control the narrative. If they ask you a question you don't like, you can say, 'I don't know about that, but I *can* tell you *this . . .*' Or you can talk up how well one of your teammates played. You can just answer in a positive way."

He looked puzzled. "What do you mean?"

"Well," I said, "they might say, 'Hey, Rasheed, we heard one of your teammates was smoking dope last week,' right after we won a playoff game. And you can say, 'Hey, I'd like to talk about the game. It was amazing. Both teams played hard. It was really well fought.'"

So he went into the press conference and answered every single question, 10 or 20 of them, the exact same way: "Hey, man. Both teams played hard."

"Rasheed, what was that play designed in the last couple of minutes?"

"Hey, man . . . both teams played hard."

"Rasheed, what were you thinking when so-and-so blocked that shot?"

"Hey, my man, both teams played hard."

It became national news. Rasheed got fined for it. And so did the Blazers.

To this day, every now and then, a professional athlete who's dodging a question will wink and say, "Hey, my man, both teams played hard."

Another Rasheed Wallace quote became the stuff of NBA legend. Every time an opponent he fouled missed a free throw, he'd shout, "Ball don't lie!" Depending on the referee, he might get a technical for *that*—or thrown out of the game entirely.

I loved Rasheed. His teammates did, too, though some grew tired of all the negative attention his tantrums generated. The media had a

field day writing about infighting, the Blazers' apparent lack of a defin-
itive leader (as if an NBA team needs just one of them), and chemistry.
I didn't make anything better when I spent 15 minutes talking about
how critical chemistry is for any team and how tricky it can be to come
up with just the right mix of all the qualities that make a team great.
You can assemble a team with the right balance of skills, and you can
make educated guesses about how they'll get along, but ultimately, you
have no idea until they start playing together. Players can like each
other but not play well together, and players cannot get along off the
court but be in sync on the hardwood. Sometimes, I've put players on
a team thinking they would get along famously, and all they did was
feud. Most people thought everyone on our 1994-95 Blazers team got
along great, but veteran players Jerome Kersey and Clifford Robinson
couldn't stand each other. Once, they threw such fierce punches at
training camp that they looked like they belonged more in a boxing
ring than a basketball court. Jerome hated Cliff's lack of work ethic—
and that he'd taken away Jerome's starting role.

Sometimes, I cross my fingers that all hell won't break loose, and
they get along great. My first season with the Sonics, everyone warned
me that Maurice Lucas—on his third team in three years—would balk
at being a role player and never share his basketball wisdom with his
younger teammates. None of that came true. Luke was a positive influence on and off the court and played an instrumental part in our
underdog team making it to the conference finals. I concluded my
comments by saying, "I'm not a chemistry major," and the media never
let me live it down.

I made the chemistry comment after bringing Rod Strickland back
to the Blazers in March 2001 to back up Damon Stoudamire as a point
guard. I try to make most of my roster moves during the off-season
to minimize the potential for midseason disruption. But in this case,
I felt it was in the team's best interests to release Gary Grant (a guard
who had lost his quickness and rarely played) and put backup point
guard Greg Anthony on injured reserve (to give his right shoulder time
to heal). We were able to pick up Rod on a prorated minimum contract for the remaining two months of the season. Paul wanted us to
strengthen our depth at point guard so we could have a better chance
in the playoffs. We told Dunleavy that if the Strickland addition didn't

improve the team or if it created a problem, he had the authority to cut Strickland. Rod played in the final 21 games, averaging 5 points and 3 assists in 16 minutes. Mike was happy with Rod because he embraced the role of backup to Damon Stoudamire. But Portland sportswriters seemed collectively obsessed with the theory that I neither knew anything nor cared about team chemistry. Why else would I have assembled a team with "too many good players"?

Meanwhile, Shawn continued to play poorly throughout the season. The turnaround that we were hoping for wasn't happening. Back in his Sonics days, Shawn would routinely arrive early (or at least on time) and stay late after practice, putting in extra time any chance he got. He was hungry. That Shawn was gone by this point in his career. Anytime I'd talk to him, I'd ask him how he was doing, and he'd insist everything was fine, not to worry. We all wanted to see Shawn get healthy and turn things around, and not just so he could play better basketball. We were as worried about him as we would be for a struggling family member.

I had been talking to Shawn's agent about his problems for months, and finally, Shawn agreed to seek help. He voluntarily checked himself into drug and alcohol treatment—eight days before the end of the 2000–01 regular season.

Our 2000–01 season ended with a 15–17 fizzle after the All-Star break, but because we had started strong, we finished the season 50–32, a solid performance, though it was nine shy of our record the year before. We faced the reigning champions in the first round of the 2001 playoffs. The Lakers swept us, and this time, Paul didn't have to tell me to fire Mike Dunleavy. There was no question it was time for a new coach.

A clear front-runner emerged as I reviewed coaching candidates with our key players: Maurice Cheeks, who had played an instrumental role in Philadelphia's 2001 run to the NBA Finals, where they lost in five games to Shaq, Kobe, and the Lakers. "Mo" had played for the Sixers, himself, as starting point guard for Philly's 1983 NBA championship team. Rasheed grew up in Philadelphia cheering for the Sixers when Mo played alongside Dr. J and Moses Malone. Players loved and respected Mo as a coach. He had mentored Allen Iverson, who was named the NBA MVP in 2001. "The Answer" did not like to practice and was often late to games. He played with passion and had a short fuse—130 career technical fouls. Iverson would often feud with head coach Larry Brown, but Mo would intervene and act as the peacemaker. Our team liked Mo because he made the game fun again.

It always takes time for a new coach to implement their system. The team struggled in December and January, losing 11 of 15 games. In previous seasons, a losing streak like that would have continued as players tuned out Dunleavy. But with Mo at the helm, we got back on track. A month after our losing streak, we won 12 in a row and 15 out of 16. The players really *wanted* to play for Mo. They appreciated that he stayed in the gym until the last player left the court. He would use the time to shoot free throws with them or rebound their missed shots—anything to make an interpersonal connection.

After going through rehab, Shawn came back, but his work ethic still lagged. He never stuck around after practice. He'd arrive a minute before practice started. Mo knew Shawn was having problems and had the wisdom to realize that no matter how much we wanted to help, that could only happen if Shawn got to a place where he recognized he needed help. We'd talk to Shawn—always discreetly—and he'd politely say, "I hear you," "I got you," "I don't need that, but thank you," "I'm doing better." We knew that was the disease talking.

One day, I got a call that the NBA would be suspending Shawn for at least five games for falling out of compliance in his rehab aftercare program. I never learned exactly what had happened. The details didn't matter to me. The only thing that mattered was Shawn doing what needed to be done to get healthy again. No one wanted him to succeed more than I did. I had brought him into the NBA when no one else had believed in his potential. I had watched him rise from wide-eyed rookie to sensational superstar. And there he was, struggling with the demons of addiction. Shawn made no excuses. He apologized and assured me he would get back into compliance, which he did in short order. He missed only five games in late February and early March because of the suspension.

When the 2001–02 season ended, it was time to let Shawn go. I wouldn't just cut him loose and say, "Have a nice life." I explained that I would be waiving him, which would drop him from our roster but still require us to pay him for the remainder of his contract unless another team acquired him and picked up the rest of the tab. I encouraged him to dedicate his time and energy to his recovery so he could get healthy and stay healthy.

He felt awful about the whole situation and agreed when I said it wouldn't be fair for the Blazers to have to pay all of his remaining $45 million contract. I talked him into renegotiating the remainder of his contract down to $20 million. No player had ever given back that kind of money before. The deal was so good (for the Blazers) that the National Basketball Players Association tried to block it. In the end, the league and the union approved the deal, which spread out payments to Shawn over a ten-year period, as I had proposed. The last thing someone struggling with addiction needs is a huge payday. (Shawn wound up signing with the Orlando Magic as a free agent in 2002–03, then got replaced by Juwan Howard and never played another NBA game.)

Paul felt so badly about how the Shawn trade turned out for the Blazers that he wanted to publicly admit he had insisted on the deal and that I had argued against it. He didn't think it was fair for me to take the blame for a bad idea I had tried so hard to talk him out of. But ultimately, I convinced him to let me remain the lightning rod. A lot of guys in my spot wouldn't have done that, because their egos are so big. We've all got egos, but I've always felt my ego needs to stand down when it's time to protect my owner. It's just part of the job. Try to give your owner as much credit as possible when things go well, and when things don't go well, make no excuses, take responsibility, and focus on moving forward.

We finished the 2001–02 season 49–33, just one win shy of our previous season. Once again, we faced the Lakers in the first round of the playoffs. The fans always loved it when we played the Lakers. Kobe and Shaq each averaged 26 points during that series, just one ahead of Rasheed, our leading scorer. Pippen held his own, averaging 16 points, nine rebounds, and six assists per game. The fans went wild in Game Three when we were up by two points with three seconds left in the game. But an NBA game is never over until the final horn sounds. "Big Shot Bob" Horry proved that to be the case, draining a game-winning triple with two seconds to go. With that 92–91 victory, the reigning NBA champs swept us, clinched the series, and went on to win their third consecutive NBA title. It was a brutal loss but an unforgettably exciting game. I always hated going into the locker room after a playoff series loss. No matter what I said to convey how proud I was of their effort, everyone still felt terrible.

In the fall of 2002, I let Paul know my ninth season with the Blazers would be my last. I had been doing too much for too many years—running two pro sports franchises in two different states and so many of Paul's other business interests, it was hard to keep track. Every time I list them, I almost think I'm leaving an enterprise or three off the list: First and Goal (Seahawks Stadium and Exhibition Center), Oregon Arena Corporation (Rose Garden Arena and Memorial Coliseum), Portland Fire (WNBA), Rose City Radio (KXL and 95.5 FM), Radio Northwest (network of 25 radio stations), Action Sports Media (24-7 cable sports channel), Action Sports Entertainment and Mobile (HDTV production truck), TBI Airports (airport advertising businesses in Portland, San Diego, Burbank), Razor Sharp Promotions (facilities events company), Blazers on Broadway (retail store).

Paul spent the entire 2002–03 NBA season in denial, either not believing I would follow through and actually resign or asking me what he could do to lighten my load, trying to get me to stay. I'd say, "Nothing, so don't try to change my mind." I assured Paul that I would happily continue my role as president of the Seahawks. The 2002 season would be our inaugural one in the new football and soccer stadium, which opened to rave reviews locally and nationally. Fans were excited. Every game was sold out, with a waiting list for season tickets. Splitting my time between Portland and Seattle allowed me no time off. I wanted more time with my family during my son's last two years of high school. I could do any number of things career-wise in a few years, but I would never get another opportunity to be there for more of Sean's football, basketball, and lacrosse games. Our daughter, Lily, was already off at college at Wesleyan, and whenever she directed a play in school, I wanted to have a chance to attend. When she was playing basketball in high school, I would hustle home from Portland, braving thick traffic on Interstate 5, to get there on time. As exhausting as those drives (and some flights) were, it was always worth the effort.

Paul could tell I was sincere, and yet he wouldn't give up hope that at some point, I'd give in and agree to stay. Whenever he'd present me with another job to do, I'd remember how hard I had worked to get into the sports business in the first place. I was just some kid from the Midwest with a good work ethic. Nobody had helped me get a job in sports. So why would I say no if my boss saw a job that needed to be done and assigned me to do it? Eventually, I *would* tell him that he had me doing too many things and encourage him to hire more people in the front office—which finally happened after I left.

One of the most unforgettable moments during my final season in Portland had nothing to do with basketball. It started out with a painfully awkward silence. A 13-year-old girl who had won a contest to sing the national anthem at a Blazers game had clammed up and forgotten the words.

In swooped Mo Cheeks, leaning into the microphone to pick up where she had left off, "Twilight's last gleaming . . ." Mo was not a singer. He never would've gotten up there on his own. But without even thinking about it, he rushed to the girl's side because he wanted this to be an experience she remembered for good reasons, not as an embarrassment. They finished the song together, with the crowd singing more loudly than usual. Then the entire arena gave the loudest round of applause I have ever heard after a national anthem. Mo didn't do it because he was hungry for credit; he just always wanted to bring out the best in the people around him. That's the kind of guy and coach Mo was—sincere and genuine to the core.

We made it to the playoffs in 2003 and faced the Dallas Mavericks in the first round. It was looking like we were on our way to getting swept, then we did something that only three teams in NBA history have ever done. Just one game from elimination, we came back from a three-to-zero deficit and took the series to seven games. Injuries prevented four of our starters (Scottie Pippen, Arvydas Sabonis, Dale Davis, and Derek Anderson) from playing all seven games. Bonzi Wells had a really good regular season and played even better in the playoff series with Dallas. He led the team in scoring, averaging 19 a game, including a franchise playoff record of 45 points in Game Two. Zach Randolph, drafted in the first round (19th pick) in 2001, also had an amazing series. "Z-Bo" averaged 14 points and nine rebounds while playing only 29 minutes a game. He shot 52 percent from the field and a blistering 89 percent from the charity stripe. It was one of the most exciting series I've ever been a part of, fueled by a remarkable team's grit, competitive spirit, and never-quit attitude.

Then I did what I said I'd do at the beginning of the season. After 25 years in the NBA, I stepped down as Portland's president and GM, proud of the team I had turned around. We made the playoffs all nine years, averaging 50 wins per season. Fans consistently filled the Rose Garden, where attendance had jumped more than 60 percent to nearly 21,000, the third highest in the NBA. During our last ten years as GMs, Jerry West and I had the top two records in the NBA. My teams won 62 percent of our games, averaging 51 wins per season, and Jerry's teams won 59 percent of the time, averaging 48 victories. My Sonics and Blazers teams made the playoffs ten times, while Jerry's Lakers and Grizzlies made it to the postseason eight times.

After I left the Blazers, they missed the playoffs for five straight years. They cycled through three presidents and four GMs and plummeted to *last* in attendance in the NBA. Paul tried to get me to come back—many times. I always said no. I had made my break and knew it was time to narrow my focus to the Seahawks.

I had never aspired to lead two pro sports teams at the same time. There was nothing power hungry about it. I took on too much and agreed to serve as Seahawks president because I had worked so hard to get the deal done for a new stadium. I couldn't bear the thought of Paul pulling the plug because the only guy he was willing to work with (me) wasn't up to one more job.

CHAPTER 14

END ZONE

After more than six years of Seahawks-Blazers double duty, I felt like I was on vacation being in charge of just one team. Instead of three-plus-hour commutes back and forth between Seattle and Portland, I had a quick 15-minute drive from my house to Seahawks headquarters in Kirkland. I could be home for dinner. I could actually *enjoy* being team president. We sold out every home game for the first three years (2002, 2003, and 2004). The community was ecstatic about their Seahawks again. And we had a Super Bowl–caliber coach at the helm.

It took a lot of work and creative behind-the-scenes maneuvering over the better part of a year to close one of the highest-profile deals I've ever done: signing Mike Holmgren as head coach of the Seahawks. I worked closely with the Green Bay Packers to amend his contract, adding a condition that allowed him to leave Green Bay if another team offered to hire him as both head coach and general manager. Privately, Paul Allen and I talked frankly about how difficult it would be for Holmgren to do both jobs well. Mike wanted the power to pick and choose his players, as some coaches do, but few do a good job at it. Nevertheless, if it would take both titles to get a Super Bowl–winning coach to Seattle, we were willing to go for it. The Packers agreed to release him under those terms, along with a second-round pick. Holmgren's $32 million, eight-year contract made him the highest-paid coach in the NFL, signaling that the Seahawks were serious about becoming a Super Bowl contender.

I had considered several other candidates, including George Seifert, who had coached the 49ers to several Super Bowl championships; Jim Haslett, a defensive coordinator for the Pittsburgh Steelers, who would soon become head coach of the New Orleans Saints; Ray Rhodes, the head coach of Philadelphia (who later joined our staff as a defensive coordinator). None of the candidates blew me away in their interviews. What Paul wanted more than anything was a marquee name. Mike Holmgren definitely led the pack of candidates when it came to name recognition.

Mike first came on to my radar in early 1998, about a year before I hired him, at Super Bowl XXXII, where he was coaching the Packers for their second consecutive shot at the NFL title. I was there to watch the game. It was my second year as the Seahawks' president. The Packers were reigning NFL champs, and I was surprised when Green Bay's general manager, Ron Wolf, sought me out and encouraged me to hire Holmgren, who was still under contract for a few more years. Why would the GM of the defending Super Bowl champs be looking to get rid of his head coach? Then Holmgren's agent asked to meet with me, too, and told me Mike wanted to coach the Seahawks. Apparently, Mike felt that Ron was getting too much credit for the Packers' success. Mike wanted more recognition for the positive impact his coaching had on the team.

Coaching a team with a quarterback as talented as Brett Favre is like having the fastest car on earth and lucking out by being the driver. Probably plenty of other drivers out there could drive that car pretty well, too. And yet a lot of coaches with egos as big as Mike's think if they're not driving the car, it'll never even get out of the garage. Don't get me wrong—I have no problem with big egos. I've never met a coach who didn't have one. And I would never hire a coach who didn't have an abundance of self-confidence. You need swagger to command respect in a locker room full of highly paid athletes, most of whom have giant egos themselves. Some coaches get into problems because they lose control of their egos. They think they're the star, the reason people buy tickets. If their team is having success, they think they're the reason why. They're wrong. At the end of the day, *the* most important thing, in any sport, is the players. Coaches can make a good team great or a great team even better. But if you don't have good players, you won't win. Period. End of story.

Green Bay lost Super Bowl XXXII to the Denver Broncos. Even though Mike wanted out of Green Bay and his GM didn't want him anymore, Packers president and CEO Bob Harlan wouldn't let go of his coach right after their second straight Super Bowl appearance. Instead, he said he would amend Mike's contract so he could only get out of it if another team offered to give him dual roles as coach and GM.

Fast forward to January 1999: Paul was scuba diving in the Great Barrier Reef when I let him know I'd chosen Holmgren. Although I'd been talking to Mike's agent for the better part of a year, Paul had never met Holmgren. That wouldn't look good if it came up at the news conference where we announced Mike as coach, so we either needed to delay the news conference or Paul had to come home early. He agreed the optics were important and cut his vacation short, traveling for almost 24 hours before we met at his house the night before the news conference. Wiped out from jet lag, Paul said very little during the dinner. He was not a very social guy to begin with. Add extreme fatigue to the mix, and he was probably mustering every ounce of energy he had just to keep from nodding off as Mike; Mike's wife, Kathy; my wife, Jan; and I chatted for a good hour and a half.

The next day, at the news conference, Mike made it sound as though Seattle's notoriously elusive billionaire had been wining and dining him for months, culminating in an exquisite feast the night before at his palatial estate. It was the first of many times I would hold my tongue about a story Mike spun, exaggerating to make himself look good. The media gobbled it up. And Mike loved it. The center of attention was his favorite place.

Despite the big name and high expectations that Holmgren brought to Seattle, the Seahawks struggled under his watch for the first few years. He had coached the Packers to a 75–37 record and two Super Bowl appearances during his seven seasons in Green Bay. During his first four seasons in Seattle, the Hawks won 31 and lost 33 games. With the team Mike inherited, we won the division his first year, then lost 20–17 at home to the Miami Dolphins (led by an injured Dan Marino) in the wild card playoff game. Mike made all personnel decisions from 1999 to 2002; we missed the playoffs each of those three years.

Mike's biggest problem during his first four years in Seattle was that he was spending too much time in the office. And for as much time as he spent in the office, he didn't have a lot to show for it. Sometimes, I'd pull him into meetings about the business side of things—a big part of a GM's job—and his eyes would glaze over. He didn't take notes, as if everything sounded so unfamiliar that he couldn't tell what he should be writing down. One time during preseason training camp, after watching the offense and defense practice in sweltering heat, he walked off the field when special teams practice started and went to have lunch in his air-conditioned office. Special teams was one of our weaker areas, so I stayed and watched, then went to talk with Mike. When I asked him why he didn't watch the special teams practice, he basically said it wasn't his thing. I couldn't believe it. Kickers, punters, long snappers, and other players on special teams (both offense and defense) are involved in roughly a third of all plays during a game. Special teams often make the difference between a win and a loss.

"When you walk off the field, you're saying they're not important," I told Mike. "I'm not even the coach, and I'm out there watching. You need to be out there, Mike. You don't have to be screaming and yelling, but your presence matters." From then on, he stayed for special teams practices—at least when I was there.

Mike routinely left the office between 5:00 and 5:30 p.m. and was done for the day much earlier than most NFL coaches and general managers. Getting ready for the next game always requires more than an eight-hour-day's worth of work. Mike loved the glitz and talking to the media, but he wasn't big on things like watching film. Mike leaned on his assistants for their take and left it at that. I'm not saying that's wrong. If it works, great. But it's not what most coaches do. And for Mike's first few years in Seattle, that approach clearly wasn't working.

As big as his ego was, Mike had remarkably thin skin. Anytime he faced criticism about losing games or draft picks that weren't working, he would point the finger my way, though I never made player or personnel decisions as Seahawks president. I never even suggested which players to pursue. I trusted our football staff to present strong recommendations, which I'd take to Paul, get his thumbs-up or thumbs-down, then relay the decision. Paul and I never prevented "Team Holmgren" from getting any player they wanted. Nevertheless, he would blame his mistakes on me, accusing me of meddling. The media ate it up. I didn't correct Holmgren. It would've been unprofessional to contradict him publicly. If Mike stretched the truth and it made him look good, why make a thing of it? I had neither the time nor the interest in squabbling with the coach I had worked so hard to hire.

Over time, a lot of people speculated that Mike and I didn't get along. We got along just fine. In fact, I fought for and saved his job a few months into the 2002 NFL season. Paul wanted me to fire him, but I proposed a compromise: to have Mike relinquish his GM title and focus solely on coaching. I assured Paul that I would be in the Seahawks office every day and keep a close eye on Mike. I wanted him to succeed. I felt responsible. I was the one who had hired him and had convinced Paul to pay him more than any other coach in the NFL.

I scheduled a meeting with Mike in my office at Seahawks headquarters. I was prepared to start looking for a new coach and a new general manager if Mike wouldn't accept his demotion. I had serious doubts Mike's ego would allow him to relinquish the GM title and no longer be in charge of football personnel decisions.

"We need to restructure things a little bit, Mike," I said. "We really need you to start working more and to concentrate solely on coaching. We're going to hire a new general manager so you can focus on your coaching duties. You're not spending as much time in the facility as other coaches. You *were* a great coach, and we think you *can* still be great. But you've got to put your energy into it. And if you don't, we're going to make a move."

At first, he didn't get it. He said, "Well, I'm not going to do that. I'm the coach *and* the general manager. I've got four more years and $20 million remaining, so I'm untouchable."

The look on his face and the tone of his voice took a dramatic shift toward fear and disbelief when I made it clear this wasn't a negotiation.

"Mike," I said, "I don't think you understand. To Paul Allen, $20 million is not a big deal. Paul told me to *fire* you. I'm trying to save your job here!"

It was a wake-up call for Mike. He knew that getting fired would tarnish his legacy. It might even cost him his shot at getting into the Pro Football Hall of Fame. He asked if he could spin the restructure so it didn't sound like he was getting demoted.

"Of course," I said. "You can spin it like it was your idea, that both jobs were too much, you want to focus on coaching, and we'll go find another general manager. Every other organization has two guys doing it, and you need to go do what you do best."

The Seahawks improved remarkably when Holmgren zeroed in on coaching. Whatever energy he had left in him, he put it in gear and really started coaching. At the end of the 2003–04 season, we finished second in the division, made the playoffs, and lost to the Packers in overtime (33–27) at Green Bay. We finished first in the division the next two seasons, too, on our way to the Seahawks' first Super Bowl appearance in franchise history.

Bob Ferguson (no relation to Washington State's 18th attorney general) took over as the Seahawks' general manager after Holmgren shed the GM title. Ferguson had local ties to Seattle, earning All-Pac-8 honors as a linebacker for the University of Washington Huskies. He was an "NFL lifer," having worked in the personnel departments of the Buffalo Bills and Denver Broncos for 11 years, during which those two teams went to six Super Bowls. He had just completed seven years with the Arizona Cardinals, the last four as general manager. "Fergy" knew Holmgren. They had both served on the NFL competition committee. Bob knew how to massage Mike's ego and was willing to let the coach have the spotlight.

And Tod Leiweke joined the Seahawks leadership team as CEO. I first met Tod (and his brother Tim) in the early 1980s, during my time as vice president of the Kansas City Kings. The Leiweke brothers (including Tracey and Terry) were running the Kansas City Comets, an indoor soccer team. We all had offices inside Kemper Arena. Nobody hustled more than the Leiwekes. They were young, aggressive showmen. After Kansas City, Tod had successful stints with the New York Arrows (a Major Indoor Soccer League team); the NBA Golden

State Warriors; and two NHL teams, the Vancouver Canucks and the Minnesota Wild. Tod knew the sports management profession very well. Because of my contract, Paul had to get my permission to bring in that high level of an executive. I gave him an enthusiastic thumbs-up. Paul made a point of noting how adding a GM and a CEO to the staff would significantly lighten my load—enough, he hoped, that I would change my mind about the clean break I had made from Portland.

"Tod would be terrific," I said. "I have no problem with him coming on board. But don't think this will make me go back to Portland. It's not happening."

Paul had tried to enlist my help in finding my replacement before I left the Trail Blazers, but I had declined. I did not want to get caught in the middle. He might try to have the new Portland people report to me instead of him, the owner, which would effectively be the same as me having to do the work myself.

In 2003–04, the first season after I left Portland, the Blazers missed the playoffs for the first time in Paul's 16 years as owner. He was pissed. Before the 2004 NBA draft, Paul called me asking for help in narrowing down their list of prospects. I said no, but he persisted. He kept asking if I would study some video footage and give him my opinion. I reluctantly agreed. He sent me DVDs of about a dozen draft prospects, many full games for each player. I spent two weeks studying the tapes. I finally called him, and we had a long talk. He promised not to tell anyone I was his "deep throat." I listed eight players from the 12 he had asked me to evaluate that struck me as good prospects, ranking them in order:

1. Andre Iguodala (University of Arizona)
2. Al Jefferson (Prentiss High School in Mississippi)
3. Anderson Varejao (Brazil)
4. Kris Humphries (University of Minnesota)
5. Kevin Martin (Western Carolina University)
6. Tony Allen (Oklahoma State)
7. Trevor Ariza (UCLA)
8. Jameer Nelson (Saint Joe's)

Paul asked me what I thought of Sebastian Telfair, a point guard touted as one of the hottest high school players in the country. I told him Telfair was not as good as the eight players I had ranked. They drafted him anyway. Not only that, they used a coveted lottery pick to get him (13th overall). Telfair went on to have a rather pedestrian career, playing for eight different teams during his ten years in the NBA.

Paul maintained a full-court press throughout the 2004–05 season, hoping I'd give in to the pressure and help him fix the Blazers. The Seahawks were on autopilot, and Portland was a mess. Paul had hired two top executives to replace me in Portland: Steve Patterson as president and John Nash as general manager. They made mistake after mistake. In 2005, the Blazers held the third pick in the draft and passed on future Hall of Fame point guard Chris Paul, in part because they had filled that position by drafting Telfair the year before. Instead, they selected Martell Webster, a high school player from Seattle who became an NBA journeyman, out of the league by age 29.

The Blazers ended the 2004–05 season with a 27–55 record. The next season they fell even further to 21–51, the worst record in the NBA. They also had the worst attendance in the league that year. No matter how many times I told Paul that I would not return to Portland, he wouldn't accept it. At a certain point, it started to become clear that I had two choices: 1) say yes to the Blazers or 2) get fired from the Seahawks.

Privately, Paul gave me a lot of credit for "righting the Seahawks ship" and reigniting Holmgren's fire as a coach. Paul was relieved he wouldn't have to eat a "$32 million mistake." As happy as he was about that, he was deeply unhappy about my refusal to return to the Blazers. I had made my choice, so he followed through with his. He fired me, with two years left on my contract, not long after the Seahawks' 2004 season ended with a 27–20 playoff loss to the St. Louis Rams.

It was my last job on staff at a professional sports franchise and the first time I had ever gotten fired. Disappointing as it was to have that chapter in my career end this way, I left the team in great shape—much better than when I had joined it. A year after I left, with 20 of the 22 starters on the roster acquired during my watch, the Seahawks finished the regular season 13–3, won their first playoff game in more than 20 years, and clinched the NFC Championship, making it to the Super Bowl for the first time in franchise history. The Hawks led the league with the highest-scoring offense going into Super Bowl XL. Many fans bitterly blamed Seattle's 21–10 loss to the Pittsburgh Steelers on questionable penalties. Even so, a crowd of 15,000 Seahawks faithful threw their team a spirited welcome-home party in Seattle, cheering loudly when Mike griped, "We knew it was going to be tough going against the Pittsburgh Steelers. I didn't know we were going to have to play the guys in the striped shirts as well."

Mike coached another three years in Seattle, leading the Seahawks to first place in the NFC West in 2006 and 2007. He made his last NFL playoff appearance as a coach in Green Bay in the infamous "Snow Bowl" at Lambeau Field in January 2008, when two inches of snow dumped down as the Hawks lost to the Packers 42–20.

Holmgren served his final season as a "lame-duck" coach; the Seahawks had already decided that his defensive back coach, Jim Mora, would succeed him the following season. Holmgren's next NFL job didn't go so well. The Cleveland Browns hired him as their president in late 2009, hoping he could turn around a team that had lost more than twice as many games as they'd won the previous two seasons. They learned the hard way that being a great coach doesn't necessarily mean someone's up to the challenge of running the front office of an NFL franchise. During Mike's two years in Cleveland, the Browns remained just as dismal as before he got there. You'd think they couldn't have gotten worse, but they did his second year, finishing the season 4–12, one more loss and one fewer win than the two years before, making them the worst team in the league. The Browns changed ownership in October 2012, and that was it for Mike; for the remainder of his five-year contract, Cleveland paid him handsomely *not* to be their president.

Mike's forgettable performance in the front office doesn't detract from his achievements as a coach. Green Bay named a street after him. His final year with the Seahawks, he became the only coach in franchise history to receive the Steve Largent Award, given annually to the player or coach who best exemplifies the spirit, dedication, and integrity of the former Seahawks wide receiver and Hall of Famer. In 2021, Mike was inducted into the Seahawks Ring of Honor. I'm happy for him because he truly deserved it.

CHAPTER 15

WAKE-UP CALL

I WOULDN'T BE HERE TO SHARE these stories about my life and career in the sports business if I hadn't gotten a routine health screening two years ahead of schedule. I was 48 at my annual physical, and everything looked great. My doctors had always kept a close eye on my heart because coronary disease runs in my family, but there was no sign anything was wrong with my ticker. I exercised a lot, ate a healthy diet, and I was dealing with a lot less work stress than usual now that I had just one job, as Seahawks president.

As my appointment was wrapping up, I asked if I should be looking out for anything health-wise. My doctor said no, other than getting a colonoscopy when I turned 50. On a lark, I asked if I could get it done early. My family had no history of colon cancer, so insurance wouldn't cover it, but my doctors said I could do the screening early if I wanted to. I scheduled the procedure, went in thinking I was being extra proactive, then woke up to news that I needed surgery ASAP. They had removed a few polyps during the colonoscopy, but one was so big—larger than a golf ball—that they needed to operate to get it out. The doctor feared I had colon cancer. I was confused, and not just because the colonoscopy anesthesia hadn't worn off yet. I couldn't understand how I could feel as healthy as I did and have life-threatening growths in my digestive tract.

"I'm not even supposed to *be* here!" I said, reminding them I wasn't due for this test for another two years and that I felt perfectly healthy. I got second opinions from two other specialists who agreed I needed the surgery, so I went ahead with it. Once they removed the mass, lab results confirmed it was a precancerous adenomatous polyp, which would soon have become cancer. All three doctors agreed that if I had waited to get a colonoscopy until I was 50, the cancer would have broken through my bowel wall and killed me.

Talk about a wake-up call! It was major surgery, and there were complications, so I spent two weeks in the hospital instead of the usual four or five days. After the colon resection surgery, I was left with a 12-inch incision and metal sutures running down my abdomen. My stomach became very distended postsurgery while I was still in the hospital. It felt like I was going to explode. Although about 18 inches of my colon had been removed, the post-op bloating was abnormal. The doctors discussed a second surgery but decided to try a less invasive procedure first, inserting a thin plastic tube into my nostril, down my esophagus, and into my stomach. The nasogastric tube would bring up air, bile, and other fluids causing the bloating. For two days, I could feel the tube rubbing against the wall of my stomach and throat. The smell of food made me nauseous. It was all I could do not to gag just about every time I took a breath.

In mid-January, about six weeks after my surgery, Paul Allen asked me to meet him at his house on Mercer Island. That was when he told me I was being fired. Paul had a very difficult time getting the words out. He was emotional and had to read the words from a signed document he gave me.

I actually finished the words for him, then asked, "Paul, are you firing me because I decided not to go back to the Blazers?"

He said it was the best thing for everyone, especially because of my current physical condition. We talked for a few minutes. He told me I was the best NBA executive he had ever seen and thanked me for the role I had played in keeping the Seahawks in Seattle. He encouraged me to get back into the NBA when my health allowed it. I thanked Paul for the opportunity and told him I was proud of what we'd accomplished together. When I asked what he would tell the media, Paul responded that his public relations team had decided "someone had to take the fall because the Seahawks lost in the playoffs."

Although I had no energy to engage in a long conversation, I did remind Paul it was the coach's job to win playoff games. I then asked if he could wait until later in the day to make the announcement because I wanted to tell my family first. He promised me he would. As I drove up his driveway on the way out, the news was already on sports talk radio because Paul had issued a news release. I was disappointed he didn't honor his promise, but I wasn't surprised. The business of professional sports can be very cutthroat.

My family had only one concern—my health. They asked if I was OK (yes) and encouraged me to get some rest. We didn't discuss any future career plans that day or for many weeks to come. I focused all my time and energy on resting and recovering, making it from one doctor's appointment to the next, each one a critical step in determining what the right medical course of action might be.

The healing process dragged on for a grueling year. The pain felt like I was being knifed in the stomach 24-7. I could barely eat and had no appetite and little energy to do anything but recover. This was the first and only serious health scare I'd experienced. The pain was agonizing, but I felt eerily grateful that I'd dodged this life-and-death bullet. It was also the first and only time in my life I was forced to slow down. It would've been nice to enjoy it more than I was able to. When you feel as terrible as I did, day in and day out, for weeks and months on repeat, it's hard to summon the energy or concentration to read books, watch movies, or any number of relaxing activities people turn to when they're recovering from surgery.

During that difficult time, it meant a lot to hear from so many friends I had made in the sports world over the years—GMs, coaches, commissioners. Two people called me numerous times, always eager to hear how I was doing, how my family was doing, if there was anything they could do: Jerry Krause (GM of the Chicago Bulls) and Tim Grgurich (who had worked with me as an assistant coach in Seattle and Portland). Every now and then, someone would say, "Hey, if you want back in, let me know." But for the most part, people just wanted to tell me they were thinking of me and respected that I would need time to get healthy enough to even think about working.

I had spent my entire life on the go, playing sports nonstop as a kid, then through high school and college, working whenever I had room in my schedule. I had gone straight from grad school to the Pacers internship that had launched my career in pro sports, playing hoops any chance I got—whether subbing in practices or competing in amateur leagues. As my work life got busier, I played less and less basketball but always exercised a lot, hopping on the treadmill after the first part of my workday, going home for dinner with the family as often as I could when the team was home, then heading back to the arena for that night's game. I put in that time on the treadmill as much for my mental health as for the physical workout. I needed that time to release stress, which I always carried in my stomach. A lot of people over the years have told me how calm I seem all the time, even in stressful situations. They have no idea of the beatdown my GI tract probably took at the same time. Sometimes, I wonder if stress had anything to do with my cancer scare. I have no idea and likely never will.

My father handled stress in a totally different way—outwardly— usually by yelling, pounding his fist on a table, or with facial expressions that made it look like he had just downed a bottle of vinegar. He was wound as tight as a drum. He had his first of seven heart attacks at age 41. I'll never forget coming home from an afternoon of playing hockey on a flooded, frozen-over baseball field to see an ambulance in our driveway. My dad was strapped to a stretcher, and as medics wheeled him toward the ambulance, all I remember my mom saying was "Go to the neighbors!" I was ten years old and had no idea what was going on. My dad had never had health problems. He didn't drink or smoke. He exercised. He had low cholesterol and low blood pressure. Long before it was a thing among health-conscious types, my dad would eat egg whites only. My mom kept the yolks in for everyone else in the family. She and my dad would make special trips to Illinois to buy margarine in bulk—considered a heart-healthier alternative to butter back then and not sold in stores in the Dairy State.

My dad definitely did not look the part of a guy at risk of a heart attack, but coronary disease ran in his bloodline. His father had died of it at age 66, his older brother at 59. Back then, we knew a lot less than we know now about how bad stress is for your health. Reading a book about type A personalities years ago, I found it startling to learn how many studies have linked stress to life-threatening health issues: cancer, cardiovascular disease, a weakened immune system, anxiety, depression, and many more.

We all experience stress, and we all have to figure out how to manage it. In my case, throughout my career, I tried to keep in mind that no matter how stressful the job got, it was something I chose to do. I worked really hard to get the opportunity to do it. Does it matter if I do a good job or a bad job? Of course. Is it worth letting the process tear me up? No. Even today, four decades into my career, I still try to catch myself, take a step back, and think, *OK, this is a problem that can be solved. This or that may not have worked, but there's always another way to approach it.*

Some leaders fly off the handle with wild abandon, wielding their temper like a weapon. Having started at the bottom rung of the front-office ladder, that would not have motivated me. It probably would've gotten me started working on my résumé. I've always found it a lot more effective to communicate with a positive and collaborative tone. You want people to *want* to work with or for you. As a president or GM, you don't tell them everything going on behind the scenes.

At times, the full truth was that the owner was on a rampage and wanted certain employees fired. Instead of scaring people by saying their jobs might be in jeopardy, I'd say something like "Hey, the owner's concerned. I'll be dealing with him for the next couple of days. You guys just work on this." I've spent a lot of time managing owners over the years, talking them out of terrible ideas, like canning a coach the day after a bad game, trading a player, or not allowing select media members to attend games.

Of course, I could never say, "You have no idea what I prevented the owner from doing today!" On the flip side, I never said everything was fine when I was trying to keep the sky from falling. Whatever you do tell your employees, it has to be the truth. Over time, you get a sense of what information is important to share and what's best held close to the vest.

Especially early on in my career in front-office leadership, I recognized that I needed to earn respect from players and coaches, employees and owners, colleagues and community partners. The last way you do that as a young leader is to be a yeller. You've got to show people you know what you're doing but also be a little deferential. If you have to tell people you're the boss and have to order employees to do their jobs, you probably won't earn their respect. It never hurts to listen before you talk.

All the leadership skills I honed during my 27 years in the pro sports business served me well when I was ready to get back to work. Though a handful of teams had reached out about bringing me in to run their front office, I wanted to stay close to home, working in a way that would afford me ample time to watch my son's football, basketball, and lacrosse games. During his senior year at Lakeside School, he was named the *Seattle Times* Male Athlete of the Year. He served as captain of every team he played for. Of all the accolades he earned, I was especially proud that his basketball coach, Stan Emert, said this about him: "In my 17 years of coaching, I've never had a kid work as hard at practice as Sean." Jan and I never pushed our kids to play sports. Sean started later than a lot of his friends and always knew that the most important thing to his parents was that he have fun. Sean went on to play lacrosse at Harvard, where he studied government.

Our daughter, Lily, played basketball in high school and enjoyed it, but her true passion was theater directing, which she did a lot of at Wesleyan, where she studied English and theater.

In addition to his athletic talents, Sean had a bit of an artistic side. He designed the logo for Whitsitt Enterprises LLC. I started the business about a year after moving on from the Seahawks. I didn't set out with a detailed road map. It was more of a hub with the potential for a lot of spokes, which I figured out one opportunity at a time. I did a lot of public speaking early on, something I really enjoy and usually do several times a year. I consulted with both buyers and sellers in professional sports team acquisitions. It's given me a chance to stay current with the business side of sports, tapping into the many connections I made in the NBA and NFL, while also branching out to other sports, including soccer (English Premier League), lacrosse (National Lacrosse League), and hockey (National Hockey League).

Team sales and acquisitions are incredibly complex deals. Sometimes, we'd spend more than a year talking, analyzing data, crunching every number you could think of, only to find the price wasn't right, market conditions had shifted, or the potential owners' or investors' financial circumstances had changed. In a lot of cases, the hurdle was what I call tire-kicker syndrome. A lot of wealthy people *think* they want to own a team, but as soon as they figure out how much it costs, how expensive pro sports teams are to run, they get a lot less excited.

In 2007, four years after I left Portland, the Blazers were still struggling. They'd missed the playoffs for the fourth consecutive season, finishing 32–50. They were on their fourth general manager in five years. For all that was dragging them down, they had a huge opportunity to turn things around. They owned the number one pick in the upcoming draft. They had to get this selection right. Paul Allen had a Blazers scout call me to gauge my opinion on two players: Greg Oden and Kevin Durant. I agreed to a meeting and spent an entire day dissecting the two players. I had watched Oden and Durant play in person in college and many times on television.

Oden was a seven-foot, 250-pound center with limited offensive skills. The NBA game had become similar to international basketball, which required all players, including centers, to be able to shoot the ball. Oden was slow footed and an offensive liability. He was a solid defensive rebounder with good shot-blocking skills, but he was injury prone. And he lacked passion for the game.

Kevin Durant was one of the greatest shooters I had ever seen. He had unlimited range and the ability to get to any spot on the floor. His seven-foot wingspan made it impossible for defenders to block his shot. He had a passion for the game. The most coveted players in the NBA were players who could shoot with range. I told the scout that Kevin Durant would easily score 25,000 points in his NBA career—a feat achieved by fewer than 30 players in league history. The scout took copious notes of my detailed analysis and planned to present my scouting report to Paul and Blazers management. I made a clear and compelling case that there really was no decision to make. It wasn't even a close call. Kevin Durant was by far the best player entering the NBA that year. No question.

The Blazers selected Oden.

Days after the draft, I called the scout and asked what had happened. The scout told me the meeting had started with GM Kevin Pritchard and President Larry Miller telling everyone in the room, including Paul, that the Blazers would select Oden. Paul had quickly agreed with their reasoning. When the scout had finally been asked his opinion, he'd felt intense peer pressure and had simply agreed with the Oden selection with no counterargument.

Many NBA observers feel the Oden selection was the biggest draft-day mistake in the history of the NBA. Kevin Durant will go down as one of the top players *ever* to play in the NBA. Greg Oden washed out after just two seasons. Paul fired the GM (and some of the scouts) two years later, after he realized the colossal mistake. As I continue to watch the brilliance of Kevin Durant, I feel terrible for Trail Blazers fans.

I also feel terrible for Sonics fans. In the early 2000s, the team was struggling and losing money. Seattle's Key Arena was no longer cutting it for NBA crowds, with its small concourses, limited concessions and merchandise sales, and other inadequate revenue-generating capabilities. Onerous lease terms prevented the Sonics from capturing as much game-day revenue as other NBA teams. The team was not very good—Gary Payton, Shawn Kemp, Detlef Schrempf, Sam Perkins, Nate McMillan, and others from the team that almost won the 1996 NBA championship were gone—so the arena rarely sold out.

An ownership group led by Starbucks chairman Howard Schultz and Sonics president Wally Walker, which had bought the team from Barry Ackerley, spent years trying to secure public funding for a new arena to no avail, then put the Sonics up for sale. Behind the scenes, I met with some people to see if I could get any local buyers to step up, but I couldn't convince anyone to invest. In the absence of Seattle-area buyers, the Sonics' owners talked to multiple out-of-state investment groups, eventually selling the team to the Professional Basketball Club, led by Oklahoma City businessman Clay Bennett. As part of the $350 million sale—a big number back then, more than the Sonics' owners thought they could get from anyone else—the new owners agreed to make "a good faith effort" to secure a new arena and keep the Sonics in Seattle.

Who did they think they were kidding? The New Orleans Hornets had been playing in Oklahoma City after Hurricane Katrina and were about to move back home. Clay Bennett's group had tried to buy the Hornets and keep them in Oklahoma City, which loved hosting an NBA team, even temporarily. Of course they wanted their own team. But the New Orleans owners had only wanted to sell a minority piece of the franchise to the Oklahoma City group, which said no. They wanted the whole thing. Less than a year after buying the Sonics, the new owners gave up on a tepid effort to get public funding for an arena in suburban Renton, south of Seattle. About six months later, they announced they would move the team to Oklahoma City as soon as they could get out of the remainder of their Key Arena lease.

There was no good reason to believe the new Sonics owners told the truth when they claimed they would do their best to keep the team in Seattle. Emails later revealed their goal all along was to move the team to Oklahoma City, even when they publicly insisted otherwise. A lot of people hate them for that. I don't. They wanted an NBA team to call their city home, and they got one. Bad on us as a city and the previous ownership group for allowing it to happen. Seattle got screwed in that deal.

The Sonics became the Oklahoma City Thunder when they moved. They kicked off their inaugural season in 2008 by losing 11 of their first 14 games. Their head coach (remember P. J. Carlesimo?) got fired less than two months into the season.

Howard Schultz would go on to call the sale of the Sonics "one of the biggest regrets of my professional life. . . . I should have been willing to lose money until a local buyer emerged."

To Barry Ackerley's credit, that's exactly what the Sonics' former owner had done when he'd sold the team in 2001. In fact, he gave a substantial discount to Schultz's ownership group to ensure the Sonics stayed in Seattle. Years later, another group of investors, led by hedge fund millionaire Chris Hansen, made a splashy bid to bring the Sonics back.

At a certain point, an influential member of the local business community—Dwayne Clark, founder and CEO of Aegis Living and a huge Sonics fan—asked me to meet with Hansen and offer my input on the vision he had been heavily promoting to buy the Sacramento Kings and move them to Seattle. Chris talked nonstop for the first hour of the meeting, offering nothing that I hadn't already read in news accounts of the big rallies he'd held, getting the community all fired up about the return of their NBA team. When I asked Chris if he had any specific questions for me, I was a bit surprised that he said no. Then I surprised *him* with my frank assessment: "You have no chance of pulling this off."

I explained how extremely hard it is to move a team. I wasn't sure if he knew I had been the guy in charge of moving the Kings from Kansas City to Sacramento, so I described the round-the-clock work it took to pull off the move. He didn't seem to fully grasp how political and relationship-driven leagues like the NBA are. And I think he underestimated what a strong and fiercely loyal NBA market Sacramento was. They had been since the day the Kings played their first game in the capital of the most populous state in the US, with an economy bigger than most *countries* in the world. Oh, and Seattle didn't even have an arena where an NBA team could play.

Hansen insisted he had the committee votes of NBA team owners who held the power to approve or deny his proposal. Days before the vote, a member of Hansen's group reached out to ask me if I could make some calls to rally some yes votes.

"Are you kidding me?" I asked. "I can't do that. I'd come across as a used car salesman. You guys have been working on this for a long time. If you don't have the votes, you don't have the votes."

And they didn't. The NBA made sure the Kings were sold to a local group that would keep the team in Sacramento, even allowing a local group to buy the team for $100 million less than the Hansen group had offered.

The business leader who had asked me to talk to Hansen later told me I was the only person who had told Hansen that his plan would never work. "We should have listened to you!" Dwayne Clark said.

People often ask me when an NBA team will come back to Seattle. I like that they ask when, not if. Only the NBA can answer that question, of course, but Seattle is in a much better position now compared with 2008, when its antiquated arena was not only too small for the

NBA but also configured so NHL hockey couldn't be played there, either.

Barry Ackerley had made sure of that. He hadn't wanted hockey competing with basketball. I'd sat in on the coliseum renovation meetings (which later became Key Arena), and it had been hard not to shake my head when Barry had insisted that the remodel be done in a way that would not accommodate NHL games. Though I'd thought an NHL team would be great for Seattle, I hadn't fought Ackerley on it, because I'd worried he might move the Sonics out of Seattle if the coliseum didn't get remodeled.

How ironic that Seattle would eventually become NBA-ready *because* of an NHL arena. It helped that the managing partner of a group that paid $650 million to get an NHL expansion franchise in Seattle was a minority owner of the Boston Celtics. David Bonderman's company Wildcat Capital Management hired me as a consultant in 2018. My main focus was to make sure the $1.2 billion NHL arena was built to also meet the many facility requirements for an NBA franchise. Honestly, I felt a bit like the Maytag repairman. I had little to do because there was nothing to fix. Climate Pledge Arena opened in 2021, the Seattle Kraken's inaugural season. The community has embraced its new hockey team as enthusiastically as it clamors for the Sonics to come back. Seattle supported the Sonics for 41 years, and I wholeheartedly believe they will sell out every game when the NBA returns to the Emerald City.

My guess is the NBA will award two expansion franchises by 2025. The price tag won't be cheap—probably somewhere in the neighborhood of $3 billion to $4 billion. Starting a team from scratch requires a lot of work and know-how. I experienced it firsthand as the point person in Sacramento, building the entire organization from the ground up. As challenging as it is to properly staff the business operations, making mistakes on the basketball side of the organization could set a franchise back for years. It takes commitment, vision, and experience to develop a championship-caliber team. Seattle deserves nothing less.

When the right time comes to relaunch the Sonics, I will do anything I can to support the effort. My commitment is absolute. I am willing to take on any role, whether it's behind the scenes, out front leading the charge, as part of the new ownership group with a financial investment, as an executive, or as a consultant. At the very least, I will buy tickets, grateful to once again belong to the enthusiastic fan base of a storied NBA franchise that's back where it belongs: at home in Seattle.

CHAPTER 16

NEVER TOO LATE

THE FIRST NBA GAME MY parents got to see with me as the team's president and general manager could not have been more exciting. It was Game Three in the first round of the 1987 playoffs. The Sonics were tied 1–1 with the Dallas Mavericks and playing our first game in Seattle to a sold-out crowd. My parents loved the game. The arena was loud and filled with Sonics energy. I could not have wished for a more thrilling vibe. We were the underdogs, without question, hungry to prove we belonged in the playoffs. And we did! We held Dallas to fewer than 20 points in the first quarter of Game Three, led by almost 20 at the half, and won the game 117–107. That victory gave us a huge surge in momentum. We had everyone in Seattle and in the basketball world talking about the Sonics, shocked that a team run by a 30-year-old president and GM, with almost all new players, was playing so well in the postseason.

Even so, my dad still wasn't sure about the wisdom behind the career I had chosen. On the ride home from the game, he asked me if the Sonics made money. I told him they were losing millions of dollars a year before I got the job, but we would make money this year if we won the playoff series against Dallas. He cautioned me to focus on making money because "rich guys don't like losing money, and that's a sure way for you to get fired." Between his hardworking nature and deep sense of duty to provide for his family, my father had always encouraged me to keep financial stability at the top of my mind. The NBA was a much bigger business in the late 1980s compared with the late '70s, when I'd started. Growing audiences were filling up arenas and tuning in to live TV coverage of games, especially when Magic Johnson, Larry Bird, or Michael Jordan was on the court. But because I was running a franchise that had fallen on hard times, my father worried that my family and I might suffer financially right alongside the team I was working so hard to turn around. I didn't take offense at his skepticism. I looked forward to alleviating his fears.

During the off-season, I scheduled a preseason game for the Sonics in Madison, Wisconsin, my hometown and where my parents still lived. We were going to play the Bucks in the Dane County Coliseum— the same venue where I'd played high school basketball tournament games. I was really excited. I planned to take a week off and spend it in Madison with my parents. The week before the game—October 10, 1987—my father died after his seventh heart attack. He was 62. I went to Madison and spent my vacation week planning my father's funeral, where I spoke in front of a church full of family and friends. It was the worst week of my life.

I'll always wish my father could have seen the long arc of my career in pro sports. And I'll always be glad that the one and only game he saw was so exciting. He may not have realized it, but he saw more than a thrilling victory. He saw a preview of the success I would go on to achieve. He saw how the first of many carefully calculated risks I took (trading away all but a few players on the team) had worked out well. My mother loved how I managed to channel my passion for sports into a career as an NBA and NFL executive. She enjoyed sharing "proud mom" stories with her friends.

She sure had an interesting tale to tell after attending the Sonics game in Milwaukee when I was forced into action as assistant coach. Remember that time, when Coach Bernie Bickerstaff was hospitalized with a bleeding ulcer, another was out with an arthritis flare-up, and a third was on a scouting trip? What were the chances that a) I'd wind up having to fill in on the bench and b) my mom would get to see her son coach the only NBA game of his entire career as a president and GM?

Looking back, I'm confident that my dad would have eventually shaken off any doubts he'd harbored about the career I chose. I bet he would have appreciated the indelible impact he'd had on me with his stern but supportive lesson on the operating cost of a neighborhood lawn-mowing business. He would have seen the dutiful midwestern work ethic he'd instilled in me—to put in whatever time and effort any job required—and then some. He still might not quite understand what it is about sports that I'm so passionate about that I've dedicated my entire career to it.

This was the man who had once witnessed a no-hitter only to complain about how *boring* it was. The hometown Milwaukee Braves won the game 1–0 against the San Francisco Giants—and Warren Spahn became the second-oldest major league pitcher to throw a no-hitter behind Cy Young. My dad never did develop an appreciation for baseball, not even when it became my favorite sport to play—the only one I played all four years in college.

I'm sure my father would have been proud (as my mom has always been) of all I accomplished during my 27 years in professional sports, especially these feats that top my list of professional thrills:

1. **Negotiating the deal that kept the Seahawks in Seattle,** leading the charge to win voter approval for a new stadium, and getting the stadium built on time and on budget.
2. **Rebuilding three championship-caliber teams,** revitalizing the fan base for each. The Sonics, the Trail Blazers, and the Seahawks were all struggling when I arrived, improved remarkably under my watch, and became serious championship contenders.
3. **Drafting four NBA All-Stars far outside of the lottery:** Shawn Kemp (17th pick for the Sonics in 1989) made the NBA All-Star team six times; Dana Barros (16th pick, one spot ahead of Kemp, in 1989), All-Star team once; Jermaine O'Neal (17th pick for the Trail Blazers in 1996),

All-Star team six times; and Zach Randolph (19th pick for the Trail Blazers in 2001), All-Star team twice.

4. **Leading the first pro sports franchise to ever win the Points of Light Foundation award** for corporate and community service in 1999, for the good deeds and positive impact the Blazers Community Builders made in Portland.

5. **Being named NBA Executive of the Year in 1994.** I was 38, and it meant a lot to be honored the same year the Sonics had the best record in the NBA.

There's more to a career than accomplishments. Ultimately, the longest lasting impact you have—in sports, in business, and in life—comes down to the relationships you nurture, the trust and respect you earn, and the character you build through the highs, the lows, and everything in between. I will always consider it a great privilege to have made a living in the NBA and NFL for so many years. It gave me countless opportunities to get to know so many people—athletes and their families, agents and lawyers, coaches and trainers, league officials and referees, fans, media, CEOs, ushers, parking lot attendants.

Every now and then, something happens that reveals the true strength of a relationship, like when Rasheed Wallace called me from his hotel room looking out on the smoldering Twin Towers on September 11, 2001. The Blazers were still on summer break. The season wouldn't be starting for another month. It had been a while since we'd spoken or seen each other, so I was surprised he was calling me. He sounded terrified, asking me what he should do and where he should go. I didn't have a lot of answers, but we talked and talked anyway. The fact that I got a call like that tells me that Sheed really trusted me, like a lot of players did. They respected me. They believed in me, as I respected and believed in them. They don't ever pull you aside and say, "Hey, thanks for being in my corner," but they know you've been there with them, day in and day out, in the trenches, whenever it mattered. They know they can count on you.

Not too long ago, I crossed paths with Shawn Kemp, Gary Payton, and others from my NBA past at a full house at Seattle's Climate Pledge

Arena for a preseason game between the Clippers and the Blazers. It had to be a quick hug and hello with Shawn, who was swallowed up by a ring of fans as we spoke. It was great to see him looking good, doing well, and smiling ear to ear as a growing throng of Reign Man fans swarmed around him. When we parted ways, he said, "I love you, man!"

When I talked to Gary, I told him I was committed to helping bring the Sonics back to Seattle and asked if he wanted to be involved. "Anything you're involved with, I'm in," he said, then grabbed my phone to make sure I had his current contact info. All these decades later, we still have a strong bond. It means a lot. More than any award or accolade ever could.

I'm a big believer in lifelong learning and venturing outside your comfort zone—which is why I enrolled in law school at age 61. In a letter I later sent to close family and friends, I joked, "I knew I was too old to be having a midlife crisis because my graduation from college was a faint memory, which had occurred 40 years earlier. Therefore, I soldiered on."

I had considered going to law school early on in my career. During my fourth year with the Indiana Pacers, acting GM Bob Salyers had suggested I get a law degree. An attorney himself, Bob respected how hard I worked, saw leadership potential in me, and planned to let me take evening classes while running the Pacers during the day. I had taken the LSAT, applied, and gotten into two schools—IUPUI (Indiana University–Purdue University Indianapolis) and William Mitchell College of Law—then a promotion requiring me to work at every game had made it impossible to go, so I'd put law school on hold indefinitely.

During all my years in professional sports, I never felt at a disadvantage for not having a law degree, even with the countless legal issues I had to deal with as the top executive of three franchises. Most times, our in-house counsel (typically the owner's corporate attorney) could handle any legal matters that came up. Sometimes, I hired an attorney with more specialized knowledge of a particular topic. Along the way, I learned a lot about scare tactics lawyers like to throw at you, like the time a certain player fired his agent, who then threatened to sue me for tortious interference to a contractual relationship—basically accusing me of sabotaging his agreement with the player he represented. The agent thought I had convinced the player to change agents because our negotiations were at an impasse. There were a few threats and lots of whining, but the agent never followed through and sued me. The player had wanted his deal done weeks earlier, was tired of waiting, found a new agent, and got a contract in short order—with the same terms the previous agent had rejected.

In another legal dispute, I negotiated a broadcast rights deal with the NBC affiliate in Sacramento—KCRA. At some point during the term of that agreement, the station was sold, and the new owners tried to terminate our deal based on ambiguous contract language. The agreement was extremely lucrative for the Sacramento Kings—not so much for the TV station, which was why the station's new owners took us to court. I served as the lead witness and got grilled by the station's lawyers ad nauseam. They asked me the same set of questions seven or eight different ways. I answered the questions the same way each time, and the judge ultimately ruled in our favor.

At no point in my career did I ever tell myself, *As soon as I have time to get a law degree, I'm gonna go for it!* My itch to go to law school didn't surface until I noticed some people my age had become slugs in their retirement. They weren't reading books. They weren't staying up on current events. I've seen 90-year-olds who carry on sharp conversations, barely break a sweat on a brisk hike, and live their lives joyfully. And I've seen 70-year-olds wither into dull, bored, lazy versions of their former selves. I've always enjoyed trying new things that test my limits and keep my mind engaged.

Back in 2006, once I started feeling more like myself after my colon surgery, I wanted to do something fun and new before I got back to work, so I enrolled in a couple of art classes—which I'd never done before but had always wanted to. I wanted to do something creative. I was the only real beginner in my introductory drawing class at the Pratt Fine Arts Center. Nothing I drew was worthy of being framed, but I enjoyed learning the fundamentals of shapes and edges, shading, perspective, and proportions. We drew a lot of fruits and vegetables. After each class, I'd get home and say, "Jan, I'll give you a dollar if you can tell me what this is!" Sometimes, she'd guess right. And I never held it against her when she got stumped.

The next semester, I took a hot-glass class. We would heat glass until it melted and then mold the liquid into amazing shapes. I found it far more enjoyable than drawing. I had watched Dale Chihuly do a much more intricate version of the same thing at his studio on Lake Union, and the class gave me a deeper appreciation of the world-famous glass blower's artistry.

Then I audited a class on business law at a nearby community college. I thought I might want to teach at the university level, so why not spend a semester being a student to see what a college class looked like from their perspective? The class was interesting and required a lot of reading. I decided my teaching would focus more on student participation and real-world learning.

I did end up teaching here and there, first at Seattle University. Inside the Front Office was the title of a graduate school class I co-taught there with my wife. I also teach at the Milgard School of Business at the University of Washington, Tacoma, where I give a lecture or two, along with other professors, in a Sports Enterprise Management class. My law school, Mitchell Hamline, has also invited me back to be a guest lecturer. Teaching is a lot of work, but I enjoy it. I learned a lot throughout my career, and it feels meaningful to share the lessons I've learned with future sports executives.

I don't recall exactly what got me thinking about going to law school in my 60s, but I do remember when I first broached the topic with my wife. Jan and I were driving to Whidbey Island one day in January 2017, when I turned to her and said I really wanted an intellectual challenge.

"What, like taking immersion Spanish lessons?" she asked.

"No," I said. "I want to go to law school."

She may have thought I was kidding. Or out of my mind.

"Law school is the *hardest* thing I have ever done," she said, "and a *huge* commitment of time and work." Jan had graduated from the University of Virginia School of Law in 1978 and had first practiced at a Wall Street firm but had never enjoyed practicing law. She'd moved on to a job she loved in business and legal affairs at ABC Sports, and later she'd become VP of marketing and broadcasting at the Sonics.

Jan and I talked about my law school aspirations for the remainder of the drive until I finally convinced her I was serious. Within days, I started the law school application process, which was both time consuming and difficult. I had to submit my transcripts from college (1977) and graduate school (1978) along with my résumé. I was fortunate my grades had been archived (thank goodness for microfiche). In addition, I had to write a personal essay and submit two letters of recommendation. I thought I could submit my LSAT scores from the early 1980s, until I learned scores were only valid for five years.

The first time I took the LSAT, in the 1980s, I just showed up the day of the test and took it. No studying. Things are a lot different today. The LSAT is the single most important element in the application process, so a bad score guarantees your application will be rejected. It's graded on a national curve, and it's become standard for law school wannabes to hire a tutor and study for several months. So that was what I did. I took lots of practice tests, timed just like they are for the actual exam. I felt as ready as I would ever be the day I lined up with several hundred other aspiring law school students (mostly in their 20s) packing into the law school on Seattle University's campus to take the three-hour exam.

The only thing I remember about my score was that it was good enough to get me into Seattle University School of Law. It was the only law school I applied to—until I learned about a program that would fit better with my work schedule. Instead of commuting to Seattle University's campus, Mitchell Hamline School of Law in Saint Paul, Minnesota, offered a full-time law school curriculum tailored for both new college graduates and working professionals. It combined online classes with several weeks of mandatory intensive on-campus coursework each semester. It was early August 2017, one of the most reliably beautiful times of the year in the Pacific Northwest. But instead of enjoying the sunshine and bright blue skies, I flew to Minnesota to start law school in sweltering Saint Paul, staying at a dinky Holiday Inn, reading and writing nonstop, with classes starting at eight every morning and ending at six every evening. Nothing about the on-ramp to law school is gradual. They hit you with reading and writing assignments in every class right off the bat. The hardest part for me: I could barely type. Throughout much of my career, I'd had assistants (at times two, each full time) who would do all the typing for me. Things always moved at a fast pace, so I would dictate to them, and they'd write it all up.

In law school, I had to figure it out on my own. Fortunately, I had a lot of help. My cohorts were younger and enjoyed helping me navigate the technology platforms we had to use. Along the way, they helped me get more comfortable with Microsoft Word. Early on, we'd get an assignment, go to an exam room, and have to submit it before we left. Most of my classmates would finish around 5:30 or 6:00 p.m., and I'd always be the last one to wrap up—often three hours later. Other exams were timed, and at the three-hour mark, the computer would automatically submit whatever you'd written up to that point. Those weren't my best grades, but I studied hard and gradually improved.

I always knew the material. I read every page of every assignment, never skipped a case, and never turned in an assignment even a minute late. My favorite classes touched on aspects of the law that felt rather familiar to me: contracts, deals and disputes, and transactions and settlements. The online classes were all recorded, and you weren't required to tune in live, but I always did so I could ask questions and have full access to my professor for a couple of hours.

I've always done well in school, not because I'm the smartest guy in the room but because no one works harder. No one is more prepared. You might get a better grade, you might out-negotiate me, but you will not outwork me. That's the one thing I can tell any employer, any colleague, any fan—when I work with or for you, you will get everything I've got.

I've always felt an inner drive to work or do something productive. If given the choice, I'll tackle the challenge that seems more complex. The more impossible a task feels, the more I love it. I'll admit, at times during law school, I wondered what the heck I had gotten myself into. I spent eight to ten hours most days on law school, on top of my work as a consultant. Before the pandemic, when I'd go to campus, I'd think, *What am I doing sitting in a classroom in Saint Paul ten hours a day when my friends back in Seattle are all out playing golf?* In the winter, I'd slog through the snow, telling myself, *I should be enjoying this—* then I'd realize I *was* enjoying it, slog and all.

One of my favorite experiences was a one-week on-campus class, open to a select few students, taught by some of Minnesota's most esteemed litigators. The Expert Witness Advocacy class was an immersion program that brought scientists in from all over the world. We had one week to prepare these witnesses for depositions and direct and cross-examinations. They all knew their area of expertise well, but they spoke in a language that most laypeople would struggle to understand. We gave them guidance on how to present complex data to a judge or jury with straightforward and compelling clarity. The course required an enormous amount of preparation ahead of time, in my case, lots of reading about the science related to hydraulic fracking.

Throughout the week, we got help fine-tuning our opening statements, trial strategy, and closing arguments. We were defense attorneys representing a client accused of contaminating groundwater through the company's fracking operation. The class culminated with two groups of students conducting a mock trial and putting our expert witnesses on the stand in front of a judge and jury. Most cases end with a jury unable to reach a unanimous verdict. The team I was on won our case. After the trial, we got to meet with jurors, who said the ultimate advantage that won them over was our strong storytelling. Convincing a jury is another form of negotiation. Speaking style, tone, appearance, messaging, eye contact, understanding circumstances, and body language are all important communication skills in a courtroom, just like in any negotiation. I loved the courtroom and will consider litigation in the future if I practice more law.

I wouldn't recommend law school to most people. It's *that* hard. One of my classmates was a practicing cardiologist who wanted to get into hospital administration. He had obviously worked hard to get where he was, but he struggled in law school so much, he got "invited" to leave. Law schools set extremely high expectations and won't hesitate to bounce you out if you show any signs that you're not up to it. By the time I finished my 27th and final class, earning the requisite number of credits for my law degree, I had submitted graded written assignments and exams exceeding 750,000 words. (I didn't know it at the time, but that's almost ten times longer than this book!) I graduated magna cum laude on January 10, 2021, my 65th birthday. It was a virtual ceremony, like most graduations that happened during the pandemic. My family tuned in to the ceremony, and my toddler grandsons, Dylan, Liam, and Clancy, got a kick out of seeing themselves seated on my lap in the picture I chose for the graduation slideshow.

"It took a village," I wrote in my graduation letter to my family. I thanked my wife, Jan, who "gave me strength and encouragement on the many days I was exhausted from 12 hours of study" and "never complained when I missed social events to work on school assignments and exams. Jan sacrificed a great amount over the past four years, and without her, this feat would not have been possible."

I signed off with two reminders: 1) Jan and I had graduated from law school 43 years apart, and 2) it's never too late.

The bar exam is one of the most stressful experiences I've endured. It's an extremely difficult series of tests spread over multiple days. Each section is timed and proctored. You have to memorize all aspects of the law, identify issues, write proper rule statements in essay format, and make convincing legal arguments. To make the exam even more nerve-racking, it takes over half the allotted time to just read the question you have to answer. A single exam question can go on for multiple pages. I studied six to eight hours a day for almost a year to prepare for the bar exam. I know many brilliant lawyers who failed the exam multiple times. I was determined to take it only once. Much to my relief, I passed the bar exam and became licensed to practice law in the state of Washington on April 22, 2021, when I took the oath of attorney. I attended the virtual ceremony from my home. With Jan and Sean proudly watching, I raised my right hand, repeated the oath, and was sworn in along with a dozen or so others. This was a very proud moment for me.

I didn't go to law school with a major career shift in mind. I just wanted to gain a deeper understanding of how the law works and the role it plays in the work I do as a sports management consultant, and to have the knowledge and credentials to work with selected clients and potentially do some pro bono work here and there. Interestingly, it wasn't my law degree in and of itself but the fact that I had gone to law school in my 60s that became a deciding factor when I got hired to the board of Diamond Sports Group, which runs Bally Sports (formerly Fox Sports Networks). The group of regional sports networks broadcast MLB, NBA, and NHL games in almost 20 markets across the country. During the interview process, the depth and breadth of my front-office leadership and negotiation experience impressed the Diamond Sports Group's hiring committee. But it was my late-in-life law school experience that convinced them I still had a fire in my belly as well as the energy and enthusiasm to work long hours when needed.

I knew it would be a big job to join a newly restructured board charged with turning around a company that had a lot of distressed debt, much of it from revenue lost during the pandemic, when there were no basketball, baseball, or hockey games to broadcast. It's a lot of work, but I'm learning and gaining valuable knowledge about technology, direct-to-consumer applications, and other innovations in broadcasting. It's exciting to have a seat at the table with a company at the center of an industry that's evolving with the growing number of fans who watch sports on streaming services.

I look forward to more challenges on the horizon, potentially a new leadership role in pro sports. I would love to be a member of an ownership group. The skills and expertise I'm gaining in sports broadcasting will serve me well when an ownership opportunity arises. The same is true for the negotiating know-how I've developed over the past 40-plus years.

Some wisdom bears repeating, especially when you're reading (or writing) the final pages of a book like this one. With that in mind, allow me to go into overtime and recap my top 12 negotiation tips.

1. **Do your homework.** Overprepare. Research everything, on your side and the other side. Take good notes. Know the other side's arguments better than they do. And know your stuff so well that you can look your fellow negotiator in the eyes while negotiating.
2. **Map out your strategy.** Outline the key points you'll make. Rehearse. Practice comebacks and counteroffers. Condense your outline to one-word bullet points. Find out who has the final decision-making authority *before* negotiations begin.
3. **Set a timeline.** Set your own deadline if you can. Stick to it. And don't blink. Timing can be everything in a negotiation. A lot of decisions are made when time is running out. Without a time constraint, deals get stuck, gather dust, and go nowhere.

4. **Listen with focus.** Active listening requires more than hearing the words. Pay attention to body language, tone of voice, demeanor—any aspect of what the person on the other side is communicating.

5. **Ask smart questions.** It might surprise you how much information the other side is willing to share. All you have to do is ask the right question the right way, at the right time.

6. **It's not all about what you say.** Getting the results you want often has less to do with what you say than how you say it. Sometimes, silence works even better. When an offer is made, look your opponent in the eye, don't say a word, and they'll likely improve their offer.

7. **Always be ready to negotiate.** Any time. Any day. A lot of the back-and-forth in negotiations happens over text or email these days, which makes this a lot easier than early on in my career, when I would pretend to be wide awake if an agent jolted me out of a dead sleep in the middle of the night.

8. **Keep calm and empathize.** When negotiations get heated, hang on to your composure, especially when the other side comes unglued. Show how you not only *hear* the other side's position but *understand* it.

9. **Be creative.** Look for alternatives. Chart your own course. Try different ways to get where you want to go, and you'll figure out how to close the deal. Even when you think you've exhausted every option, there are always others.

10. **Get to the handshake.** At a certain point, it becomes clear that a deal is close to happening or falling apart. Whenever you get to this point, make sure you've saved something valuable to offer at just the right moment. It can give you the last bit of leverage you need to seal the deal.

11. **Know when to walk away.** Sometimes, no matter how hard you try, you just can't make a deal. You might think

it's worth chasing, but in all likelihood, you'll just be wasting your time.

12. **Study your mistakes.** Take the time to analyze what didn't go your way and why. Seize mistakes as valuable opportunities to sharpen your skills, change things up, and negotiate more effectively the next time.

Finally, I'll leave you with some lasting lessons learned that have kept me grounded, focused, and confident that I can get results as long as I stay true to these guiding principles, all rooted in doing what's right for my team. These words of wisdom go far beyond negotiation. I hope they inspire and motivate you, whatever challenge you face in life and leadership.

- **It takes courage to make unpopular decisions.** Media hype usually lasts a week. The impact of a bold, well-thought-out decision can lead to a transformation that lasts years, if not decades.
- **Great deals won't find you, so make them happen.** Only time will determine the greatness of a deal, so chart a vision, and make it happen. Shawn Kemp was part of my vision, but it took years before he became a star.
- **There is always a solution if you look hard enough.** Create an environment where all parties agree that they want to collaborate to find a solution, and a solution will be found.
- **Momentum is real.** Don't always focus on the "how" if you're getting positive results. Sometimes, it's best to abandon the game plan and let events unfold. Feel it, don't force it. If a poor three-point shooter has made three in a row, let him keep shooting!
- **Give 100 percent effort, and others will do the same.** Actions always speak louder than words. The Chicago Bulls won six championships in part because their best player was also the hardest worker. Michael Jordan conducted his own strength-and-conditioning workout *before* practice, and soon the whole team joined him.

- **Confidence comes with preparation.** Great athletes perform when the game is on the line because they have practiced for that moment for years. Great litigators and negotiators get the job done because preparation allows success at each twist and turn.

- **Think through every logistical detail.** If someone says "Don't worry" or "Yeah, I've got it," that's a red flag that they're more likely to screw things up than get the job done. Make sure you have a checklist clearly spelling out who's doing what. And use it.

- **Always have a backup plan.** People get sick. Technology fails. Deliveries arrive late. Whatever falls through, make sure you have a plan B to keep the show going. It will keep your stress level manageable and the people you serve happy.

- **Don't fake it; ask questions.** You can't fix it if you don't understand it. Telling someone you don't understand an issue is a sign of confidence, not weakness.

- **Give credit to those who have earned it.** People love to be recognized, and a simple acknowledgment for a job well done motivates and energizes individual and company morale.

- **Don't complain if you get no credit for a job well done.** It can be frustrating to work your butt off and get no recognition for it. Or worse, to have someone else try to take credit for the good work you did. Ultimately, the only thing that's worth your time and energy is getting the job done, then building on that achievement.

- **Call someone when you say you will.** No matter how high powered your position is, show people the respect they deserve, and get back to them when you promise to follow up. Even if it's just to say you haven't made your final decision yet.

- **Be curious and honest about your mistakes.** Great leaders view mistakes as exciting opportunities to learn and get better. Embrace failures as valuable mileposts along the twists and turns on the path to achieving your goals.

- **It's never too late.** If I knew how hard it would be, I might never have gone to law school. Especially not at age 61. I didn't *need* a law degree. What I needed then was a rigorous challenge to broaden and deepen my understanding of the world. If you live, work, parent, and play with that in mind, you'll never "get old." You'll just keep discovering new and meaningful ways to achieve your goals—even, and especially, when people say you won't succeed. That's when you know you're living and leading courageously.

HOW TO GET A JOB IN PRO SPORTS

A LOT OF PEOPLE ASK ME for advice about how to get a job in professional sports. There is no certain path. If you ask ten different sports executives how they got their start, you'll probably get ten different answers. To help you navigate your journey, I can offer this advice:

Educate yourself. Understand that the industry requires long hours and offers low pay for entry-level jobs. Learn the responsibilities of the various departments within an organization. The variety of functions on the business side of professional sports includes ticket and suite sales, sponsorship sales, customer service, game operations, marketing, community engagement, promotions, public relations, finance, legal, information technology, and human resources.

Know your goal(s). Saying "I want a job in pro sports" is not helpful. Be as specific as possible when applying for a job. The required skill sets vary greatly depending on each department.

Formal education. Consider enhancing your formal education to become more qualified and attractive to employers. Some organizations require a sports administration degree. Others may require a law degree. Getting a legal internship for a sports team or law firm representing a sports team is a good strategy because teams are usually inundated with legal work.

Internship. An internship accomplishes two things. It gets your foot in the door, and it provides a firsthand look at how a sports organization operates. This is an ideal way to help you decide if a job in professional sports is really what you want. Internships are hard to get because hundreds, if not thousands, of people apply for each one. Most teams award internships to students in a sports administration program at a nearby college.

Sales job. Sales jobs are usually easier to get than internships because teams hire more people to fill these roles. This is a results-oriented opportunity and compensation is commission based. A good salesperson usually has an opportunity to advance within the organization. All businesses love people who generate revenue.

Attend conferences. Attend sports business conferences such as those sponsored by the *Sports Business Journal.* Consider traveling to the annual league meeting site for the chance to bump into influential people at the headquarters hotel. Join professional organizations and workshops. Stay current on sports industry innovations.

Network. Meet people who could be helpful to you. Start by befriending people already working for sports teams, because they have inside knowledge of upcoming jobs and internships. Develop and sustain these relationships because opportunities arise when you least expect them. Be persistent, and be polite.

Expand your search. Don't limit your search to one sport. Consider the NFL, NBA, MLB, NHL, MLS, event management, facilities management, sports media, gaming, sports betting, sports podcasts, social media, collegiate athletics, and others.

Stay positive. This isn't easy, and you are not the only one trying to get a job in sports. I was rejected by over 100 sports teams and organizations before I landed my internship with the Indiana Pacers. "No" just means "Not now."

ACKNOWLEDGMENTS

W RITING THIS BOOK ALLOWED ME the opportunity to take a four-decade journey down memory lane. Although this project was a labor of love, it could not have been accomplished without the inspiration and support I received from so many.

I want to start by thanking my amazing wife, Jan, who has been by my side from day one. At the beginning, she was a senior executive with the Sonics. Her understanding of the sports business allowed me to follow my passion, which included long hours and many family sacrifices. At the end, she was my strongest supporter when I decided to go to law school at age 61. She is my biggest fan and my most truthful critic. I am lucky to have her as a partner—her contributions to this book as an editor and advisor were essential. Thank you so much!

I am so happy my children were able to enjoy some of my sports moments growing up, without getting caught up in the glamour. My proudest experience was watching Lily and Sean become outstanding adults and parents. My four grandsons—Liam, Clancy, Wyatt, and Dylan—provide me endless joy. I hope each of them enjoys this book—once they learn to read.

I was so fortunate to have parents who modeled the values of honesty, integrity, and work ethic. Ray and Lorrie Whitsitt set the table for future generations.

Paul Allen was the best owner I worked for, and our shared passion for basketball was the superglue of our friendship. Paul's confidence in me was my fuel, and I'll always appreciate that he kept an open mind about owning the Seahawks.

I'm grateful Barry Ackerley took a chance on a 30-year-old

first-time president and GM. Our rise from "the outhouse to the penthouse" is something we both will always be proud of.

I learned a lot from Gregg Lukenbill's can-do attitude and ability to think outside the box. Thank you for the class you displayed by letting me out of my Sacramento Kings contract to become president of the Sonics.

Bob Salyers showed unmatched confidence by allowing a 25-year-old to lead the Indiana Pacers franchise. In hindsight, I would have been thrilled just to be a passenger on the Pacers' bus.

Nothing good can happen without a great team of people. The sold-out games, community engagement, and success on the court and field were a result of everyone's hard work in each organization. It is impossible to mention all the talented and dedicated people I worked with over the years, but I would like to name a few.

Thanks to my assistants, Sally Simonds, Sarah Furtado, Tia Hughes, and Kim Lindbeck. Each of you managed my hectic schedule and provided me with valuable input on a daily basis. I owe a debt of gratitude to the many talented senior executives—including Rick Benner, Julie Fie, Jan Sundberg Whitsitt, Shelley Morrison, Jim Marsh, Scott Patrick, Jim Rupp, Gary Spinnell, Bill Ackerley, Glen Christofferson, Bert Kolde, Erin Hubert, Harry Hutt, Jay Isaac, Tim McNamara, Mike Fennell, Bill Christensen, Joe Vaughn, Duane McLean, Gary Wright, Chuck Arnold, Mickey Loomis, Mike Flood, Cindy Kelley, Sandy Gregory, Mike Reinfeldt, Tod Leiweke, Lance Lopes—for helping make the businesses run smoothly.

I also want to thank Mark Warkentien, Gary Wortman, Frank Furtado, Jim Paxson, Tates Locke, Herb Livsey, Chico Averbuck, Jay Jensen, Bobby Medina, Randy Mueller, Ted Thompson, and Bob Ferguson for helping make our teams win many more games than they lost.

I'm thankful to Kevin Calabro for accepting my offer to be "the voice" in Indiana, Kansas City, and Seattle. Your calls were nothing less than a magic carpet ride!

Throughout this book, I wrote about the head coaches I worked with. I would be remiss not to mention the assistant coaches that were instrumental to our success over the years—Tim Grgurich, Bob Kloppenburg, Terry Stotts, Tom Newell, K. C. Jones, Dick Harter, Rick

Carlisle, Ron Adams, Bill Musselman, Jim Eyan, Johnny Davis, Tony Brown, Elston Turner, Jim Lynam, Herb Brown, Dan Panaggio, Neal Meyer, and Caldwell Jones.

I want to give a special thanks to five iconic commissioners—Paul Tagliabue, Roger Goodell, Larry O'Brien, David Stern, and Adam Silver. Each of you helped make me a better sports executive. Under your leadership, the NFL and NBA have grown to unthinkable heights and continue to be culturally relevant, exciting, and fan friendly.

I am grateful to Bill Koenig, NBA president of global content and media distribution, and the entire NBA family.

Professional sports are centered around chasing a championship. To win, you need talented, dedicated, hardworking, and passionate players. I've been fortunate to work with hundreds of such athletes over the years. Thanks to all of you for giving everything you had. Special appreciation to the many doctors and health providers who cared for these athletes.

I owe a debt of gratitude to Liz Murtaugh Gillespie, a talented writer, editor, and researcher. Her participation in this book was essential, as was the expertise of Girl Friday Productions.

And finally, sports teams are nothing without dedicated fans. The fans in the Pacific Northwest are second to none! From the Seahawks "12s" to sold-out Sonics and Blazers arenas, our home crowds were *game changers*. Thank you to all the fans for being part of the team.

—Bob Whitsitt
Whitsittenterprises.com
November 1, 2022

REFERENCES

PREFACE

Byers, Justin. "NBA Tops $10B in Revenue for First Time Ever."
Front Office Sports, July 14, 2022. https://frontofficesports.com
/nba-tops-10b-in-revenue-for-first-time-ever/.

CHAPTER 1: Reign Man

Abrams, Jonathan. *Boys Among Men: How the Prep-to-Pro Generation
Redefined the NBA and Sparked a Basketball Revolution.* New
York: Three Rivers Press, 2016.
Nelson, Glenn. "The Post-X Factor: Kemp Set to Make His Mark."
Seattle Times, December 11, 1990.

CHAPTER 2: The Intern

Pluto, Terry. *Loose Balls: The Short, Wild Life of the American
Basketball Association.* New York: Simon and Schuster, 2007.

CHAPTER 4: Train Wreck

Carlson, Chris. "Carrier Dome to Get Name Change as Syracuse
Reaches Settlement on Naming Rights, Sportico Reports."
Syracuse.com, April 15, 2022. https://www.syracuse.com/orange
sports/2022/04/carrier-dome-to-get-name-change-as-syracuse
-reaches-settlement-on-naming-rights-sportico-reports.html.
Eddy, Terry. "Why Naming Rights Deals in College Athletics Are
Complicated Business." Athletic Director U, https://athletic
directoru.com/articles/naming-rights-tipping-point/.

Novy-Williams, Eben. "Syracuse Terminates Carrier Dome Deal, JMA Wireless to Take Over." Sportico, April 15, 2022. https://www.sportico.com/business/sponsorship/2022/syracuse-exits-carrier-dome-deal-jma-1234672962/.

CHAPTER 5: Cleaning House

Corr, O. Casey, and Alex Tizon. "The Trouble with Barry—Ackerley: An Enigma Who Attracts Negative Publicity His Critics Say Is Well-Deserved, but Others Say Is Wrong." *Seattle Times*, June 12, 1994. https://archive.seattletimes.com/archive/?date=19940612&slug=1915216.

CHAPTER 6: Cinderella Surprise

Associated Press. "Chambers, Ellis Guide Sonics Past Rockets for 3–1 Series Lead." *Dallas Morning News*, May 10, 1987.

Associated Press. "Fitch Says Sonics Are 'Putting Dirt in Our Faces.'" *San Francisco Chronicle*, May 7, 1987.

Associated Press. "Sonics Heading Home—Sort Of." *Lexington Herald-Leader*, April 28, 1987.

Blinebury, Fran. "Sleepwalking to a Win—Despite Inadequate Rest, Sonics Looked Good in Victory." *Houston Chronicle*, May 3, 1987.

"Ex-Mav Ellis Sinks Late Free Throws as Sonics Even Series with Dallas." *Houston Chronicle*, April 26, 1987.

Galloway, Randy. "No Excusing Mavericks' Hardest Task." *Dallas Morning News*, April 30, 1987.

Hanson, Eric, Harry Shattuck, and Alan Truex. "Two SuperSonics Arrested in Mets-Type Lounge Tussle." *Houston Chronicle*, May 4, 1987.

Hubbard, Jan. "'Incredible' Effort Paid Off for Sonics." *Dallas Morning News*, April 27, 1987.

Hubbard, Jan. "Sonics Looking for Answers After Embarrassing Opener." *Dallas Morning News*, April 25, 1987.

Kelley, Steve. "Sonics Slam Door on Doubters." *Seattle Times*, April 26, 1987.

Kelley, Steve. "Turn Out Lights on This Series; It's Just Reruns." *Seattle Times*, April 24, 1987.

Kelley, Steve. "When All Goes Well, Team Anonymous Gets Sidetracked." *Seattle Times*, May 8, 1987.

Longman, Jere. "From Unappreciated to All but Unstoppable: Dale Ellis, an Afterthought in Dallas, Is an NBA Force in Seattle." *Philadelphia Inquirer*, May 14, 1987.

Nelson, Glenn. "Ellis Delivers Clutch FTs to Tie Series." *Seattle Times*, April 26, 1987.

Nelson, Glenn. "History Straddles Sonic Bench in Houston." *Seattle Times*, May 12, 1987.

Nelson, Glenn. "Lakers D-fuse Sonics in Game 1—Showtime Canceled in 92–87 Laker Victory." *Seattle Times*, May 17, 1987.

Nelson, Glenn. "Rally Gains Hope, Not Victory—Sonics Close 21-Point Gap, but Lose at End." *Seattle Times*, May 13, 1987.

Nelson, Glenn. "Sonics No Longer Destiny's Darlings—Lakers Write Final Chapter on Playoffs." *Seattle Times*, May 26, 1987.

Nelson, Glenn. "Sonics to Charge into Playoffs on High—X-Man's 39-point Spree Keys Victory over Lakers." *Seattle Times*, April 20, 1987.

Nelson, Robert T. "Suddenly, Seattle Loves the Sonics." *Seattle Times*, May 14, 1987.

Newnham, Blaine. "Hey, Red, What Can You Tell Us About Sonics Now?" *Seattle Times*, May 5, 1987.

Owen, John. "Incredible Sonics Keep Shooting the Eyes Out of Texas." *Seattle Post-Intelligencer*, May 6, 1987.

Parietti, Walt. "Sonics Surprise Chambers, Too." *Seattle Times*, May 7, 1987.

Richardson, Kenneth. "Ellis-Led Sonics Jolt Dallas Again: Ex-Mav's Career-High 43 Points Give Sonics 117–107 Win, 2–1 Lead." *Seattle Post-Intelligencer*, April 29, 1987.

Richardson, Kenneth. "Nightclub Episode Hyped, Didn't Hurt Ellis in 2nd Game." *Seattle Post-Intelligencer*, May 6, 1987.

Richardson, Kenneth. "Pressure Is on McMillan to Handle Harper's Best." *Seattle Post-Intelligencer*, April 24, 1987.

Richardson, Kenneth. "Pride Wounded, Clemon Climbs Back into Series." *Seattle Post-Intelligencer*, April 27, 1987.

Richardson, Kenneth. "Sonics (0–5) Have to Be Super Against Dallas—McDaniel Wants to Turn Series into War." *Seattle Post-Intelligencer*, April 24, 1987.

Richardson, Kenneth. "Sonics Blasted by 151-Point Mavs." *Seattle Post-Intelligencer*, April 24, 1987.

Richardson, Kenneth. "Sonics Polish Off Mavs with Rout." *Seattle Post-Intelligencer*, May 1, 1987.

Richardson, Kenneth. "Sonics to Try and Topple More Texans Today." *Seattle Post-Intelligencer*, May 2, 1987.

Seven, Richard, John Peoples, and Glenn Nelson. "Rejuvenated Sonic Fans Undaunted by Loss." *Seattle Times*, May 8, 1987.

Sherrington, Kevin. "Ellis' Revenge Comes to Pass, or Was It Shoot?" *Dallas Morning News*, April 26, 1987.

Smith, Sarah. "X Puts Solving Worthy Riddle over Career High." *Seattle Times*, May 24, 1987.

"Sonics Beat Rockets 128–125 in 2 OTs." *Mercury News*, May 15, 1987.

"SuperSonics 117, Rockets 102: Chambers' 38 points, Ellis' 32 give Sonics 3–1 Advantage over Rockets." *Orlando Sentinel*, May 10, 1987.

Thiel, Art. "Hec Ed: Sonics Return to Site of 1980 Disaster." *Seattle Post-Intelligencer*, April 28, 1987.

Truex, Alan. "Rockets vs. Sonics–Game 1–Sonics Power Past Rockets." *Houston Chronicle*, May 3, 1987.

Underwood, Roger. "To Say the Seattle SuperSonics Encountered Turbulence Thursday Night While Cruising with a Five-Game Playoff Win Streak Would Be to Suggest That the *Hindenburg* Had a Rough Landing." *USA Today*, May 8, 1987.

Watson, Phil. "NBA Power Rankings: 10 Biggest 1st-Round Upsets." FanSided, April 24, 2014. https://hoopshabit.com/2014/04/24/nba-power-rankings-10-biggest-1st-round-upsets/8/.

CHAPTER 8: The Glove

"Gunman Robs Payton of Cash, Jewelry." *Seattle Times*, February 23, 1993. https://archive.seattletimes.com/archive/?date=19930223&slug=1686926.

Kirkpatrick, Curry. "'Gary Talks It, Gary Walks It': Oregon State's Gary Payton, a Loose-Jawed Kid from the City, Has Quietly Become the Premier College Basketball Player of the Season up in the Woodsy Precincts of Corvallis." *Sports Illustrated*, March 5, 1990. https://vault.si.com/vault/1990/03/05/gary-talks-it-gary-walks-it-oregon-states-gary-payton-a-loose-jawed-kid-from-the-city-has-quietly-become-the-premier-college-basketball-player-of-the-season-up-in-the-woodsy-precincts-of-corvallis.

Moriello, John. "Former No. 1 Draft Pick Derrick Coleman Led the NBA in Arrests." Sportscasting, July 31, 2020. https://www.sportscasting.com/former-no-1-draft-pick-derrick-coleman-led-the-nba-in-arrests/.

Smith, Jack. "Payton Agrees to Six-Year Sonic Contract." *Seattle Post-Intelligencer*, October 10, 1990.

Smith, Jack. "Payton, Kemp Impress at Scrimmage." *Seattle Post-Intelligencer*, October 11, 1990.

CHAPTER 9: The Right Coach

Aldridge, David. "This Is No Odd Couple of Coaching." *Los Angeles Times*, December 17, 1989. https://www.latimes.com/archives/la-xpm-1989-12-17-sp-1524-story.html.

Arthur, Ben. "George Karl: Clyde Drexler Trade to Seattle SuperSonics 'Almost Happened.'" *Seattle Post-Intelligencer*, June 11, 2020.

Aschburner, Steve. "Humility, Appreciation Mark George Karl as His Hall of Fame Moment Nears." NBA.com, September 7, 2022. https://www.nba.com/news/george-karl-hall-of-fame-profile.

Associated Press. "Slumping Sonics Fire Jones." *Sun Sentinel*, January 16, 1992.

Beard, Curt. "Courting an NBA Title: The Chemistry Between Whitsitt, Bickerstaff Is Helping the Sonics Develop a Formula for Success." *Everett Herald*, November 5, 1987.

Bonk, Thomas. "The Bernie System: Bickerstaff Is Trying to Put the Super Back in Sonics." *Los Angeles Times*, May 21, 1987. https://www.latimes.com/archives/la-xpm-1987-05-21-sp-1374-story.html.

Cotton, Anthony. "Bickerstaff Named by SuperSonics." *Washington Post*, June 21, 1985. https://www.washingtonpost.com/archive /sports/1985/06/21/bickerstaff-named-by-supersonics/adf0b82f -940a-4da0-bea1-f05cb123e6bd/.

Goldaper, Sam. "Wilkens and K. C. Jones Elected to Basketball Hall of Fame." *New York Times*, February 11, 1989. https://www.nytimes .com/1989/02/11/sports/wilkens-and-k-c-jones-elected-to -basketball-hall-of-fame.html.

Kahn, Mike. "Sonics Embark on the K. C. Jones Era." *Los Angeles Times*, May 20, 1990. https://www.latimes.com/archives/la-xpm -1990-05-20-sp-378-story.html.

Karl, George. *Furious George: My Forty Years Surviving NBA Divas, Clueless GMs, and Poor Shot Selection*. New York: Harper, 2017.

CHAPTER 10: Paul Allen Calls

Aldridge, David. "Scarred by Incident, Trail Blazers Face Trouble in Many Directions." *Washington Post*, March 2, 1993. https://www .washingtonpost.com/archive/sports/1993/03/02/scarred -by-incident-trail-blazers-face-trouble-in-many-directions /cd7efedf-bf7f-4e4a-97c5-6e6918e6b691/.

"Clyde Drexler Felt Trail Blazers Rebuild." NBC Sports Northwest, https://www.nbcsports.com/northwest/portland-trail-blazers /clyde-drexler-felt-trail-blazers-rebuild-his-trade-was-premature.

"Drexler Gets His Dream Trade: Blazers Send Him to the Rockets." SFGate, February 15, 1995. https://www.sfgate.com/sports/article /Drexler-Gets-His-Dream-Trade-Blazers-send-him-3044732.php.

Freeman, Joe. "A Look Back at Past Trail Blazers General Managers, from Harry Glickman to Kevin Pritchard." *Oregonian*, July 20, 2010. https://www.oregonlive.com/behindblazersbeat/2010/07 /a_look_back_at_past_trail_blaz.html.

Goldberg, Jamie. "'Original Trail Blazer' Geoff Petrie Became 'Dynamic' Star Before Injuries Cut Short His Career: Rip City 50." *Oregonian*, November 6, 2019. https://www.oregonlive.com /blazers/2019/11/original-trail-blazer-geoff-petrie-became-dynamic -star-before-injuries-cut-short-his-career-rip-city-50.html.

"Petrie Leaves Blazers' Front Office." UPI, May 18, 1994. https://www
.upi.com/Archives/1994/05/18/Petrie-leaves-Blazers-front
-office/5349769233600/.

"Portland's Adelman Fired After Playoff Letdown." *Chicago Tribune*,
May 19, 1994. https://www.chicagotribune.com/news/ct-xpm
-1994-05-20-9405200212-story.html.

"Rider Traded to Blazers for 2 Players." UPI, July 24, 1996. https://
www.upi.com/Archives/1996/07/24/Rider-traded-to
-Blazers-for-2-players/8450838180800/.

"Washington, Portland Make Major Trade." UPI, July 15, 1996.
https://www.upi.com/Archives/1996/07/15/Washington
-Portland-make-major-trade/8592837403200/.

West, Brian. "Troubles Aren't over Just Yet for 4 Players from Portland."
Deseret News, February 11, 1993. https://www.deseret.com/1993
/2/12/19031900/troubles-aren-t-over-just-yet-for-4-players-from
-portland.

Winn, Luke. "The Old College Try." *Sports Illustrated*, https://www
.si.com/longform/sabonis/index.html.

CHAPTER 11: Saving the Seahawks

"About the Kingdome." Seahawks.com, https://www.seahawks.com
/team/facilities/kingdome/.

Associated Press. "Seahawks Owner Has a Super Goal." *Spokane
Chronicle*, August 30, 1988. https://news.google.com/newspapers
?id=xUJYAAAAIBAJ&sjid=2vkDAAAAIBAJ&pg=5731
%2C2103897&safari_group=9.

Farnsworth, Clare. "Dark Days: 10 Years Ago, the Seahawks Nearly
Moved to California." *Seattle Post-Intelligencer*, February 1, 2006.
https://www.seattlepi.com/sports/football/article/Dark-days-10
-years-ago-the-Seahawks-nearly-1194634.php.

Henderson, Brady. "How Paul Allen Saved the Seahawks from
Leaving Seattle." ESPN, October 18, 2018. https://www.espn
.com/blog/seattle-seahawks/post/_/id/31584/how-paul-allen
-saved-the-seahawks-from-leaving-seattle.

"King County Council Recognizes 20th Anniversary of 'Save Our

Seahawks' Campaign." Seahawks.com, October 30, 2017. https://
www.seahawks.com/news/king-county-council-recognizes
-20th-anniversary-of-save-our-seahawks-camp-197721.

Romero, Jose Miguel. "Whitsitt Fired." *Seattle Times*, January 14,
2005. https://www.seattletimes.com/sports/whitsitt-fired/.

"The 'Concrete Cupcake' Crumbles in Seattle." *Washington Post*,
March 27, 2000. https://www.washingtonpost.com/archive
/sports/2000/03/27/the-concrete-cupcake-crumbles-in-seattle
/194e3f98-d27e-4b93-873c-752d95d9d775/.

Wilma, David. "King County Voters Reject a Stadium for the Seattle
Mariners on September 19, 1995." HistoryLink.org, July 5, 2001.
https://www.historylink.org/File/3429.

CHAPTER 12: Rip City Revival

Addy, Steve. "J.R. MIA." *Las Vegas Sun*, August 4, 2000. https://
lasvegassun.com/news/2000/aug/04/jr-mia/.

Associated Press. "Pippen Comes to Portland Blazing." *Los Angeles
Times*, October 5, 1999. https://www.latimes.com/archives/la
-xpm-1999-oct-05-sp-19084-story.html.

Associated Press. "Stoudamire Finally Traded to Portland." *Los
Angeles Times*, February 14, 1998. https://www.latimes.com
/archives/la-xpm-1998-feb-14-sp-19093-story.html.

"Dunleavy Named Coach of the Year." *New York Times*, May 22, 1999.
https://www.nytimes.com/1999/05/22/sports/nba-roundup
-portland-dunleavy-named-coach-of-the-year.html.

Golianopoulos, Thomas. "'An Unmitigated Disaster': An Oral History
of the Lockout-Shortened 1999 NBA Season." The Ringer,
February 19, 2019. https://www.theringer.com/nba/2019/2/19
/18228706/lockout-1999-season-san-antonio-spurs-new-york-knicks.

Kirby, Chris. "Was Brian Grant the Blazers' Greatest Free Agent
Signing?" Rip City Project, July 24, 2015. https://ripcityproject
.com/2015/07/24/brian-grant-blazers-greatest-free-agent-signing/.

NBA.com Staff. "NBA J. Walter Kennedy Citizenship Award Winners."
NBA.com, September 13, 2021. https://www.nba.com/news/history
-citizenship-award-winners.

Nelson, Glenn. "Blazing New Trails: Finding Right Mix of Talent Portland's Biggest Roadblock to NBA Title." *Seattle Times,* November 1, 1999.

Open Court. "21 years ago today, the Portland Trail Blazers received the Points of Light Foundation 1999 Award for Excellence in Corporate Community Service." Facebook, October 25, 2020. https://www.facebook.com/TheOpenCourt/posts/21-years-ago -today-the-portland-trail-blazers-received-the-points-of-light -found/1806367062846814/.

Puma, Mike. "Sprewell's Image Remains in a Chokehold." ESPN Classic, https://www.espn.com/classic/biography/s/Sprewell _Latrell.html.

"Rider Gets Cut Quickly by Nuggets." *Los Angeles Times,* November 21, 2001. https://www.latimes.com/archives/la-xpm-2001-nov -21-sp-6774-story.html.

Rohlin, Melissa. "All Things Lakers: Isaiah Rider." *Los Angeles Times,* February 12, 2011. https://projects.latimes.com/lakers/player /isaiah-rider/.

Chapter 13: Too Much

Arnold, Geoffrey C. "The Toughest Coaching Job in the NBA." *Oregonian,* April 19, 2001.

Associated Press. "Kemp to Portland, Grant to Miami in 3-Team Deal." *Los Angeles Times,* August 31, 2000. https://www.latimes .com/archives/la-xpm-2000-aug-31-sp-13198-story.html.

Associated Press. "Trade-Happy Trail Blazers Get Davis from Pacers for O'Neal." *Los Angeles Times,* September 1, 2000. https://www .latimes.com/archives/la-xpm-2000-sep-01-sp-13781-story.html.

Ence, Jason. "Top 10 Players with the Most Technical Fouls in NBA History." TwinSpires Edge, March 30, 2021. https://edge.twinspires .com/nba/top-10-players-with-the-most-technical-fouls-in-nba -history/.

Fish, Mike, and Associated Press. "Donaghy Sentenced to 15 Months in Prison in Gambling Scandal." ESPN, July 29, 2008. https://www .espn.com/nba/news/story?id=3509440.

Hughes, Grant. "Rasheed Wallace's Unbreakable NBA Technical Fouls Record." Inside Carolina, July 14, 2020. https://247sports .com/college/north-carolina/Article/Rasheed-Wallaces -Unbreakable-NBA-Technical-Fouls-Record-149133056/.

Jackson, Barry. "Blazers Struggle for Answers Despite $86 Million." *Miami Herald*, March 18, 2001.

Quick, Jason. "Blazers Are at a Crossroads, and the Clock Is Ticking." *Oregonian*, March 11, 2001.

Quick, Jason. "Strickland Steps into the Crowd." *Oregonian*, March 6, 2001.

Thomas, Mike. "Maurice Cheeks' Biggest Assist of His Career Came During the National Anthem." Sportscasting, April 12, 2020. https://www.sportscasting.com/maurice-cheeks-biggest-assist-of -his-career-came-during-the-national-anthem/.

CHAPTER 14: End Zone

Cabot, Mary Kay. "Mike Holmgren Out as Cleveland Browns President After This Season; Joe Banner Taking Over Under New Owner Jimmy Haslam." Cleveland.com, October 16, 2012. https:// www.cleveland.com/browns/2012/10/mike_holmgren_joe_banner _jimmy_haslam_cleveland_browns.html.

Chodos, Ben. "Mike Holmgren Steps Down as President of Cleveland Browns." Bleacher Report, November 25, 2012. https://bleacher report.com/articles/1421795-mike-holmgren-steps-down-as -president-of-cleveland-browns.

Clayton, John, and Associated Press. "Holmgren Says He's Fine with Reduced Duties." ESPN, December 31, 2002. http://a.espncdn .com/nfl/news/2002/1231/1485140.html.

Digital Editors. "Brett Favre Owes All of His NFL Success to Packers General Manager Ron Wolf: 'He's Like a Grandfather to Me.'" Sportscasting, May 29, 2021. https://www.sportscasting.com /brett-favre-owes-nfl-success-packers-general-manager-ron-wolf/.

Drosendahl, Glenn. "Seattle Seahawks Play in the Super Bowl on February 5, 2006." HistoryLink.org, November 1, 2012. https:// historylink.org/File/10219.

Farnsworth, Clare. "Fired: Seahawks Can Whitsitt." *Seattle Post-Intelligencer*, January 14, 2005. https://www.seattlepi.com /sports/football/article/Fired-Seahawks-can-Whitsitt-1164230.php.

LV. "Mike Holmgren Hired as New Cleveland Browns Football Czar." Bleacher Report, December 22, 2009. https://bleacherreport.com /articles/313047-the-browns-hire-holmgren-to-be-their-football -czar.

Marmor, Jon. "Bob Ferguson, '73, Lands Dream Job with the Seahawks." *UW Magazine*, September 1, 2003. https://magazine .washington.edu/bob-ferguson-73-lands-dream-job-with -the-seahawks/.

O'Neil, Danny. "Alexander Registers a Seahawks First: MVP." *Seattle Post-Intelligencer*, January 5, 2006. https://www.seattlepi.com /sports/football/article/Alexander-registers-a-Seahawks-first -MVP-1191944.php.

Obee, Maliik. "Mike Holmgren Named a Finalist for the Pro Football Hall of Fame." Seattle Seahawks, July 28, 2022. https://www .seahawks.com/news/thursday-round-up-legendary-seahawks -coach-mike-holmgren-among-dozen-coaches-con.

Smith, Corbin K. "Mike Holmgren's Coaching Legacy Goes Full Circle Joining Seahawks Ring of Honor." FanNation: All Seahawks, October 30, 2021. https://www.si.com/nfl/seahawks/news/mike -holmgrens-coaching-legacy-goes-full-circle-joining-seahawks -ring-of-honor.

"The Amazing, Heartbreaking, Ugly Super Bowl History of the Seattle Seahawks." NBC Sports, https://www.nbcsports.com/northwest /seattle-seahawks/amazing-heartbreaking-ugly-super-bowl -history-seattle-seahawks.

CHAPTER 15: Wake-Up Call

Brunner, Jim. "The Secretive World of Sonics Owners." *Seattle Times*, April 5, 2006. https://archive.seattletimes.com/archive/ ?date=20060405&slug=sonicsowners05m.

Haggin, Patience. "Top 10 Most Hated Sports-Team Owners: Clay Bennett." *Time*, July 18, 2012. https://keepingscore.blogs.time .com/2012/07/19/top-10-most-hated-sports-team-owners/slide /clay-bennett-the-reviled-relocator/.

Hughes, Frank. "Why Schultz Tuned Out and Sold Out the Sonics." *ESPN*, July 20, 2006. https://www.espn.com/nba/columns/story ?columnist=hughes_frank&id=2525634.

Schultz, Howard. *From the Ground Up: A Journey to Reimagine the Promise of America*. New York: Random House, 2019.

Smith, Craig. "*Seattle Times* Prep Male Athlete of the Year, Sean Whitsitt." *Seattle Times*, June 14, 2005. https://www.seattletimes .com/news/seattle-times-prep-male-athlete-of-the-year-sean -whitsitt/.

Chapter 16: Never Too Late

Huber, Mike. "April 28, 1961: Braves' Warren Spahn Pitches Second Career No-Hitter." Society for American Baseball Research, 2016. https://sabr.org/gamesproj/game/april-28-1961-braves-warren -spahn-pitches-second-career-no-hitter/.

ABOUT THE AUTHOR

© 2023 Jeffrey Fong

BOB WHITSITT HAS BEEN CALLED the "most influential figure in Northwest professional sports" by *Washington CEO* magazine and "one of professional sports' sharpest executives" by the *Seattle Times*. In seventeen seasons as an NBA president and general manager, "Trader Bob" built teams that made the playoffs sixteen times. He was selected NBA Executive of the Year for transforming the Seattle SuperSonics from a nonplayoff team into the team with the best record in the NBA. In nine years as president and general manager of the Portland Trail Blazers, he built teams that averaged fifty wins per season, and he played a key role in the successful completion of the Rose Garden Arena. President of the Seattle Seahawks from 1997 through the beginning of 2005, he negotiated the acquisition of the team for Paul Allen and led a successful statewide referendum that secured $300 million in public funding for the Seahawks' new football and soccer stadium and exhibition center. Whitsitt is a sports business consultant and attorney. He and his wife, Jan, have lived in the Seattle area for the past thirty-seven years.